**Presented
To**

....

From

....

Date

....

the Financial Crossroads
The Intersection of MONEY and LIFE

Published by Companion Enterprises, Inc.

5840 South Memorial Drive, Suite #312

Tulsa, OK 74145-9082

Companion Enterprises, Inc. books may be purchased in bulk for educational, business, fundraising, or sales promotional use.

For information email jim@jimstovall.com or call 918-627-1000.

The Financial Crossroads:

The Intersection of Money & Life / by Jim Stovall & Timothy J. Maurer

1. Finance 2. Personal Growth

13 digit ISBN: 978-0-967-24270-5 (hardcover)

10 digit ISBN: 0-967-24270-3

Printed in the Republic of South Korea

09 10 11 12 13 8 7 6 5 4 3 2 1

Jacket by Judy McHenry – Tulsa, OK

Interior layout / design by Liquid Lotus – Colorado Springs, CO

dedication

As always, I would like to dedicate this book to Dorothy Thompson, who, once again, turned my words into sentences and paragraphs that have become this book. Also, I would like to dedicate this effort to my mother and father, George and Florene Stovall, who taught me that money is important but is only one element of a successful life.

Jim Stovall

I dedicate this book to my beautiful wife, Andrea, and my remarkable sons, Kieran and Connor, collectively my inspiration and reminder that money and material possessions serve no greater end than the furtherance of relationships.

Tim Maurer

Endorsements

"Jim Stovall is one of the most extraordinary men of our era."

Steve Forbes
President and CEO
Forbes magazine

****

"Jim Stovall is one of the greatest and most inspiring authors of all time. I love reading and re-reading his brilliance. If you are ready to make your life work magnificently and have money flow into your experience – read this masterpiece and share it with those you love & care about."

Mark Victor Hansen
Co-creator
Chicken Soup for the Soul®

****

"In my 38 years of banking, I saw thousands who could have avoided financial and life problems by reading the material in *The Financial Crossroads* by Jim Stovall and Timothy J. Maurer, CFP®. This could be the best investment you ever made in yourself."

Don M. Green
Executive Director
Napoleon Hill Foundation

****

"*The Financial Crossroads* is a useful guide to help readers build financial plans that will support their own unique life goals. Jim Stovall and Timothy J. Maurer, CFP®, provide detailed financial information in a readable, storytelling style that addresses more than just the mechanics of managing money."

Rick Kahler, CFP®
Co-author of *Conscious Finance, The Financial Wisdom of Ebenezer Scrooge, Facilitating Financial Health,* and *Wired for Wealth*

****

"Timing is everything, especially concerning your personal finances. As you face your own crossroads in life, this excellent book (like a GPS road map) gives you the timeless, as well as timely truths you need to reach your ultimate financial goals."

Denis Waitley, author
The Psychology of Winning

****

"*The Financial Crossroads* is very conversational and it is just spilling over with excellent information. Where most personal finance books are all hat, no cattle, Jim and Tim have really delivered with a lot of actionable, quality advice. They've hit the nail on the head when it comes to life and money—they're so intertwined—they do a great job of illustrating that your life comes first, and your money should simply fall in line."

Jesse Mecham
Founder and Creator
You Need A Budget (YNAB)

****

"*The Financial Crossroads: The Intersection of MONEY and LIFE* is a must read book for individuals and families that are looking for guidance with the ways money and life are always connected. From easy to understand real world examples to worksheets, readers are guided through multiple topics including budgets, insurance, investing and retirement. Stovall and Maurer's approach to these topics allows readers to apply the information outlined in the book to their everyday lives immediately. Their insightful information about retirement will make you rethink your goals and the way you save. They get readers focused on actions on fulfilling retirement wishes rather than a number. This book should be on everyone's holiday gift list."

Ezra Kucharz
CEO
FiLife.com

****

"*The Financial Crossroads* is a book for our times. The authors demystify the financial industry, explain the financial crisis, and provide readers with a financial road map for navigating each financial milepost of their lives. Stovall and Maurer have artfully combined their personal stories and a healthy dose of inspiration along with a step by step plan for mastering the complexities of our financial lives. However, their greatest gift in assembling this comprehensive and insightful guidebook is reminding us all of the importance of building 'true wealth.'"

Carol Anderson, President
Money Quotient

****

"Practical, personal and fun, grounded in the wisdom of life's realities, promises and possibilities, *Financial Crossroads* puts our personal relationships with money in living perspective without nagging, harping or preaching. It will give you much to talk about and even more to think about. Highly recommended."

Richard B. Wagner, JD, CFP®
WorthLiving, LLC

****

"The severe recession and financial crisis of 2007-09 have shaken the foundations of the American economy. Its rebuilding and restoration won't come from looking elsewhere for help, but will take shape through the accumulated actions of individuals and families. To help, Tim Maurer and Jim Stovall have produced a book filled with insight and utility. We would all do well to heed their lessons."

Carl J. Schramm
President and Chief Executive Officer
Ewing Marion Kauffman Foundation

Acknowledgements

I would like to thank Jim Stovall for his willingness to consider, support, and undertake this collaboration. I learned very quickly why Jim is a highly sought after speaker and prolific writer, as his words and actions breathed life into this project when it was little more than a hopeful notion.

Every word and phrase in this book benefited from the review and critique of Dorothy Thompson, Jim's right and left hand, and Robin Maurer. The latter also answers to Mom when I or my brothers are around and helped ensure that the book's content was technical enough to teach but fluid enough to read.

I so value and have internalized Drew Tignanelli's thoughts in the study of money and life that they most assuredly have been presented as my own throughout this book in addition to where he is quoted. I thank him for his selfless contributions to the book's content, and to me and my family, personally.

Many colleagues and industry experts have contributed their comments and encouragement, such as Dick Wagner, Rick Kahler, Carmen Wong Ulrich, Pat Goodman, Addison Wiggin, Marcus Harris, Aaron Patzer, Jesse Mecham, Odysseus Papadimitriou, Dan Singer, Sean Kelly, Russell Lagreca, Manash Ray, Eric Pines, Matt Rakerd, and Josh Itzoe, lending considerable strength to this project.

Thought leaders in the arenas of money and life who unknowingly lent their wisdom and humor to this book are

Stephen Covey, Dave Ramsey, Ted Klontz, Warren Buffett, Richard Foster, Rob Bell, Bono, and, of course, Chevy Chase.

Companion Enterprises as well as Tim Tomlinson and the Global Procurement Solutions team have helped Jim and me transform this content from words on a computer screen to the product in your hands while Ben Lewis, Kelly Morrison, Beth Sharp, and Jessy Smith have aided us in bringing our message to the print, radio, television, and online media.

Finally, I'd like to thank everyone at The Financial Consulate for their support of this initiative, and especially Bob Hayden, Chuck Bender, Kelly Allen, and Roger Bair, as well as Mike McCarthy, who has worked tirelessly to create the online exercises for the Timely Applications in each chapter.

Table of contents

Endorsements 6

Acknowledgements 9

Foreword by Jim Stovall 13

Introduction 17

Chapter 1: **The Power of Money** 24

Chapter 2: **Cart Before the Horse** 33

Chapter 3: **How to Spend $1 Million at Starbucks** 47

Chapter 4: **More vs. Enough** 64

Chapter 5: **Don't be Sold Insurance! Manage Risk** 90

Chapter 6: **Life Insurance, Part I: Why?** 103

Chapter 7: **Life Insurance, Part II: How?** 115

Chapter 8: **15 Minutes Could Cost You a Fortune** 137

Chapter 9: **Money and Health** 152

Chapter 10: **Risk Management Investing** 182

Chapter 11: **Portfolio Management: All Things Considered Equal** 196

Chapter 12: **The "A" Word** 221

Chapter 13: **Wag the Dog** 244

Chapter 14: **If Cost Were No Object** 263

Chapter 15: **~~Retirement~~ Fulfillment Planning** 286

Chapter 16: **The Ultimate Gift** 319

Chapter 17: **Everyone is Biased** 348

Chapter 18: **Your Story, Your Plan** 376

Foreword

I have written a dozen books prior to this one. These books have included autobiographies, motivational books, business books, and several novels. As a blind person, I write in a totally unique and quite unusual way. I dictate each of my books to a very talented colleague, Dorothy Thompson, who is the best grammarian I have ever known. As I dictate, she puts the books into sentences, paragraphs, and chapters. We write very quickly and rarely make any changes or edits. With over 8 million books in print, we must be doing something right.

I have a number of unwritten rules that I follow when I am writing. I never plan or outline my work. I don't title a book until it's finished. And I rarely read what I've written until it is completed. Another of my unwritten rules involves never collaborating with anyone else in authoring a book. I've had a number of very flattering offers to co-write a book with some very well-known and talented people. I have never accepted one of these offers because of the unique and unusual way that I work.

Now, for the first time, I find myself collaborating on a book. This goes against everything I have done to date, but I'm willing to alter my successful system for one very important reason: It is best for my readers and the overall project.

I've never considered collaborating on my novels as they merely require me to tell the story that is in my mind. Authoring autobiographical books would not lend themselves to collaboration, because I am still the world's leading and undisputed authority on me and my opinions. But now, as I seek to write something meaningful about financial matters and the current economic conditions that affect every area of our lives, I find myself facing some new challenges that I have not dealt with before.

When I write a motivational book, it is simply a matter of telling my readers why they should do the things that they already know to do. In these matters, we don't fail because we don't know what to do—we fail because we don't do what we know; however, as I face the daunting task of attempting to lead my readers through the turbulent times we are facing in the economy and in our own personal finances, I recognize it's not only a matter of motivating individuals regarding why they should undertake a financial strategy, but additionally, they must know what it is that they should do.

We are facing an economic landscape that is totally unique and unprecedented. Furthermore, it is changing daily. These factors combined to convince me that the only way to address this effectively is to collaborate with an individual who has the expertise and track record of helping real families in the real world.

As an author, columnist, platform speaker, and founder/president of a television network, I have been interviewed on literally hundreds of radio and television programs. Only a handful of these stand out in my mind over the years. I remember the day when I arrived at my office, and I was told, among many other things, my calendar called for a one-hour interview on the radio to promote my book, *The Ultimate Gift*. I deplore long interviews as most radio and TV hosts neglect their homework, leaving you floundering to fill the time on their program. When you are facing even a 10-minute interview with one of these unprofessional interviewers, it can seem like a transcontinental flight just getting through a few moments on the radio.

When I sat down to do what was to be an hour interview with Tim Maurer, I will admit that I was filled with a bit of dread; however, when Tim and I began talking about *The Ultimate Gift* book and movie, as well as life in general and the things that matter to real people, the hour flew by before I knew it. I will admit that I was actually excited when Tim called the following year and asked me to do another full hour to discuss my business book, *Ultimate Productivity*. He was positive, upbeat, and—unlike most of his radio colleagues—had actually read the book. Talking with Tim Maurer is like talking with an old friend, while you let the radio listeners eavesdrop.

When Tim called and asked me to collaborate on this book project, my initial reaction was not positive, as it violates all of my rules to date; but since I had already built up so much respect and esteem for Tim, both personally and professionally in our radio encounters, I was willing to listen and give him the benefit of the doubt.

I came to the conclusion that if I'm going to write about anything at this point in time that will make a difference in people's lives, it's going to have to deal with financial matters and the economy as a whole. The current trends on Wall Street and on Main Street are affecting every area of daily life. Money is far from the most important thing in life, but it affects each of the areas that are the most important things in life.

I'm very proud to collaborate with my friend, Tim Maurer, as I tell you why money is important and how you should prioritize it as Tim tells you what you should do and when you should do it. I feel as if I'm the travel agent or tour guide, encouraging you to go to a marvelous destination and enjoy everything it has to offer, while Tim is the captain of the airliner that will get you there safely, no matter how turbulent the conditions may be.

Being motivated to act is useless unless you know what to do. Conversely, knowing what to do is irrelevant unless you are motivated to act. Together, Tim and I will endeavor to help you plan your financial destination and help you get there safely and on time.

Just as I have offered the readers of my other books, I want to offer you the following opportunity. If this book raises questions that it does not fully answer to your satisfaction and comfort, or if somehow you don't believe financial success and wellbeing is within your grasp or meant for you, pick up the nearest phone and call me at 918-627-1000. As always, I want you to know that you have one guy that believes in you, your dreams, and your financial success.

Jim Stovall

July 2009

Introduction

Timeless and Timely

"**I**t really is an economic Pearl Harbor," said Warren Buffett, speaking of our current economic crisis. What brought us to this point? There is certainly no shortage of blame being spread around. Opportunistic, self-serving companies deserve their fair share of the blame. Their dedication to profit over service led them to create and sell products that were destined to hurt consumers in the future. Additional blame cast on us, as consumers, is also justifiable. Corporate greed would not have gained a foothold had we not cast aside the financial wisdom of generations past, instead seeking to have more sooner and save less, or never, while suckling off of our over-inflated home equity. Much has been said, and more will be, of the actions (and inaction) of companies and consumers that led to this historic economic demise.

However, our actions are only symptomatic of our thought processes. A thought precedes every action, yet we rarely even recognize our thoughts about money. Indeed, talk of money and things financial is pervasive in our society, yet we address money as though it is purely objective, dollars and cents—an end, not a means. How then can we alter our money behavior without examining what we believe about money?

What you believe about money will determine what you will do for and with it.

This is a personal financial planning book exploring the intersection of money and life. We explore the connection between our actions and thoughts regarding things financial. We'll reintroduce timeless financial truths, many of which were forgotten in the run up to our current economic crisis, and offer the timely practical application of these truths that can improve your life today. We'll offer you an insider's look into the recently humbled "Big 3"—the banks, brokerage companies, and insurance companies—and the inner workings that often set their proprietary goals and objectives over our own. These findings are not speculative but based on my experience working as a financial advisor in each of them. We'll examine the role of all of the various financial sales people, advisors, planners and consultants and educate you on the economic bias of each to make you a better consumer of their product and service offerings.

Economic Bias Alert!

Economic Bias is a term we'll use throughout the book to point out a conflict of interest where one party may have the motivation to alter its behavior for the reason that it will benefit financially based on your action or non-action. Some Economic Biases are obvious. When we purchase a new or used car, we understand that the selling agent a) wants us to purchase a car and b) would prefer that we purchase it for a higher, rather than lower, price. When we purchase life insurance, we expect that the agent wants to sell us more so that he or she can make a larger commission. But many Economic Biases are not so easy to spot. Did you know that the Economic Bias of a home and auto insurance agent is actually to sell you LESS insurance?

We are well served to recognize that Economic Bias exists in every service or transaction, corporation or non-profit entity. Car salesmen and insurance agents exhibit it, but so do financial advisors, lawyers, universities, authors, pastors, and doctors. Economic Bias in and of itself is not bad, and it is not our objective to make you paranoid or judgmental of every interaction involving money, but you are a better educated consumer if you know how to spot it, bring it to the forefront of your business dealings, and minimize it to the greatest degree possible. Throughout this book, we'll offer Economic Bias Alerts to point out examples of Economic Bias in the financial services realm.

Timeless Truths

These truths are recognizable, but they're shrouded among a host of equally timeless falsehoods. These falsehoods are reincarnated in each generation, like Gordon Gekko's proud mantra in Oliver Stone's movie, *Wall Street*, "Greed is good." Or, as my three-year-old son is apt to cry at the top of his lungs, "But... but... I NEED it!" (I'm quite sure that Adam, the first man, heard this when his first son, Abel, reached the ripe old age of 20 months.) Throughout this book, Jim Stovall will represent the foundational truths upon which a successful financial plan is built.

Jim is the internationally recognized author and speaker whose brilliant fictional account of how money interrupts and corrupts relationships, *The Ultimate Gift*, has sold over 4 million copies and was turned into a major motion picture. The reason for Jim's success with *The Ultimate Gift* is his uncanny ability to personalize a story. In this book, he employs his wisdom in an even more personal way, in the form of a financial guidebook to be employed in your story.

Jim also has a unique ability to offer his helpful directives and have us receive them. We all have a unique history that we bring into our decision-making, but we often rely on our uniqueness to offer justification for our actions. "Yeah, that may have worked for you, but my situation's different...it's harder... it's worse." Few of us can say that when Jim asks us to consider an alternative course of action, because virtually all of his success has come despite incomprehensible odds.

When Jim, a promising college athlete with aspirations to play professional football, went to the doctor for a routine physical, he was told that he had a degenerative condition that would rob him of his sight completely. He's human, so be assured he was extremely disappointed, but he took that disappointment and redirected it at a new competitive endeavor, becoming an Olympic weightlifter. He couldn't read with his eyes, so he began listening to books. Though he wasn't a big reader prior to his loss of sight, he now reads one book each day with the aid of a high-speed listening device. When told that blind people had nothing to gain from television, he responded by starting the Narrative Television Network, an Emmy Award-winning network serving the nation's visually impaired.

Jim's deep level of understanding regarding money issues isn't superficial, it's experiential. His first job was as a stock broker, and although his message has broadened over the years, he has always lived the fundamental financial disciplines and inspired others to do the same. Jim doesn't recognize "can't" or "hard" or even "impossible," and I hope that the confluence of his wisdom and his story will make it easier for you to find freedom in the Timeless Truths he shares.

Timely Application

Timeless truths may be simple, but they're not easy to apply. All the education and motivation in the world will do very little unless you know how and where to apply it. I'll offer concrete steps designed to help you accomplish your financial goals. But before you start implementing to accomplish those goals, you have to know what the goals are. I'll give you practical steps designed to help you create your goals. And before you can set goals, you have to have a foundation upon which those goals are built. Let's call that foundation your values, or simply the stuff in life that you want to be about. I'll give you practical steps to help you articulate them. The book's website, www.thefinancialcrossroads.com, will have resources that you can download for each chapter's Timely Application to complete your own personal exercise.

Most financial plans speak of goals and occasionally values, but the recommendations often focus only on the final phase of your plan—the implementation—and most of the goals and values are dictated to you, instead of drawn from you. I'll help you understand how to save for retirement, but before you do that, I'll help you understand how to define retirement in your personal terms, and whether or not a traditional retirement is even a goal that is consistent with your values. I'll show you how to determine how much insurance you should purchase—if any—but I'll also teach you to become a risk manager, instead of simply a consumer of insurance. I'll tell you which essential estate planning documents you should consider having drafted, and I will also tell you how to spot signs that an attorney is giving you a sales pitch to buy an expensive document that you don't need.

I'll act as your buffer to and from the financial services industry. I'll be drawing on my experience working with clients and teaching the financial planners of tomorrow, as well as the experiences of my mentors and the thought leaders of the personal financial planning profession. I'll also share eye-opening stories from the training I and other planners received growing up professionally in each of the aforementioned "Big 3," exposing the techniques used that you need to know in order to effectively manage your cash, invest, and insure in the way that is best for you.

One of the greater frustrations with the Timely Application of financial planning recommendations is the perpetual state of flux in the industry, regulatory organizations, and governmental bodies. Financial information is moving at a rate faster than at any time in history. If I were writing this introduction a year ago, I may have spoken of the impenetrable walls of the financial industry fortress and how the industry would take the passing of a generation before necessary change would take place, bringing the industry into alignment with the best interest of the consumers it serves. In reality, it took only a matter of weeks to see the entire financial services industry brought to its knees!

In the 4th quarter of 2008, we witnessed the undoing of the country's largest bank, brokerage firm, and insurance company, and that is likely to have reverberations through future generations as the purveyors of financial products remake themselves. A massive political shift will also bring even further change in the financial industry and in your personal realm. We'll show you what is likely to change and how it will impact you, and the website, www.thefinancialcrossroads.com, will keep you up to date on major changes that may have an impact on your life.

Again, this is a personal financial planning book examining the intersection of money and life. Our financial lives are embedded in our...lives. We're not educating for the sake of philosophizing—all the information contained is held to the standard of practical application. The following pages are designed to help you reframe the way you look at money and then build a foundation of education upon which a specific, personal plan of action can be created and implemented.

Timeless and timely. We need it now more than ever.

Tim Maurer

Chapter one

The Power of Money

> If money be not thy servant, it will be
> thy master. The covetous man cannot
> so properly be said to possess wealth,
> as that may be said to possess him.
>
> *Francis Bacon*

> Money is a terrible master but an ex-
> cellent servant.
>
> *P.T. Barnum*

Money is the most misunderstood commodity in our society, even on our planet. People today understand the price of everything and the value of nothing. There have been more conflicts, divorces, and disputes over money than anything else. In order to begin to have healthy attitudes toward money, we must understand that it is nothing more—or less—than a neutral tool or vehicle.

It is also critical to understand that money is not inherently bad, unimportant or irrelevant. Many have misquoted and misused ancient wisdom proclaiming that "...money is the root of all evil." The context here is imperative. "For *the love of* money is the root of all evil," is the actual quote, and the difference is profound. Nothing can take the place of money in the things that money does, but outside of the scope where money is useful, it has no value.

When it comes to your health, family relationships, or personal well-being, for example, money is of little importance. It serves us best when it is a facilitator of relationships, not an end in and of itself. This understanding will keep money and its detrimental pursuit in check. Once you see money with new eyes, you'll use it better and more effectively.

Timeless Truth

There are only four things you can do with your money: Acquire stuff, buy security, create memories, and make the world a better place. There is no right or wrong place to put your money regarding these four areas. As in most life decisions, balance is the key.

Acquiring "stuff" has become our national pastime and obsession. Most people spend more time working than necessary so they can acquire stuff that they don't have time to use because they spend so much time working to get it.

Security is an admirable pursuit. But if you're not careful, you will fall into the group of people who spend their whole lives preparing for a rainy day, and it never so much as sprinkles.

Creating memories is a vital component in a fulfilled life. Those memories can never be taken from you, but if all you do is pursue memories, you will spend your entire life looking in the rear view mirror. It's nice to look back there every once in a while, but if you drive through life very long looking only in the rear view mirror, you are bound to get a rude awakening.

And, finally, money, like any other tool, can be used for good or for bad, but it can, indeed, help to make the world a better place when it is put in the hands of the right people. We must be cautious here as well, because among those sincere souls who seek your money for admirable pursuits, there are many who, under the guise of good works, are prepared to rip you off.

Apply the following litmus test for proper money usage: Money used wisely enhances relationships; money used poorly is a relational stumbling block.

How would your life be different if money were no object? This is a difficult question to consider, because we seldom make any decisions that are not based upon money. This is a poor way to look at the world. Decide what is good or right or meaningful, and then worry about the money.

Jim Stovall

You may be interested to know there has never been a money shortage. There is, however, from time-to-time a creativity, service, or value shortage. Money is nothing more or less than a result of creating value in the lives of other people. If you stop worrying about money and concern yourself instead with creating value in the lives of those around you, you will have more money than you need.

What is the actual, literal value of the dollars in our pockets? Nothing. There was a time when that was not the case. The Bretton Woods Agreement, forged after World War II, pegged the value of a U.S. Dollar to 888.671 milligrams of gold. Other currencies were then pegged to the dollar, and the U.S. pledged to convert dollars to gold, but the U.S. went off of the gold standard in 1971 never to return. Now, as Dick Wagner puts it, "we have traded money of intrinsic value for perceived value." While some claim that perception is reality, perceived money is simply more easily manipulated, for better and for worse. Prior to our current recession, the value of a U.S. dollar steadily declined relative to other world currencies. The U.S. dollar, however, is still the currency used to conduct business around the world, so as the recession deepened, the inherent need for dollars to transact business around the world helped the dollar increase in value again.

The primary method used by the U.S. government to combat our current recession is "printing money"—making cash more easily available to financial institutions in the hope that they make it accessible to the consuming populace in the hope that they spend it. (Hmmmm... Sounds eerily similar to the problem that put us here in the first place, doesn't it?) The drastic increase in money supply is an attempt to avoid the deflationary downward spiral that occurred in the Great Depression. It will inevitably, however, play a role in a further devaluation of the U.S. dollar when we emerge from the "Great Recession." The increased supply of dollars will result in a lower value for each dollar.

Therefore, money has no value other than that which we attribute to it. Academically, this makes sense, but why does it actually matter how we view money? Isn't it only splitting hairs over semantics? How then does the once almighty dollar have such a hold on us in our daily lives? Over 50% of first marriages end in divorce. The majority of those suggest financial disputes as the primary impetus for the break-up, and not one of us can attest to money not playing a primary role in some relational disruption with family or friends. We must then be giving money power over us.

How do we give money power, and how do we recognize when we're doing it? Let's first examine the symptoms. My wife and I were on one of our first dates many years ago at a restaurant in the northern suburbs of Baltimore. While enjoying the romantic, candlelit environment, I displayed my chivalry by inviting Andrea to be the first to give our server her order. She ordered the crab cake; I don't remember what I ordered. The reason I'll never forget her crab cake is because, as the waiter walked away, I scoffed at Andrea's foolishness to ever order a menu item at the rate of "Market Price"—like the crab cake—without first asking what the market price is! I thought I was doling out financial wisdom, but Andrea heard that I thought money was more important than she. Romantic, huh? After what happened there, I'm lucky to be married! What was my money belief that brought about that embarrassing snafu?

Rick Kahler and Ted Klontz, a financial planner/psychologist duo, collaborated on the topic of personal finance culminating in the must read, *The Financial Wisdom of Ebenezer Scrooge*. Note their explanation on how our beliefs about money and our actions surrounding it are likely to correspond.

> *Very early in life, people begin to internalize messages about money's purpose...how it works, what it promises, its overall significance....[T]hey translate what they see and hear into unconscious rules about life, including any internalized messages about money....[E]very financial behavior, no matter how*

seemingly illogical, makes perfect sense when we understand the underlying beliefs.

In my first date example, it was not that I actually believed that money was more important than my wife, but that is certainly the message she received. And sadly, I think she's received that painful message many times since then even though I've never intended to send it. What then could help us better understand our own beliefs about money and how they were formed?

Timely Application
Personal Money Story

Write your own "Personal Money Story." Sit down with a piece of paper and write the earliest memory you have of money and your best guess of your age. For many, it will involve some combination of a piggy bank and an allowance or birthday gift somewhere between ages 3 and 6. Then rate this experience numerically between +10 for a great experience and -10 for a scarring memory. Continue this pattern, marking all of the notable experiences you had with money, good and bad, throughout the course of your life. Then, with the +10/-10 continuum on the vertical axis and the timeline on the horizontal, plot out a visual picture of your history with money.

If you're single, consider journaling on your experiences and/or sharing your conclusions, and any resolutions you make as a result, with a close friend or family member. If you're married or heading in that direction, conduct this exercise individually and then share it with your loved one. You may have a "light bulb moment" that changes the course of your life, but at the very least, you and the people that love you will better understand your background with money.

With that greater level of understanding, my wife will be less likely to see me as a greedy monster when she shares passionately about an improvement that she envisions for our home and I respond, "How much?" Conversely, I'll be less likely to utter those words at that moment in the first place!

Visit www.thefinancialcrossroads.com to find a template to use in creating your own Personal Money Story.

Tim Maurer

What you believe about money will determine what you will do for and with it. Right thinking leads to right actions, but those outward actions do not spring from nowhere. In his 1902 work entitled *As a Man Thinketh*, James Allen said, paraphrasing Proverbs 23, "Every action and feeling is preceded by a thought." Ralph Waldo Emerson postured, "The ancestor of every action is a thought." This isn't esoteric philosophy without application; it is practical advice that leads us to a better understanding of our interaction with money, and thereby, a better life.

The name of the weekly radio show that I co-host is "Money, Riches and Wealth." It's not what you think. Actually, the host of the show, Drew Tignanelli, derived the name from a study that he did on the origination of those three words, and his findings are powerful. "Money" means something very close to what we believe it to mean today—currency. "Riches" in its original context implies what you'd expect—money, with an extra helping of extravagance and a pinch of greed. "Wealth," however, has a far different meaning than that which is attributed to it today. The closest meaning to a modern word would be contentment. And isn't that what we desire when we're at our best? Contentment may be acompanied by money and even riches, but there are plenty of rich people who aren't wealthy by this definition. Contentment is attainable for any of us at any moment.

Money has no power other than that which we give it. It's hard to find contentment in a financial world that is filled with jargon, marketing, and economic bias. Let us show you the wisdom and knowledge that you need to give you a better understanding of things financial so that you can be *truly* wealthy.

Personal Money Story

Age	Description	Score
5	Birthday money received from relatives	10
5	Had to put the birthday money in bank	-5
9	Used money saved to buy bike	10
13	Spent $100 on game gear	5
15	Received money for services provided (pet sitting)	5
16	Opened own bank account	10
16	Crashed car had to pay $500	-10
18	Crashed car again had to pay deductible	-7
19	Paid mom back for air fare to/from spring break ($810)	-10
21	Bought car 0% interest $16k	10
21	Got part time job	10
22	Lost job	-10
22	Got married (no job)	0
23	Got small jobs	5
25	Got job with government contractor	10
27	Got job with US Government	10

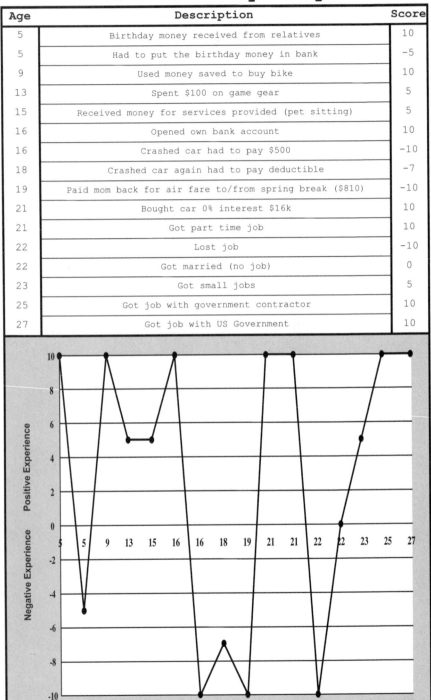

CART BEFORE THE HORSE

> Not only must we be good, but we
> must also be good for something.
>
> *Henry David Thoreau*

> The great and glorious masterpiece of
> man is how to live with a purpose.
>
> *Michel de Montaigne*

Most of us do not achieve our goals, financial or otherwise. The primary reason we fall short is not that we have unrealistic goals or a lack of ability to achieve them. It is because we have not completed an exercise of far greater importance than goal setting. Prior to establishing goals, we must understand the stuff in life that we want to be about. Stephen Covey calls them values, Ben Franklin called them virtues, but we'll call them Personal Principles. What are the underlying principles that guide you, and how do you want to make a mark on this world?

Establishing goals that are not supported by our Personal Principles can only achieve one of two dissatisfactory results. Either we feel the inadequacy of falling short of our aim, or we change our value system to conform to the goal. For example, if I'm reading a financial magazine that tells me that I need to have

$3 million dollars saved to retire comfortably by the age of 55 and I take the steps necessary to meet that goal, I may work two jobs that I hate and be perpetually absent from family functions and my kids' sports events. If "Being present physically, intellectually, and emotionally for my family" is one of my Personal Principles, you can imagine how difficult it would be to achieve the early retirement goal without compromising the underlying value. Goals that are prescribed to us by a parent, teacher, book, or financial advisor that are not supported by our Personal Principles have little chance of success. Conversely, when we align our goals in life with our Personal Principles, we have a very high success rate.

Ah...success. Is that ultimately what we desire? I don't think so. We long for fulfillment and contentment. Remember our definition of the word wealth? In the financial services industry, on television, and in books—even text books—wealth means one thing...dollar signs! If this is true, many among us would never have the opportunity to be wealthy and, therefore, would not enjoy the satisfaction of being financially "successful."

Stanley and Danko did an excellent job in their classic, *The Millionaire Next Door*, helping us better understand what financial success looks like. Their conclusion is that it doesn't really look any different than financial mediocrity. Most millionaires don't actually fly around in corporate jets and drive Maseratis. They drive pickup trucks and live in nondescript houses, and they don't see the benefit in bidets. They're successful in their dealings with money because they've put money in its rightful place as a means to an end, not the inverse. Success, then, is a natural byproduct of a contented life lived fulfilling your unique purpose.

Consider the slight difference in the two words *compelled* and *impelled*. The former you hear often, but not so much the latter. To be compelled is to have an external force move us to action. "I was *compelled* by my self-righteous sister to give up the family party on Thanksgiving to serve at the local homeless shelter." One who is impelled acts on a force that comes from within. "I was *impelled* to sacrifice food and football this Thanksgiving and, instead, serve those at the local homeless shelter who don't have the privilege of choice."

You're the only you, but most of us are so busy fulfilling an endless series of external requests on our time, talent, and treasure that we never take the opportunity to reflect on what our purpose really is. As often as is possible, be impelled to fulfill your own purpose in life, not compelled to live out someone else's.

Timeless Truth

Money will not make you happy. I hasten to add that neither will poverty make you happy.

In a recent study on happiness, it was determined that, beyond basic food, clothing, and shelter (approximately fifty thousand dollars in the U.S.) adding more money to the equation did not necessarily make one happy. Money without purpose is like fuel without a destination. It is useless if not dangerous to have around if you don't have a purpose.

I have written a dozen books, and I will never forget the day when an eminent financial planner and estate attorney called me to compliment me on my "book on finance." He said he had given over 1,000 of the books away, and he wanted me to know how much the book meant to him. I was flattered but baffled at the same time. I was glad that one of my books had found meaning in his life and in the lives of the clients he served; however, I wasn't aware that I had written a book on financial planning or estate planning.

When he told me he was referring to my book The Ultimate Gift, I had to stop and think about why that book was considered by this renowned professional to be a breakthrough in estate and financial planning.

The Ultimate Gift and the subsequent movie from 20th Century Fox based on the book, is a story about life, principles, goals, and values. Money is not the major theme of The Ultimate Gift or the sequel book, The Ultimate Life. I only used a billionaire character in the stories to try to put money into perspective. Then I realized the ultimate lesson about money is not about money. It's about life. The lesson is as personal and individualized as you and I.

We cannot do planning by looking at a financial statement any more than we could fit you with the perfect pair of shoes by talking to you on the telephone. Always remember, when you're talking to a financial planner, a lawyer, a CPA, insurance salesperson, banker, or anyone else you call upon to help you with your personal finances, the most they can accomplish is to make your money do what you want it to do in the context of your life. Letting them drive your future is like letting the gas station attendant tell you where to drive your car.

> Resource without direction, wealth without planning, and money without destiny is the height of human folly.

Jim Stovall

Once you have established your Personal Principles, it is then time to move on to setting your goals. Without goals, life is lived at the behest of a collection of circumstances. You're compelled to do so much by so many outside forces that you've no time for your personal, purposeful impulsions.

In order for a goal to be valid, it must meet the following four criteria: *specific, measurable, attainable,* and most importantly, *meaningful.*

"Go to the gym" is a specific enough goal, but without determining how many times per week you intend to go to the gym, the goal is not measurable. "Go to the gym seven days per week" is both specific and measurable, but with a spouse and three small children, it may not be attainable. And without a meaningful purpose, such as improving your self image or relieving stress, the most specific, measurable, and attainable physical fitness goal will go on unfulfilled. The meaning for your goals is found in your Personal Principles.

There are few areas where this practice of understanding your own Personal Principles and Goals is more vital than in your personal finances. Many of the people who render financial advice don't understand, or seek to understand, you and your Personal Principles. How then could they make the appropriate recommendations? They don't! And this is evidenced not in the financial plans that they write, but instead in the rate of their successful implementation.

The financial planning, psychological duo of Rick Kahler and Ted Klontz posit that over 80% of the financial planning recommendations that are made are not implemented![i] Is this because the people who have paid a financial planner to tell them what to do have somehow lost the motivation to do so? In some cases, yes, but in many cases, the planners are at fault for walking into their interaction with a preconceived list of recommendations (that work for them or someone like them) already on the tip of their tongue.

Financial planners think, talk, and act differently than most of their clients. They accidentally (and sometimes purposefully, as a sales tactic) use industry terminology that only makes sense in technical circles, shaming clients into nodding through meetings, too scared to show their justifiable ignorance and ask, "I'm sorry, what again is a QTIP trust and how is it used?" Or maybe even, "What is the difference between growth and value? Absolute or relative return? A stock or bond? A mutual fund??"

Economic Bias Alert!

Your financial planner has an economic bias that inevitably inhibits you from going through a thorough analysis of your values and goals. Most financial planners don't get paid until very late in the optimal financial planning process. This is especially true of the majority of advisors who work for proprietary product distribution companies—banks, brokerage firms and insurance companies, and even independent broker/dealers.

You see, they don't get paid until you implement the recommendations in your financial plan...which doesn't happen until you have chosen to accept a planner's recommendations...which doesn't happen until you've received the planners recommendations...which shouldn't happen until the planner has a very good understanding of your goals...which shouldn't happen until you've determined your foundation for those goals—your values.

The natural result is that most financial planners go into every meeting with a cookie-cutter mentality; in essence, they already know the goals that you "should" have and the steps that are required to meet your—their—goals. This doesn't make the planner a bad person, but if they're not going to get paid until you buy something, don't you see how they may be inclined to prefer to see that come to fruition sooner rather than later?

The solution? If you're working with a planner who seems to be putting his or her own goals above yours, make a new goal of yours to find a new financial planner.

Financial endeavors are especially hollow without goals that meet each of the four criteria. Saving for retirement in a 401k or IRA for every generation from the Baby Boomers on has become as common as brushing your teeth or tying your shoes, but these accounts are notoriously under-funded and poorly managed because the goals are not clear. Why do I want to kiss goodbye a meaningful part of every paycheck that could otherwise be spent? If you don't know the answer to that, you'll never be a good retirement saver. Or, if you deprive yourself and your family of every comfort, convenience, and luxury for the purpose of saving as much as you possibly can for retirement, you may be left with a pile of cash with no earthly idea how to spend it and no one to spend it with.

Timely Application
Personal Principles & Goals

This Timely Application also qualifies as Timeless Truth. Ben Franklin is a legendary historical figure for many reasons, not all of them noble. But there is little doubt that his was a life of purpose. He deliberately set forth to accomplish certain things, yes, but his accomplishments sprang from what he referred to as his personal virtues. These were the values and character traits that he hoped would mark his accomplishments on this earth. I encourage you to read these not to make them your own, but to get an idea of how to discern your own. If you try to make Ben Franklin's virtues and goals your own, you're likely to fall short of your unique potential and purpose, but the study of the principles that marked the life of a great man are sure to inspire as well as entertain:

Ben Franklin's 13 Virtues

Temperance: Eat not to dullness and drink not to elevation.

Silence: Speak not but what may benefit others or yourself. Avoid trifling conversation.

Order: Let all your things have their places. Let each part of your business have its time.

Resolution: Resolve to perform what you ought. Perform without fail what you resolve.

Frugality: Make no expense but to do good to others or yourself: i.e. waste nothing.

Industry: Lose no time. Be always employed in something useful. Cut off all unnecessary actions.

Sincerity: Use no hurtful deceit. Think innocently and justly; and, if you speak, speak accordingly.

Justice: Wrong none, by doing injuries or omitting the benefits that are your duty.

Moderation: Avoid extremes. Forbear resenting injuries so much as you think they deserve.

Cleanliness: Tolerate no uncleanness in body, clothes or habitation.

Chastity: Rarely use venery but for health or offspring; never to dullness, weakness, or the injury of your own or another's peace or reputation.

Tranquility: Be not disturbed at trifles, or at accidents common or unavoidable.

Humility: Imitate Jesus and Socrates.

Deliberate over that which you want to mark your life. Write down a word or phrase that will be your Personal Principle, and then give a sentence or two of explanation. These are yours, but I encourage you to share them with a good friend and your spouse, if applicable. (One of the nuanced difficulties and benefits of marriage is the necessity of allowing your Personal Principles to be folded into those of your spouse. If your spouse is a willing participant, encourage him or her to complete this exercise as well to develop a set of Unifying Principles for your family.)

Your Goals, especially your financial goals, may be better informed when you complete this book, but practice now writing down a few goals that meet the specific, measurable, attainable, and meaningful criteria, then come back to them after completing the book. Financial goals will then be broken down into specific steps to meet those goals in your Action Plan.

Visit www.thefinancialcrossroads.com to find templates to use in creating your own Personal Principles & Goals.

Tim Maurer

What does this discussion of Personal Principles and Goals have to do with money? Everything! In our modern times, money is the facilitator of virtually everything we do. If, like Franklin, frugality is something that you want to mark your life, it will impact how and when you spend money. If health and exercise is a value of yours, you'll be required to purchase running shoes, athletic apparel, and likely even make a monthly expenditure for a local health and fitness club. If artistic expression is a Personal Principle of yours, you'll be purchasing a musical instrument or easel and paying for lessons. If your aim is to serve the underserved in your community, money will aid you in your pursuit. A prerequisite for good money management is an understanding of your Personal Principles.

The only guarantees in financial planning are *surprises, change,* and *failure.* Successful application of your Personal Principles and Goals requires three important counteragents: margin, flexibility, and grace.

Surprises *require* margin.

Change *requires* flexibility.

Failure *requires* grace.

Life is not linear or predictable. In actuality, it's a downright mess! Without margin in your Personal Financial Statements (to be discussed in the next chapter), surprises can bury you, leading to revolving debt, foreclosure, and bankruptcy. Since the only constant in personal finance is change, it requires us to be flexible and adjust to the inevitable changes in our careers, government, and personal lives. Remember, that which is not flexible in a changing environment breaks. The final guarantee—failure—is a tough one to swallow. Once we've purposed ourselves to accomplish a goal, we don't want to acknowledge the possibility of failure, but if we don't give ourselves grace when we do fail, we're unlikely to set another lofty goal.

Once you have laid the foundation of your Personal Principles and Goals, you are ready to start crunching some numbers. We'll begin with an examination of the three Personal Financial Statements in the next chapter.

[i] *Facilitating Financial Health* by Rick Kahler, CFP® and Ted Klontz, PhD

Personal Principles...

Principle	Explanation
1	
2	
3	
4	
5	
6	
7	
8	
9	
10	

...and Goals

Principle	Goal	Specific Measurable Attainable Meaningful ✔✔✔✔
		☐ ☐ ☐ ☐
		☐ ☐ ☐ ☐
		☐ ☐ ☐ ☐
		☐ ☐ ☐ ☐
		☐ ☐ ☐ ☐
		☐ ☐ ☐ ☐
		☐ ☐ ☐ ☐
		☐ ☐ ☐ ☐
		☐ ☐ ☐ ☐
		☐ ☐ ☐ ☐

HOW TO SPEND $1 MILLION AT STARBUCKS

The art of living easily as to money is to pitch your scale of living one degree below your means.

Sir Henry Taylor

Pretend for a moment that your personal life is actually a business. The Board of Directors is getting together to review your stewardship of the company's finances. Would they be pleased with your performance as the company's Chief Financial Officer? For many of us, if we conducted our occupational endeavors the way we manage our household finances, we'd be fired! I encourage you to manage your household finances as though you are a business, and that management centers around three financial statements that are just as effective when used to manage You, Inc. as they are in Fortune 500 companies.

The three Personal Financial Statements are:

    1) Personal Cash Flow Statement

    2) Personal Balance Sheet

    3) Personal Budget

An easy way to remember these is to view them as representing the past, present, and future. Your cash flow statement represents your financial past; the balance sheet, your financial present; and the budget, your financial future. Many confuse these three statements, or assume that the singular statement they use is sufficient. But without all three statements working in conjunction, the value of any one of them is reduced to almost nothing.

Timeless Truth

Cash, time, fitness, and a number of other areas of our lives are easy to manage. With all due respect to my friend, colleague, and co-author Tim Maurer, it's simple to manage household cash flow. Anyone can do it. It is agonizingly hard, however, to manage ourselves.

Money, time, and fitness are governed by fairly simple equations. Most of us know what to do. We fail because we don't do what we know.

Success in the money arena or any other is a matter of being productive. Productivity is a function of determining what we want in our lives and making effective progress toward that goal.

Recently, I teamed up with Steve Forbes and legendary coach John Wooden to conduct research and write a book called Ultimate Productivity. In that book, I revealed that being productive is simply a matter of managing our motivation, communication, and implementation.

All of us are unique. We all have strengths and weaknesses that will affect our productivity. This level of productivity will show up in every area of our life, including money.

Through my productivity research, I developed a Productivity Profile that will allow you to answer 60 simple questions to reveal how you are motivated, receive and send communication most effectively, and the most productive method for you to implement. You, as well as your friends and colleagues, can take that Productivity Profile and receive a free assessment simply by going to www.UltimateProductivity.com and entering your access code: 586404.

Once you have determined how you are motivated and the best ways for you to be productive in your communication and implementation, you need to start managing today and tomorrow. Everything we do today affects the future just as everything we want in the future must be instigated today.

Jim Stovall

Recently, I learned about the results of a 20-year exhaustive psychological study conducted at Stanford. This psychological test was done on a number of preschool children who were then followed for decades to determine how they succeeded in their lives. The Marshmallow Test may be one of the most accurate and precise indicators of future accomplishment. It is simple but poignant and goes to the heart of all success principles.

In the Marshmallow Test, a preschool child is taken into a room with a small table and one chair. The child is seated in the chair, and one marshmallow is placed on the table before the child. The child is then instructed by an adult that he or she will be left alone for just fifteen minutes. During that time, the child can eat the one marshmallow or wait until the adult returns in a few minutes, at which time the child will be given two marshmallows. This seems ridiculously simple as do most great tests and lessons in life.

Those children who eat the marshmallow immediately, grow up to have all sorts of trouble throughout their lives. They are more likely to have career problems, substance abuse problems, and financial problems than their contemporaries who see the wisdom in waiting a few moments and delaying their gratification in order to receive two marshmallows. This principle of self discipline and delayed gratification, when learned as a small child and carried out through adulthood, results in better academic careers, athletic and social experiences, and successful employment and business endeavors. It's not a matter of one marshmallow or two. It's a matter of learning to sacrifice now for something better later.

Once you begin to understand success principles and compounding returns, you will understand how expensive the single marshmallow is now, and you'll also understand that if you'll delay the gratification by not eating the marshmallow instantly, your reward will be much more than two. Success doesn't add. It multiplies geometrically. As you go through your Personal Financial Statements, be willing to pay the price for that future reward.

The Personal Cash Flow Statement is an accounting of your past expenditures. Most people who say they budget are actually only tracking their cash flow after they've already spent the money. It is true, however, that you can't prepare a reasonable budget without knowing—and understanding—your cash flow. This task is made much easier with the advent of online banking and online aggregation tools which we'll discuss later in the chapter. Now you can effectively view and manage your cash flow without even lifting a pencil.

Timely Application
Personal Cash Flow Statement

Through the online banking systems of most banks, you can now view a history of your expenditures for specific periods of time in seconds. If you prefer to do things the old fashioned way, your recent bank statements will also show you your spending past. Seeing what you've spent is step one in creating a cash flow statement. Step two is categorizing your spending. What have you spent money on? This can be an eye opening experience.

Visit www.thefinancialcrossroads.com to find a template to use for the creation of your Personal Cash Flow Statement.

Tim Maurer

My good friend (Scott, we'll call him) is, by any standards, wealthy. His net worth is in the multi-millions. In early 2008, he decided to do a complete analysis of his cash flow.

What he learned so shocked him that he now tracks his monthly cash flow with religious fervor. He realized that in the calendar year of 2007, he had spent over $12,000—at Starbucks alone! You're probably thinking, "I know Starbucks is a little pricey, but it's impossible to spend $12,000 at a coffee store in one year!" Here's how it happened:

Scott lives in an affluent neighborhood in one of the most expensive cities in the world, where there is a Starbucks less than a block from his residence. In the morning, afternoon, and evening, Scott would treat himself and his wife to a Venti-mochalattesoychaifrapacino (or something like that) at the bargain price of $5.50 per. That means that he spent $33 every day. Anyone who appreciates Starbucks knows that an addiction of that nature can simply not be broken once it is well established, so after 365 days of that, Scott spent $12,045 in 2007!

If Scott was willing to break with his addiction and put the $12,045 into an investment account that earned 7% per year, in thirty years his account would be worth $1,137,780! Yeah, tracking your cash flow is important, and it is possible to spend a million dollars at Starbucks!

The Personal Balance Sheet is a snapshot of your assets and liabilities at a particular moment in time. What do you own and what do you owe? Many of my college students at Towson University will be graduating with a negative net worth. Armed with their accounting and finance degrees, they'll hopefully get good jobs to start creating consistent cash flow, but they'll be starting in the red thanks to college and auto loans. In our next chapter, we'll discuss debt in detail, but the completion of your own balance sheet will give you an aggregated view of your financial realm.

Timely Application
Personal Balance Sheet

Collect all of the statements for every bank account, investment account, 401k, IRA, etc. along with every statement detailing your debts: mortgages, auto loans, college loans, credit cards, etc. Add up your assets and your liabilities and then subtract the latter from the former. The resulting balance is your NET WORTH.

Visit www.thefinancialcrossroads.com to find a template to use for your Personal Balance Sheet.

Tim Maurer

The objective for your balance sheet is relatively simple; you want to make your net worth a positive number, and then you want to see it rise each year. The mechanism for doing so is your Personal Budget.

Most people mistake tracking their spending after-the-fact (the cash flow statement) for the Personal Financial Statement that represents the future (the budget). It's nearly impossible to create a budget without first having completed the exercise of creating a cash flow statement. With that in hand, you're ready to create your budget, the projection of what your spending should be in the future. For most of us, our income and expenses run on one of a few variants of a monthly cycle;

therefore your budget should also be computed on a monthly basis, although it is also helpful to view it on a quarterly, semi-annual, and annual basis to fully appreciate how much your personal vices and creature comforts cost you.

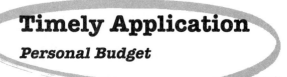

Timely Application
Personal Budget

Every dollar that you expect to receive in the coming month should be allocated to a budgetary category. Your fixed expenses are the easiest to plan for, but you must also estimate what your variable expenses are going to be. You also can't forget about those expenses that come quarterly, semi-annually, or annually. This should include things like your water bill or insurance premiums that you pay on an interval other than monthly, but it should also include those personal expenses like vacations.

Visit www.thefinancialcrossroads.com to find a template to use for your Personal Budget.

Tim Maurer

Unplanned vacation spending is the most notable culprit that throws off millions of non-budgeters every year. Each of these irregular expenses should be broken down into a monthly amount that will enter a budget category to be there waiting for you when you need it.

The key to wise and low stress management of your personal finances is margin. You've doubtless heard that you're supposed to keep a specific amount of cash as an emergency reserve on your balance sheet. This is true, but in the real world, most people making up to $150,000 per year live paycheck-to-paycheck. The first step to having adequate emergency reserves is getting one month ahead of your bills. A cash flow innovator, Jesse Mecham, developed software designed to help people do just that. I spoke with Jesse, the architect of YNAB.com (You Need A Budget), and discussed the origins of his product.

The inception of his widely used budgeting software was brought about by necessity. He and his bride-to-be were examining how their finances would be joined. Jesse, an accountant by trade, recognized the importance of analyzing and planning their cash flow together to stay on top of things financially. The first of YNAB's four rules, the foundation of his product, is "Stop living paycheck-to-paycheck." Jesse told me, "When living on the financial edge, you don't have the option to plan wisely." If your monthly income immediately exits your checking account to pay for due bills, you know this all too well. By getting only one month ahead, your income this month is set aside to pay next month's bills. This increases the ease of bill paying, reduces the stress of imminent collectors, and gets you off to a running start on that emergency reserve, which we'll discuss in greater detail in the next chapter.

In addition to being imperative in your balance sheet, margin is also a key component in your successful budget. That means that any line items or categories whose monthly allotment can be variable should be estimated in the upper portion of that range. If every category is pegged at a hopeful number that can often not be achieved, the process of budgeting will become a fearful one and will eventually be abandoned as a failed attempt.

Why do the majority of income earning Americans not budget? "It's too difficult," is a comment that I've heard. Tedious it may be, but difficult, it most certainly is not! Consider this recent interaction that I had with my three-year-old son: Connor, our second son, emulates his father's character and personality traits, for better and for worse. Even at his young age, his aversion to succumbing to authoritative direction is unmatched—that is, since I was his age. One night, Connor decided that the tedium of brushing his teeth before bedtime was simply more than he was willing to accept, and he demanded an indefinite waiver. A battle of wills ensued.

He screamed and wriggled every little muscle in his body as I brushed his teeth—by force. After three nights of this, I decided to take a new tack. I said, more than partially exasperated, "Connor! You don't have to brush your teeth if you don't want to. But, if you don't, your teeth will start to rot, causing a lot of pain, and then they will fall out!" He said, "Get out of my way; I need to brush my teeth!" Now, when in the swirl of activity surrounding bedtime, if I forget to remind Connor of his duty, he will remind me that, "Dad, I need to brush my teeth so they don't fall out!"

Most of us don't budget because we say it's too much work. It is work, but then like many other little annoyances in life, they become part of our regimen and no longer bother us. Do you despise brushing your teeth in the morning and at night? No, you just do it (now flossing, that's another matter!). These daily disciplines stop grating on our nerves and become natural and neutral, if not even a source of peace as we relish, if only for a second, checking off one of the day's to-dos.

Once you've developed your mechanism for the management of your personal financial statements, it will take little more time than brushing your teeth, but far less time than a daily physical workout, another incredibly gratifying discipline. Like all the other disciplines, you don't have to manage your personal financial statements if you don't want to...but if you don't, one day, you're likely to discover that you've fallen into fiscal ruin!

Aaron Patzer, the creator of the personal finance website Mint.com, has made this task a great deal easier for us. Mint aggregates all of your financial instruments and accounts. After the initial work of inputting your online usernames and passwords for your bank and investment accounts as well as your mortgages and credit cards, as often as you open the Mint.com page, you'll see precisely what your balances are in each—on one single page. Your personal balance sheet is updated to the minute right before your very eyes. In addition, you can create a rough budget and also track your expenses, so the site also helps you in your cash flow and budget management. The best news is that Mint brings this all to your computer, laptop and even your iPhone for the low, low price of nothing—nada!

In our discussion, Aaron acknowledged to me that they certainly do have an economic bias, and that is that they accept advertising revenue and even spotlight certain products and services from which they receive compensation, but I can attest to their relatively benign presence on the site. Frankly, I'd rather pay nothing for Mint and look past advertising that I don't need. Remember, it's not that economic bias is always wrong. It just requires recognition so that we're more informed consumers.

I was introduced to Jesse of YNAB and Aaron of Mint.com as I surveyed all of the budgeting and cash flow tools available on the market. I believe that these are two that rise to the top. As I mentioned, Mint is the best aggregator of personal financial information on the market and has received notoriety from other third party resources like *Kiplinger's Personal Finance* and *Money* magazine. The cost to utilize the service is zero dollars.

YNAB, in my estimation, is the best product for the serious budgeter. It trains and refines you and your process. The cost, as of my recent discussion with Jesse, is $49, and I have found it worth every penny. And, while we're talking economic bias, I think it's only fair that I mention that I did not accept anything from either of these young entrepreneurs, and they did not seek me out. I put them up against the biggest names in the business, conspicuously missing from our "Best Of" (Microsoft Money and Quicken), and found them to be superior in just about every way, and also better values.

Many, if not most, Americans saw their personal net worth decline year-over-year in 2008. Most of our houses lost 5-30%, and that is the largest item on most Personal Balance Sheets. The next largest item, your 401k(s) and/or IRA(s), also likely backtracked in 2008. The broader U.S. market indices lost around 40%, and with most investors following the preferred investment "logic" of the largest financial institutions, they felt the full brunt of the downturn's wrath.

These losses and their corresponding financial, emotional, and relational pain was the impetus for this book and will be discussed in much greater detail in the chapters on investing, but the origin of much of our economic calamity is found in these three Personal Financial Statements. Banks whose policies invited homeowners to take on more housing debt than is reasonable deserve significant blame and should be made accountable, but we are the Chief Financial Officers of our Personal Balance Sheets, not the loan officer at the bank or mortgage company. It was common practice for banks to offer mortgages and home equity loans and lines up to, and in some cases even over, 100% of the value of the property. What did banks or homeowners think would happen when the inevitable year or years came where their homes lost value!?

Shame on them and shame on us, but why would any of that matter so much if people just kept making their mortgage payments? The answer is that it wouldn't have, and it doesn't matter to those whose ability to make their mortgage payments is not hampered. But for those who utilized adjustable rate mortgages, HELOCs that were tied to a variable rate, or those whose compensation diminished or expired as a result of the recession, they began having trouble making their payments or chose to give up, hoping for some sort of personal bailout. This, too, is a Personal Financial Statement problem, because so many people consume most or all of their disposable cash flow, have little to no buffer or emergency savings on their balance sheet, and outspend their budget on a monthly basis, backfilling it with whatever equity was left in the home—until the unsustainable double-digit growth on their homes reversed.

Let's learn from this mess. Let's seek and find the peace that accompanies wise financial stewardship and explore the problem at the core of Americans' financial troubles in our next chapter, *More vs. Enough.*

Cash Flow Statement

Cash Flow	In/Out	Category	Period
NET CASH FLOWS			

Balance Sheet

Assets	
Asset	Value
TOTAL Assets	**$0**

Liabilities		
Liability	Balance	✔/x
TOTAL Liabilities	**$0**	
NET WORTH	**$0**	

Budget

Category	Spent Last Month	Budget This Month
Alimony		
Auto Insurance		
Cable TV		
Child Support		
Dividends		
Dry Cleaning		
Entertainment		
Fast Food		
Gifts		
Groceries		
Home Insurance		
Internet/TV		
Land Phone		
Mobile Phone		
Mortgage		
Property Taxes		
Rent		
Restaurants		
Taxes		
Utilities		
Water Bill		
Other:		
Other:		
Other:		
Other:		
Other:		
Other:		
Other:		
Other:		
Other:		
Other:		
Other:		
TOTAL	**$0**	**$0**

MORE VS. ENOUGH

> [Americans] are borrowing and spending as if there were no tomorrow, and they are investing as if there were no yesterday.
>
> *Bill Bonner and Addison Wiggin*

> ...the borrower is servant to the lender.
>
> *Proverbs 22:7*

Years of success and prosperity in our economy have created a consumer-based society. We are no longer worried about our physical or financial survival; therefore, we have undertaken a new challenge. We have embraced the illusive challenge of accumulating more. Please understand that there is absolutely nothing wrong with enjoying material possessions. It is important, however, to draw a distinction between the possessions we have and those possessions that have us.

Timeless Truth

If your goal is to acquire a certain standard of living or lifestyle for you and your family or for your future security, this is admirable; however, if it is your burning desire to keep up with the image portrayed by the commercials on television or in the glamour magazines, you have been afflicted with the dreaded disease called <u>more</u>.

More is a disease which feeds upon itself like a thirst that can never be quenched. As we rush about aimlessly trying to accumulate more, we become aware of even a greater number of things we don't have and must obtain. Instead of seeking the impossible goal of reaching more, we should, instead, seek the internal goal which is called enough.

Ironically, we can find people who are literally billionaires who have long ago lost count of all of their possessions; however, these people are still driven on that eternal quest for more. On the other hand, there are people of seemingly modest means who have attained the state of enough. They no longer judge themselves based on what they have, but instead, on who they are. They have come to the conclusion that it is more important to be someone special than to have a vast accumulation of possessions. They have reached a state of being where they understand that it is not important to be a "human having." It is only important to arrive as a "human being."

In the final analysis, many times reaching the state of enough will give you the confidence and peace of mind to be an even better person who will attract more success, resulting in the tangible possessions that have become such an addiction in our society. Focus on who you are, and allow what you have to become a result of your personal success.

Jim Stovall

"Freeeeee-dooooom!" Mel Gibson played William Wallace, in the 1995 Academy Award winning movie, *Braveheart*, set in Scotland in the year 1280 A.D. I hate to spoil the ending if you've never seen it, but Wallace does eventually get caught and is recommended to be "purified by pain," dying at the hands of a British torturer and executioner. After putting Wallace through a goodly number of physical atrocities, the executioner gives him a final chance to pledge his allegiance to the brutal king, Edward "The Long Shanks," who is, incidentally, on his death bed as well (and conveniently within ear shot). Instead of begging for mercy, Mel yells out "Freedom!" at the top of his lungs, yanking every ounce of satisfaction away from the dying King Edward.

Financial freedom and flexibility is what I want for you. Despite the multi-million dollar line-up of clever commercials from credit card companies that lure your business with the hollow promise of financial freedom and flexibility, it is the over-utilization of their products that will most assuredly lead to financial bondage and submission. Financial freedom and flexibility is found in low or no debt and plenty of liquid savings. And, since your run-of-the-mill savings account doesn't offer a whole lot of sex appeal, I hereby submit for your consideration the "Freedom Fund" or your "Braveheart Account", whatever you need to call that savings account to remember its purpose.

The inverse of freedom is bondage; the inverse of savings is debt. The two are inextricably intertwined. One is the problem and the other the solution. Before you flip to the next chapter because you don't have an ounce of credit card debt, you're comfortable with your level of savings, and you've never missed a mortgage payment, don't leave us just yet. We will be discussing the insidious enslavement of revolving debt, but we're also going to tackle the question of whether there is such a thing as "good debt." And even if you don't have any debt—not even a mortgage—I still want you to read this chapter if only to give you educational material for those under your mentorship.

Our current financial crisis may be the best thing that ever happened to us financially. It's hard for me to write that, and it may also be hard to read it if you're one of the many who have suffered in this time; but the primary lesson that American citizens, American financial institutions, American businesses, and (hopefully) the American government have learned in the last 18 months is that we must not borrow and spend as if there were no tomorrow and invest as if there were no yesterday. If you are a young professional, I hope you will internalize this truth and allow it to be a reminder when you're tempted to fall into bad spending and saving habits. If you're close to retirement, the pain will be greater and the outlook more grim, but you also have a way to benefit from this difficult lesson, if only to give strong encouragement to your children and grandchildren not to fall into the same trap.

What brought us to this point? Affluenza. As reported by PBS in a special that aired long enough ago that its website still offers to sell you a copy on VHS, Affluenza is "the bloated, sluggish, and unfulfilled feeling that results from efforts to keep up with the Joneses. An epidemic of stress, overwork, waste, and indebtedness caused by dogged pursuit of the American Dream. An unsustainable addiction to economic growth." I'm guilty. Are you?

Pat Goodman, a close friend and mentor of mine, has a number of memorable maxims that I wish I'd come up with. He encourages me to live a life of purpose when reminding me that "You go no place by accident." But it's this prophetic truism of Pat's that seems to ring especially true when taking on Affluenza-driven debt. "You not only have to want what you want; you have to want what your wants lead to."

You not only have to want that bigger house; you have to want to ruin your credit in foreclosure if your Adjustable Rate Mortgage sends your mortgage rate to the moon. You not only have to want to spend all of your discretionary income today instead of saving for emergencies; you have to want to settle for that job that you don't love when you lose the job you did because you didn't have the emergency reserves to hold out for the right position. You not only have to want to buy that flat screen TV on your 0% credit card for a year; you have to want to pay the 21% retroactive interest if you haven't paid it off in full on the 366th day. You not only have to want to take on debt to give you immediate gratification; you have to want to deal with all of debt's friends—interest payments, loss of freedom, collections, foreclosure, and bankruptcy.

It's important now to remember a fundamental theme of this book introduced in the very first chapter and illustrated throughout. Money is not the root of all evil. It's a neutral tool to facilitate the furtherance of relationships. The use of debt and the business of lending are not inherently evil either, but I struggle to write that they are purely neutral. Debt is always shadowed by an element of bondage because the indebted is contractually obligated and beholden to someone or something. Wise utilization of debt can be used to positive economic benefit, without question, but the elimination of debt grants an uncommon level of peace that is profound and prolonged. I can account for its validity from the stories of numerous clients, several of whom reported that the sense of unburdening they felt upon the dissolution of that final piece of debt—possibly even a small mortgage with a good interest rate—was visceral and lasting. Whether you've paid off your debt or not, don't you long to do so?

But what advice do many economists and politicians give us at this time, even as we are on the verge of converting the financial stress and pain we've felt to the resolute practice of living within our means? "Buy real estate! Buy cars! Buy computers and TVs! Spend, spend, spend!" It frustrates me horribly to hear economists and financial commentators on the radio or on television suggest that the only path back to economic prosperity is for consumers to get back out there spending. How could they be so short-sighted to suggest that the best course forward is for more of what got us in trouble in the first place? A newly sober alcoholic will end his painful withdrawal symptoms with the rapid consumption of a bottle of Jack Daniels, but it most assuredly will not aid him in the path to freedom.

Most of those who are indebted do not actually have a pathological debt problem. It's a cash flow problem, a budgeting problem, and most often, a savings problem. In the last chapter, we talked a lot about how to put in place a great cash flow and budgeting system. We also mentioned the importance of margin in the management of your personal finances, and there is no better example of margin than the mythical "emergency savings." Emergency savings is that financial elephant in the room. Financial writers and planners have adequately educated everyone on the need, but much like flossing your teeth, everyone knows you're supposed to do it, but no one does it!

No one does it, that is, until they feel some pain. That is how I can suggest that this current crisis is a good thing for us, on both the personal and institutional level. It gives us the opportunity to see precisely how painful it can be to find ourselves on the wrong side of the debt/savings ratio. At this moment, the market "only" fell 50%, and unemployment is "only" inching up towards the 10% mark. I say "only" here because during the Great Depression, those amounts were 90% and 25%, respectively. While later generations of Americans are chided for their short-term memories, that was not a problem for those in the Greatest Generation.

A dear friend of mine, now in her late 80s, lived in a time when she felt and saw the direct impact of the Great Depression. She is a widow who has lived most of her life in a modest Baltimore row home. She never, throughout her working years, took a vacation. Never. She worked well past retirement age, even as defined by Social Security. She has no debt—of course—and although her net worth is in the millions, she has never stopped saving. The vast majority of her savings are in investment vehicles that are guaranteed by the full faith and credit of the United States government, and she invested dribs and drabs in various banks within walking distance because she didn't trust the solvency of any one. Did I mention that she never even took a vacation?!

Her story is not uncommon. I've met with multiple Depression Babies who literally had cash buried in the back yard in Mason jars to guard against the insolvency of the American financial system. We may be able to look at their situation now and say, "That's crazy!" or "That's ridiculous!" but I assure you that if you had lived in a time where you lost 90% of your nest egg and one-in-four of your friends were out of a job, you may see financial security a bit differently.

So what have you heard about emergency reserves? Rules of thumb range from one to 12 months, and no one seems to know what they need. And, is it three months of expenses or income? This and most rules of thumb in personal finance are over-simplifications that are often tossed aside because of their impersonal feel. We'll tell you what you should have for your emergency reserves (and why you should have it) and rely on your intimate knowledge of your own finances to help dictate your ultimate course.

The three factors of which to be cognizant when determining your personal rule of thumb for emergency reserves are the following:

1) **The number of sources of family income:** whether or not a household is reliant on one or two income earners.

2) **The nature of business supporting those sources:** a tenured professor simply has more job security than a mortgage banker.

3) **The variability in those income sources:** whether the income is derived from a pure salary or based largely or completely on bonuses and/or commissions.

I do suggest that your emergency savings be computed in denominations of months, as we're generally estimating the severity or length of a job loss or income reduction. To that end, maintaining whatever number of months of your expenses is sufficient. While most people need the vast majority of their income to cover their expenses, rendering this debate largely moot, there are those who make significantly more than they spend and save. If someone is making $13,000 per month and "using" only $6,500, there is simply no need for them to warehouse twice the cash they need in a liquid account with minimal opportunity for growth. Consider the following matrix for monthly savings:

3 months' expenses for dual income household with salaried workers in stable jobs and industries.

4-6 months' expenses for single income household with salaried worker in stable job and industry.

6 months' expenses for dual income household with variable incomes in stable jobs and industries.

7-9 months' expenses for single income household with variable income in stable job and industry or salaried worker in unstable industry.

9-12 months' expenses for dual or single income household with variable income in unstable job and/or cyclical or volatile industry.

12 months' expenses or more for self-employed and business owners.

I bet no one has ever told you why some multiple of a 30 day period is used to create these rules, so let's examine that. In our three month example, if someone lives in a dual income household where both income earners work in a stable industry, probability would suggest that it is unlikely that either would lose their job; but if one of them did, it could take up to a few months to shine up the resume and find a position that meets his or her expectations. They should have three months of their combined income, though, just in case they run into one of those financial perfect storms where a job loss is followed by a leaky roof and a broken transmission in the mini-van. The additional months tacked on to other households reflects their household potential for financial risk.

The location of the above savings is generically suggested only to be in liquid, FDIC protected savings. This is a good rule of thumb, but can be overly conservative for balances that are especially large. For example, the business owner making $250,000 per year will ideally have $250,000 of liquid savings at his or her disposal, but as long as the business is well established and in a stable industry, the entirety of the savings should not be in a low interest bearing savings account. A healthy portion should be in pure cash with the remainder in a conservative, liquid investment portfolio balanced between cash and CDs as well as an appropriate (for the economic times) balance of bond and even stock exposure. This will be discussed further in our chapters on investing.

Debt, we've established, is something that you are obligated to pay another person. Someone has granted you a credit—given you goods or services for the promise of future payment—or has loaned you cash to spend on whatever you choose (a personal loan) or has loaned you money against another asset like a car, boat, or house (a collateralized loan). These consumer loans can be revolving debt or installment debt. An auto loan or mortgage is an example of installment debt. The bank loans you $25,250 to buy a car at 7% and requires you to make payments of $500 per month for 60 installments (five years). Revolving debt has no set timetable for repayment and allows you to borrow perpetually up to a maximum line of credit. Credit cards and Home Equity Lines of Credit (HELOC) are examples of revolving debt.

How then do we differentiate between "Good Debt" and "Bad Debt?" I'm tempted to suggest that bad debt is any kind that requires you to owe money to someone else—all of it! I do believe that everyone should be working in the direction of having no debt, and I can better segregate the various types of debt as Bad Debt and Better Debt. Bad debt is any kind of debt on a depreciating asset—assets that lose value over time. This is furniture, computers, stereo equipment, clothes, jewelry, boats, motorcycles, and yes—this includes automobiles.

Dave Ramsey, one of the foremost voices on the subject of consumer debt, has no time for pleasantries, sympathy, or nuance. Here's what he has to say about automobile debt in his bestseller, *The Total Money Makeover*. "Taking on a car payment is one of the dumbest things people do to destroy their chances of building wealth." But you suggest, "Dave, I can get a car these days at MSRP with a 0% rate of interest." He responds, "A new car loses 60% of its value in the first four years; that isn't 0%." If you, like Steve Martin in the Saturday Night Live skit, "Don't buy stuff you cannot afford," (watch the skit on the link provided on this book's website) have no idea how one would purchase something without using credit, here's what Mr. Ramsey has to suggest regarding an auto purchase:

If you put $464 [the average car payment] per month in a cookie jar for just ten months, you have more than $4,000 for a cash car. I am not suggesting you drive a $4,000 car your whole life, but that is how you start without debt. Then you can save the same amount again and trade up to an $8,000 car ten months later and up to a $12,000 car ten months after that. In just thirty months, or two and a half years, you can drive a paid-for $12,000 car, never having made a payment, and never have to make payments again.

You say, "But I can't buy the car I want for $12,000!" It is true that some people simply don't care about the type of car they drive. They see it as the depreciating asset that takes them from one place to another. Warren Buffett, one of the world's richest men, is known for showing frugality in the area of automobiles. I, personally, am not one of those people. I have to subvert every materialistic fiber in my being when powerful sports cars drive by—especially German ones. If it weren't for my father—the electrical engineer who fits the beloved stereotype for frugality—and his insistence that I drive cheap beater cars as I grew up, I would've made a foolish mistake many years ago that would have had a significant impact on me today. Let me explain.

My first car was a Plymouth Horizon worth $4,000. "The Horizon," as it was known by my buddies (accompanied with a sweeping arm gesture illustrating the horizon), was not a "cool" car. But, it got the job done, and may have even played a role in saving my life, as it was the car in which I had a nearly-fatal car accident. It ended up at a junkyard where the owner said he couldn't believe that the driver actually lived. After my accident, some family friends took pity and gave me a 1981 Volkswagen Rabbit. One day, gears two and four of the manual five-speed transmission ceased to function. I drove it to the junkyard only using gears one, three, and five (can you picture the sights and sounds of that drive?). My parents again helped me out and fronted me $1,200 to replace the deceased rabbit with an ailing Pontiac Fiero (not to be confused with a Ferrari, the Fiero was the two-seater death trap known for its fiberglass body and unexplainable spontaneous combustion).

In my first successful capital transaction, I sold the Fiero for $1,400 to someone else who mistook it for cool and bought a 1980 Volkswagen Scirocco for $900, putting the profit into stereo equipment likely worth more than the vehicle. While I still think that is a classic vehicle generically speaking, mine was painted in the same color scheme as the owner's Winnabago, behind which it was trailered. Again, not particularly cool. After that car gasped its dying breath in the parking lot of the same junkyard that had my Horizon and my Rabbit, I purchased a Honda Civic for $4,000. I did need a vehicle to get to and from school and work and wasn't wise enough to save up the money to purchase it in cash, so my Dad co-signed on a short-term auto loan with our credit union.

Days after my wife and I were married, her financially-frugal husband asked her to sell her beautiful, paid-for Volvo S70 T-5. Unlike most Volvos, this thing was a true sports car with a turbo enhanced engine. But, our matrimony brought with it a small amount of bad debt, so I twisted my wife's arm to sell the Volvo and buy another Volkswagen (this time stepping up into the "big time" with a Jetta) for $12,000 and use the profit to pay off our remaining credit card debt. At that point, we had no bad debt. After the Jetta hit 180,000 miles and began to show signs of its looming demise, I bought, for the first time ever, a car that I really wanted. It's a BMW 3 Series. It looks like it is worth a fortune, but I bought it used from a great friend that I knew took fantastic care of it. With around 70,000 miles already on the car, I got it for under $10,000. Both of our family's cars now have over 100,000 miles on them, but they are makes and models that should easily go over 200,000.

Let me be clear on this point. There's nothing wrong, immoral, or unethical with buying new or expensive vehicles; but when we get caught up in the plight of Affluenza, we convince ourselves that we "need" that mini-van with the leather, swivel seats, and DVD players that fold down for each row because our family has grown. Once beholden to that monthly payment on a depreciating asset, we also lose our financial flexibility. Several years back, my wife and I took what would have been our car payment money—$500 per month—and purchased one-half of a lake cabin and property with a family member. If we had a brand new Hybrid Toyota Camry instead, we may have helped reduce carbon emissions, but we'd not have been able to enjoy the environment as much as we do at the lake.

Carmen Wong Ulrich is the author of *Generation Debt* and the host of an informative personal finance show on CNBC called *On the Money*. I've had the opportunity to work with Carmen on the show, and the topic on which we spend more time than any other is debt. I recently talked to Carmen about this topic, and she offered to share some of her personal experience with us.

Carmen got herself in and out of debt—twice. She didn't come from a family of significant means, so she and her mom worked waiting tables to put Carmen through her undergraduate education. She emerged with her degree, but still with $40,000 in student loan debt and another $2,000 in credit card debt. Upon graduating, she acknowledges that she felt entitled to getting some decent interview outfits and some furniture for her apartment. It is in some of those instances that she feels she crossed the line. Carmen began to succeed professionally and shortly thereafter had eliminated her bad debt.

Then came round two. Like many young people, Carmen got swept up in a relationship that ended after a two-month marriage. She was in grad school at the time, and getting through the divorce and staying on track with her education took a significant emotional and financial toll on her. She added, "Divorce always puts you in some form of debt," emotionally and/or financially.

The accrual and repayment of debt has significant emotional and financial components. Ulrich refers to her time with substantial debt as a period in her life when she felt imprisoned. But once she mastered the emotions, it was her financial acumen and discipline that enabled her to rid herself of bad debt. The first and most important step in debt elimination is the two-fold decision you make to eliminate your credit cards as a purchase option and divert discretionary cash flow to debt repayment acceleration.

It's normally not blatant, wasteful spending that allows credit card debt to accrue; it's the aggregation of a number of individual decisions, each of which on its own merit appears benign. Some, however, do develop an addiction to excessive spending and debt itself. In these situations, you and your financial planner should be augmented by a counselor or psychologist to help delve deeper into your past to explain the actions of the present and plot a successful course for the future.

Dave Ramsey acknowledges that he's not the first to suggest it, but he might be the most ardent promoter of, the "Debt Snowball" technique for getting out of debt. In his version of the technique, you list out each of your credit cards and respective balances. The idea is to make nothing more than minimum payments on all of your cards, except one. Pay any and all discretionary income you have towards the repayment of that single card. Then, once it's paid off, apply all of that overpayment to your next card, then the next, etc.

Ramsey suggests disregarding the interest rates and paying the cards down starting from the smallest balance to the largest, allowing for the "moral victory" of paying a few cards off early to get your snowball rolling. I recognize the psychological benefit of that technique, but the number cruncher in me computes that from a purely financial perspective, you'll save more money by paying the cards off in order of highest to lowest interest rates. If you need a swift kick in the pants to get things moving, go through Dave Ramsey's Total Money Makeover, and follow his debt elimination plan. If you're already resolved to getting rid of your debt and have the discretionary income to do it, consider getting your snowball rolling starting with the highest interest rate.

Economic Bias Alert!

Most bankers and credit card executives aren't bad people, but they do have an Economic Bias to keep you in debt, which is undoubtedly bad for you and your finances. Credit card companies do make money in ways other than charging absurd interest rates. I spoke with Odysseus Papadimitriou, formerly the senior marketing director at Capital One credit card company, now the CEO and Founder of Card Hub, a website designed to help consumers choose the best credit card for them. He told me that credit card companies could survive even if every borrower paid off his or her credit cards every month, because they charge the merchants 2.5% - 4% of every credit card transaction.

But have no doubt that credit card companies also seek a profit in the rates they charge and the minimum payment cycles offered to borrowers. Although it has improved and is likely to be changing more as a result of new credit card legislation, making the minimum payment on most credit card balances with most credit card companies has historically been a joke, stretching payment schedules on balances in the thousands out over decades.

Carmen Wong Ulrich told me of an analysis that

she did for her CNBC show, *On the Money*, in which a credit card borrower owed $25,000 across seven different cards. If she kept making the cards' minimum payments, she would pay them off in 15 years and 10 months. However, if she added an additional $200 to the payment on her card with the highest interest rate, all the cards would be paid off in two years and one month!

Lenders, and especially credit card companies, have an Economic Bias to KEEP you in debt. And, as Mr. Papadimitriou, the former credit card executive told me, "Borrowers must avoid the trap of consumer entitlement and always be working towards a debt-free end."

If Bad Debt is any debt on a depreciating asset, what are permissible forms of Better Debt? Debt can be wisely used in the purchase of appreciating assets, but with varying degrees of risk. Wise investors will seek to reduce the risk of borrowing to the greatest degree possible. A business should be an appreciating asset. An education should be an appreciating asset—for the student, not the parents—and as we'll discuss further in our chapter on education planning, one must not assume that every and any expense made in the pursuit of education is wisely spent.

A house is an appreciating asset over a long stretch of time and the best example of better debt. We re-learned a lesson in the last three years that real estate can and does lose money, and additionally that real estate will likely not be increasing in value with double-digit growth. When it does, you can be quite sure that it will eventually retreat back towards a more normal growth rate nominally above inflation and not out of reach of income earners. To reduce the debt risk of a home purchase, you should make a meaningful down payment (20% or more, ideally) and lock in your mortgage to a fixed rate. Although in some environments, an Adjustable Rate Mortgage (ARM) can work to your advantage, the increase in risk is not worth the potential benefit for most homeowners.

You've no doubt heard the term leverage used to describe debt. Two dollars in your pocket can buy precisely two dollars worth of goods or services. But what if I was willing to match your two with an additional eight to make a total of 10? That would add leverage to your investment, giving you more money to spend. If you spent that money wisely, and it doubled in value—to $20—then you could pay me back the eight that I loaned you and keep the 12 for yourself. On an investment of two dollars, that is a 600% rate of return! Not bad.

What if the investment didn't pan out? What if you put up two, I put up eight, and the $10 investment lost 50% and was sold for five dollars? You've lost your two and you still owe me eight, so you need to find another three bucks to supplement the remaining investment of five just to pay me back. In that case, the use of leverage resulted in a 250% loss!

You might think I'm over exaggerating to make a point here, but the percentages used above are carbon replicas of what happened to a large number of homeowners in the last several years. In the last decade, it was not at all uncommon to own a piece of real estate that would have doubled in price. In that example, if you put 20% down on the house—the old rule of thumb—you could have seen that 600% rate of return, although it would have been diminished by the interest paid on the mortgage (your leverage) and the transaction costs of buying and selling the property.

Many neighborhoods across the country have seen the value of their real estate cut in half within the last 12 months. If in 2007, you purchased a house for $300,000 in Cape Coral, Florida, one of the highest flying real estate markets during the housing boom, it is all too realistic to expect that your home is now worth $150,000. So, if you put down $60,000 (20%) and the bank pitched in the other $240,000, you would lose all of your investment and still be writing a check to the bank for $90,000!

Now comes the answer to the age-old question, "Should I work to pay off my mortgage as soon as possible or maintain a mortgage indefinitely for the tax breaks and to invest the money that I'd use to pay off my mortgage?" It seems that most financial advisors, accountants, bankers, and economists agree that a wisely-used mortgage is always a good thing. We disagree. In order to understand why we disagree, you must understand how we look at every financial decision.

In all financial decisions, there are two genres of thought to consider: economic and emotional. The economic considerations are quantifiable and available for analysis. The emotional are difficult to quantify and, in many financial circles, are considered worthless or insignificant. That's rubbish! Economic considerations are far from meaningless, but the point of most financial decisions is to determine how to make life better, not the other way around. Therefore, if you have the means to pay off your mortgage early—or at least by the time you choose to retire—and you'll sleep better at night for having done so, you absolutely should.

Economically speaking, it should almost always make sense to hold a mortgage if it is at a reasonably low, fixed interest rate and one is dedicating the surplus liquidity to wise, long-term investing. Here's how we support that claim: Let's assume you have $300,000 of cash and you'd like to buy a house for $300,000. If you can get a mortgage at 6% and you are able to deduct a meaningful amount of that mortgage payment from your taxable income, the effective rate of interest that you are paying is around 4.5%. If you are then able to earn 6% or 7% investing your cash, you can see how you're able to act as a bank would, and make money on the spread between the amounts that you are paying and the amount that you are earning. If you are young or behind on your retirement savings, consider following this path to help grow your asset base.

But, let's assume in the above scenario that in addition to the $300,000 that you had in cash, you had another $1 million, an amount that you had determined would supplement your Social Security and pension income to maintain your desired lifestyle. Additionally, having a $300,000 mortgage—or any amount of debt for that matter—would cause you a material amount of stress. That's when I would suggest sacrificing the spread, which is not guaranteed, for the peace of mind that is.

From whom did we learn to develop poor financial habits? For starters, Uncle Sam. Since this book is geared primarily towards personal finance, I don't want to divert too far into the financial woes of our government, but be assured that although government finance seems far removed from our personal lives, it has, does, and especially will be having a very significant impact on our personal finances. If you're interested in learning more on this topic, check out the movie,"I.O.U.S.A." You can find a link to its website on **www.thefinancialcrossroads.com.**

Once your cash flow is guided by the healthy discipline of a reasonable budget and you have established sufficient emergency reserves, bad debt should be a thing of the past. Your finances will be running like a business, and you'll have the opportunity to use credit cards to your advantage. I put virtually everything on a credit card that is paid off every month, but I do accrue points with each purchase. I pay no annual fee, no interest, and each year, I get enough points to add a meaningful chunk to my Christmas present budget category!

Timely Application
Personal Debt Audit & Elimination Plan

If you refer back to the Personal Balance Sheet you created, you will have already compiled your debt information in the liabilities section. Next to each liability, put an "X" next to Bad Debt and a check mark next to Better Debt. Then, transfer the Bad Debt to the Debt Elimination form available on our website and customize your Debt Elimination Plan. List the debts in the order in which you will pay them off. If you want to get that ball rolling faster emotionally, take Dave Ramsey's advice and pay your cards off in order of smallest to largest. If you want to save the most in interest payments, list the debts from the largest interest rate to the smallest.

When you make that last payment, celebrate! Take your NEXT month's payment, a significant chunk of cash flow that you'll now be able to plough into more generous budget categories and investment for the future, and throw yourself a party. Invite family and close friends who've supported you throughout, and enjoy the peace of mind that comes with being debt free.

If you don't have any Xs on your Debt Audit because you only have Better Debt, you need not put yourself through a financial boot camp like those with Bad Debt. But, deliberate over the debt you do have and consider whether or not a debt repayment acceleration plan may be right for you. If so, use the Debt Elimination form to plan your course of action.

Visit www.thefinancialcrossroads.com to find a template to use for your Personal Debt Audit & Elimination Plan.

Tim Maurer

I have a good friend who started investing some of his spare time and cash into a residential real estate business a few years ago. He made good money on a couple of transactions, and then came 2008. In no time, he was upside down on more than one property with no additional lines of credit on which to draw. Initially, he was very distraught. How could he have gone from having more materially than the average person to a negative net worth so fast? Did this mean he was a bad husband? Father? Steward? After struggling with this reality for months, he sent me an email with some God-given wisdom—in this case, it was in the form of two symbols. The two symbols that he focuses on when he starts to ruminate on his worsening financial situation are the dollar sign and the number zero. $0, because that is precisely how much you will take with you when you leave this earth.

Do you see the irony? He brought himself to financial ruin because he was too focused on rapid material accumulation—more. My friend got all the way to bankruptcy before realizing that Affluenza is a lifeless pursuit. He's been cured of Affluenza and is enjoying rebuilding with enough, but he still has a black mark on his and his wife's credit that may make it difficult to get a car, job, or house for the next seven years. Don't wait until you're faced with $0 to address your debt demons.

Unfortunately, being on a firm financial footing in your household is not a cure-all for Affluenza and the undying quest for more, but I do have a cure to offer—giving. Here are the three reasons why:

1) Personally, you'll feel good. Apparently we are wired to receive a physiological benefit from giving. That same sense of satisfaction that you get from a compliment from your friend or a raise from your boss comes from an endorphin rush sent through your body when you give. In addition to these individual senses of satisfaction, you will gradually feel a greater sense of control over your own financial situation when you give to

others. This positive response is especially heightened when you are able to connect yourself physically—not just fiscally—in this act of giving.

2) Mysteriously, you'll actually have more money. Once in a pattern of giving, you have a heightened sense of the needs of others, and the excess in your own budget. The net effect is that you may find yourself choosing to purchase one or two fewer five dollar lattes per week, staying in occasionally instead of going out, and finding more money in your bank account.

3) Practically, you'll save money on your taxes. When you give to a qualified charitable organization, you will generally receive an income tax deduction. Talk to your CPA to see how this will affect you personally.

As the ancient saying goes, "If I give water to others, I will never be thirsty." The benefits of charitable giving—for everyone, not just the wealthy—may be just as meaningful to the giver as the recipient.

Through the first four chapters, we've provided a strong foundation for your personal finances. Next, we'll discuss how to protect that foundation and your future plans.

Debt Elimination

Liability	Balance	Interest Rate	Minimum Payment	Additional Payment	Paid Off
TOTAL DEBT			$0		

DON'T BE SOLD INSURANCE!
MANAGE RISK

> Never ask a barber if you need a
> haircut.
>
> *Warren Buffett*

I f you purchased insurance for everything for which it was created, you wouldn't have any money left. You manage risk, however, every day whether you know it or not. Do you wear a seatbelt? You're managing risk. Do you mountain climb? You've made a risk management decision. Do you look at the number of calories or grams of fat before you eat something? You're a risk manager. A greater level of understanding regarding risk management techniques will help you better understand insurance. You'll know when you need insurance or need better insurance, and you'll also know when you need less or no insurance at all. Proper risk management results in a healthier personal bottom line today and in the future.

Timeless Truth

To paraphrase the Surgeon General of the
United States, life may be hazardous to your health.

All of us know that bad things happen to good people, and none of us are destined to get out of this life alive. There are few things less sexy, attractive, or appealing than thinking about insurance. When most of us think about insurance, we have visions of dealing with people we don't enjoy, while discussing things we don't understand, and considering possibilities we don't want to think about.

When we buy a new car, new clothes, or a new house, we feel energized and want to share our new purchase with friends and family members. When we buy insurance, we get an envelope full of legalese and an endless string of bills neither of which are anything we want to share with those we care about. Unfortunately, for most people, insurance is a reality of life at least during certain times in the growth and development of your family.

There are few things less important in our minds than insurance when we don't need it and almost nothing more important than insurance when we do need it. Insurance is like an umbrella that simply gets in the way until you find yourself dressed for an evening out while getting out of the car in a driving rain. That which was useless suddenly becomes imperative.

For anything as confusing as insurance, you and I need a guide or an advisor to lead us through the process. Unfortunately, the vast majority of insurance policies were sold to consumers by commissioned salesmen instead of being bought by informed consumers. When it comes to insurance, what you don't know can definitely hurt you.

While you are building the life of your dreams with those that you care about, be sure to create a

```
layer of protection between your future and a world
full of opportunities, but also disasters, waiting to
happen.
```

Jim Stovall

There are two broad risk categories on which we will focus: personal risk and financial risk. Many single risk management decisions have both personal and financial risk components. For example, the invigorating pursuit of mountain climbing has the personal risk of injury, even fatality, and the financial risk of the cost of medical bills. Regardless of your action or inaction, you have made a risk management decision.

There are four primary risk management techniques: risk avoidance, risk reduction, risk assumption (or self-insurance) and risk transfer (or insurance). Let's analyze a real-life example to illustrate the various techniques.

The summer I was 18 years old, I was a punk. You know, a cocky know-it-all who would rather stick a hot poker in his eye than respond positively to any authority figure. I was invincible and omniscient. That's why I knew that even though police officers had given me three separate violations for driving without a seatbelt, I had nothing to fear driving around without shoes or a seatbelt. To say that I learned several lessons the hard way that summer is an understatement.

I spent part of that Tuesday working, if you can call kicking back on a platform soaking in the sun while twirling a whistle around your finger and occasionally calling out, "Adult swim!"

work. After I clocked out, I did what I did every summer Tuesday (and Wednesday, and Thursday)—find the party. I partied until a friend drove me back to her house where I slept off the day's activities. Feeling sufficiently rested at 2:00 a.m., I got in my car to drive home. Ten or so minutes later, I was awakened to the sound of my tires hitting the rumble strips, and before I could respond, the car descended over an embankment.

Since I wasn't wearing a seatbelt, I bounced all around the vehicle as it rolled down the embankment, finally resting on its wheels. My right femur (the longest bone in your body) was visibly broken. I had also suffered a broken pelvis and several internal injuries, as I'd later learn. Possibly because I had watched too many action movies, I had an irrational fear that the car would blow up, so I tried to open the driver door and then the passenger door to "escape" before the impending explosion. When they wouldn't open, I painfully crawled into the back seat. Neither of those doors would open either. I didn't know that the car metal had rolled down over the doors.

Laying there in the back seat, I moved in and out of consciousness for hours. It wasn't until 6:00 a.m. that a truck driver finally spotted my car from above and called in the accident. I can't report that I was brave and unflinching, that I fought for every breath to cling on to life. I actually gave up. The last thing I remember hearing was the sound of a helicopter and a voice saying, "This doesn't look good. I don't think this kid is going to make it."

God used Baltimore's legendary University of Maryland Shock Trauma Center to save my life. They said I was only minutes from bleeding to death in the car. Shortly after arriving at the hospital, my left lung collapsed. After fighting the machines that were providing my oxygen, they induced a coma, in which I stayed for five days. I learned later that my chances of living fell below 10%. Since this is a financial book, I should point out that those are not favorable odds.

Why do I tell you this story? Because I think it will help you remember the concept of risk management. Let's examine the personal and financial risks that I faced and the various risk management methods in the example of an automobile accident.

Risk avoidance: There is only one way to assuredly avoid the personal and financial risk of an automobile accident. Don't drive. Every time we get in an automobile, we give up the ability to avoid the inherent risks associated with that activity.

Risk Reduction: This was my biggest area of weakness on the risk management front. In the personal injury category, even if I would have insisted on doing everything else wrong, I could have worn a seatbelt. This still may have been a serious accident, but it would not have been a life threatening one. Certainly, driving at 2:00 a.m. after a day full of working and partying in the sun is a risk that could have been easily mitigated. On the financial front, all of the above foolishness applies, because when irresponsible behavior leads to a life-threatening accident, it takes a lot of money to put you back together. But, on a more generic front, a financial risk management method regarding auto usage is:

Drive cautiously. If you drive cautiously, you'll have fewer accidents costing you less money, and you'll also decrease your insurance costs significantly for having a driving record free of accidents and tickets.

Risk Assumption: Do you remember when I mentioned that doing nothing is still a choice? This was the personal risk management method I chose. Despite the seemingly blatant logical flaws, 18-year-old men seem to truly believe that they are invincible. For this reason, I chose to go without a seatbelt even after repeated violations and fines for not doing so. I self-insured my personal injury. I didn't need anyone's help to protect me. I was a competent driver and had conquered far worse than a 20-minute drive home at 2:00 a.m. I laughed off the personal risk and assumed it myself. Financial risk assumption in the case of a car accident is going without insurance.

Fortunately, I did have both auto and health insurance, but not of my own choosing. Since my father had helped provide me with my means of transportation, he refused to do so without requiring my acquisition of car insurance. And who needs doctors or health insurance when you're 18 and invincible? I was fortunate enough to still be on my parents' health insurance plan since I was enrolled in college.

Risk transfer: Insurance is the transfer of risk from one party to another. Much of the risk in life can be avoided, reduced, or assumed, but many of the catastrophic risks in life require deeper pockets. That is where insurance is very helpful. I can assume the risk of my auto insurance deductible. I can't assume the liability risk of someone suing me for $1 million if I have a car accident, so I transfer that risk with auto and umbrella insurance. I can assume the risk of replacing the hot water heater in my house. I can't assume the risk of rebuilding my house and replacing its contents if they burn to the ground, so I transfer that risk with homeowner's insurance. I can assume the risk of what it would cost to bury me if I die prematurely. I can't yet assume the risk of replacing my future income for my wife and children, so I transfer that risk with life insurance.

How does insurance work? You need to understand one word to understand insurance—pool. This is not a hole with water in it, but a risk pool. You are not the only one who has risks that you cannot avoid, reduce, and assume. An insurance company takes you and a huge number of others like you and throws you into a common risk pool. Brilliant numerical wizards called actuaries make determinations of the probability of certain risks occurring over various periods of time. After having done so, they can derive the estimated cost of claims in a set period of time. That cost, when broken down across each of the individuals in the risk pool, along with a built-in profit for the insurance company, becomes your premium. Added to that number is an additional premium if your past behavior or circumstances make you a higher risk than the average in the pool. Subtracted from that number is a discount if your past behavior and circumstances make you a lesser risk.

You say, it sounds like gambling. It is, but with people much smarter than your poker buddies. And as it applies in Atlantic City and Las Vegas, yes, the house always wins. Insurance is not an investment. Those who claim it as such are lying and may be breaking the law (the laws are different in each state). Some insurance products have internal components that accrue cash that in some cases is invested in mutual fund-like vehicles, but you must never forget that there is always a cost to the insurance and that is the primary purpose of the product. We'll get into greater detail on this in the life insurance chapters.

You say, it sounds like discrimination. It is. It's legal and appropriate discrimination, and with the exception of your race or creed, just about everything else is up for grabs. For reasons that should now be entirely apparent, 18-year-old men pay significantly more for auto insurance than 18-year-old women or even 25-year-old men. It is both sex discrimination and age discrimination. Men pay more for life insurance than women because, statistically, they have a higher chance of dying earlier (plus they drink more beer and eat more junk food). Again, sex discrimination. Women pay more for health insurance since they have the ability to get pregnant. You get the idea.

If you are the healthiest person on earth but your mom or dad died of a heart attack in their 50s or younger, you will pay more for life insurance. If you take any kind of anti-depressant, you may be denied long term disability altogether. The older you get, the more you will pay for life, disability, long term care, and health insurance. On its face, insurance is the business of discrimination, but if they didn't discriminate, insurance wouldn't exist.

Economic Bias Alert!

There are few transactions where Economic Bias is any more present than with insurance products. Most of the people who are in the business of helping people make insurance decisions are people who benefit economically from the consumer's decision to purchase said insurance (I know that's a shocker!). So inevitably, most insurance agents have an inherent tendency to prefer that the consumer buys the product or products that he or she sells or represents.

Despite the caricatures, most insurance sales people are not bad people. They are simply sales people. Their training is heavy on the sales end and light on the advice end. Most of them know their stuff and many even carry legitimate credentials (like the Certified Financial Planner™—CFP®—credential), but if they profit when you buy and don't when you don't, you need to know that. Understanding this bias will help you make a more informed decision.

If you want advice with less conflict of interest, pay a fee-only CFP® practitioner to review your various insurance coverages and make recommendations. And don't hesitate to ask the question of the salesperson that is bound to ruffle feathers, "HOW MUCH WILL YOU MAKE OFF OF THE SALE OF THIS PRODUCT?" The answer is absolutely material. The higher the commission, the more context you have to make your decision.

Many bemoan the cost of insurance and say, "See, I paid thousands of dollars into this policy that could've been growing in my investments. What a waste!" It is my fervent hope that all of your insurance premiums end up being a waste of money. You don't buy insurance for the service that is required at an auto body shop, at a hospital, or from a home builder. You buy insurance on an annual basis to transfer the risk of needing to utilize those services unexpectedly. Would you feel better if you had the car accident, became disabled or died, but got some insurance money out of it?

Even as an 18-year-old punk kid, I could have completely avoided my accident using only one technique, risk avoidance, by not driving at all that night; however, let me be clear. It is not my intent to suggest that your life should be one big exercise in risk avoidance. Many of the things that give us the greatest enjoyment in life carry with them inherent risks. And despite my nightmarish story, I actually still have a natural attraction to that which is personally risky. I love rock climbing, cycling, white water rafting, and riding motorcycles; but I climb with ropes, bike with a helmet, raft with a guide, and have agreed with my wife that I'll not own another motorcycle until my boys are adults and college is paid for. Risks are best managed when all of the techniques are used together.

Timely Application

Risk Management Matrix

The way to see activities through a risk management lens is to go through some ideas of your own, like my example of the car accident, and discuss or jot down the ways in which that risk could have been managed with each of the four methods. It doesn't have to be something as dramatic or painful. It could easily be a risk management success story that you can now better understand.

Examine both the personal and the financial risk using all four of the risk management techniques. After doing that exercise, discipline yourself to analyze a few other examples throughout the course of your days. If you're bold enough, teach the technique to a friend or family member (there's no better way to learn something than to teach it). Eventually, it won't be work, and you'll see your options more clearly. Then, when you examine your existing insurance products or new offerings, look for ways that you can reasonably avoid, reduce, or assume that risk before paying someone else to do it for you.

Visit www.thefinancialcrossroads.com to find a template to use in creating your own Risk Management Matrix.

Tim Maurer

In the following chapters, we'll specifically address the primary areas of risk that are most often associated with the purchase of insurance: life insurance, home and auto insurance, health insurance, long term care insurance, and disability income insurance. We'll make recommendations for insurance's best uses and point out its misuses and abuses.

Risk Management
Matrix

Risk Situation:

Risk Avoidance Method

Personal Risk:

Financial Risk:

Risk Reduction Method

Personal Risk:

Financial Risk:

Risk Assumption Method

Personal Risk:

Financial Risk:

Risk Transfer Method

Personal Risk:

Financial Risk:

LIFE INSURANCE, PART I: WHY?

> I detest life-insurance agents; they always argue that I shall some day die, which is not so.
>
> *Stephen Leacock*

Y ou don't even want to read this chapter, do you? I say "life insurance," and you immediately get a picture of someone in a plaid short-sleeved shirt accented with a squared-end tie and maybe even a brown corduroy jacket with the elbow pads and a serious comb-over. You picture someone sitting across the kitchen table launching a guilt blitzkrieg with a hefty price tag in your direction. You picture someone who has as much conflict of interest as the hungry lion circling the wounded wildebeest on the National Geographic show.

And, you may be partly right, but that doesn't mean you can ignore the duty of properly managing the financial risk associated with death. There are certainly times when properly managing risk warrants or even mandates the transfer of that risk with—you guessed it—life insurance. If you are already financially independent, you have self insured the financial risk that you might die prematurely. Whereas, if you are a young parent with a good income, but not enough saved to keep paying the bills indefinitely if you leave this earth, you need to purchase some life insurance. We will give you the guidelines you need to begin making this decision.

It is not easy to talk about life insurance because it's not easy to talk about death. It is especially difficult to pin a numerical value on a person, but that is precisely what we do with life insurance. It is important to recall in this chapter the lesson we learned in the first chapter: money is not powerful, but your relationships are. The point of life insurance is not to "buy off" someone's pain and suffering over the loss of a loved one; it's to provide the financial stability so that the survivor doesn't have to worry about the money and can instead properly mourn their loss. I encourage you to have deep and meaningful thoughts and discussions surrounding the topics of life and death, but when you are doing life insurance planning, an objective approach is wisest.

Timeless Truth

Life insurance is not a way to get rich, nor does it really insure your life or eliminate the risk of your death. Fear is often used to sell life insurance, and please remember that if someone mailed, emailed, or phoned you regarding insurance, they are an insurance salesperson. There's nothing wrong with being a salesperson. It is an honorable, highly-paid vocation; but it is important to realize that salespeople sell products. They don't necessarily assess needs, manage risks, or conduct financial planning. To a man with a hammer, everything, indeed, looks like a nail, and to an insurance salesman, every human being with a pulse looks like a potential customer.

I hate to be the one to tell you, but you and I and everyone we have ever met are going to die. The act of dying, in and of itself, does not create a need for insurance, but the result of your death may. Life insurance could more aptly be named Income and Expense Insurance as these are the risks it covers.

When you buy insurance, you are placing a bet or wagering against an insurance company. Much like when you put money on a table in a casino, you are wagering against the house. If you have looked at the ornate, multi-million dollar establishments where people gamble or house insurance companies, you have probably figured out that you are not going to beat the casino or an insurance company over the long haul. This doesn't mean, however, that you and I shouldn't consider our need for insurance.

Unfortunately, most families currently own several insurance policies that they were sold. They do not understand these policies, and they did not choose the best options among several choices. In too many cases, a salesperson crammed them into a one-size-fits-all insurance policy. The amount of coverage that they have was not a matter of what they truly need but, instead, a function of what they can afford.

If the doctor tells you that your child needs a lifesaving prescription, you will not decide what to do based on what you can afford, but you will focus on what you and your child need and move ahead. Once you, your calculator, and an independent financial advisor determine exactly what you and your family need, then and only then should you look at affordability. If there are two pharmacies that sell the lifesaving prescription for your child and they are both equal, you might then consider the cost involved, but only after you're convinced you are covering the life and death issues.

Jim Stovall

What is life insurance and how did it come to be? As mentioned in the previous chapter, insurance is a form of highly sophisticated gambling. You'll remember that an insurance company throws you into a pool with many others like you. In this case, the stakes are clear. The insurance company makes a bet on the probability that you are going to live—or die. They calculate how much premium they need to receive from their pool so that they have enough money to pay a benefit to the probable number of families who are likely to have their loved one pass away in a particular time frame, and collect a handsome profit on top of that. The sale of life insurance in the U.S. dates back to pre-Revolutionary times when Christian organizations created risk pools for the underprivileged in their communities.

First, let's view life insurance through the eyes of a Risk Manager.

Risk Avoidance: Regarding the financial impact of death, risk avoidance is extremely difficult. Unless you intend to go out like Elijah in a chariot of fire, I must deliver the sobering news that you (your body at least) will eventually die. This reality renders the Risk Avoidance method of life insurance quite impotent. There is a place, however, for...

Risk Reduction: You reduce the risk of the negative financial impact of an unexpected death by being proactive about your pursuits of good health. In addition to lessening the risk that you would have a heart attack at a young age, for example, you will also be significantly reducing the premiums that you do pay on any life insurance that you own. In the eyes of the actuaries, smokers have effectively submitted themselves to a virtual guarantee of an early death, and their insurance premiums can as much as double to reflect that increased risk.

Risk Assumption: It is not only possible, but probable, for any individual or family who reaches a level of financial independence to assume some or all of the financial risk of death. Although the insurance industry has tried to convince each generation that you'll always, until your dying day, have a reason to own life insurance, their postulation is self-serving and dead wrong (pun intended). If the empty-nest retired couple is debt free and completely self-sufficient with their sources of fixed income and their investment assets, they don't need any life insurance, though they might want some (more on that later).

Risk Transfer: Life insurance, the source of our discussion in this chapter, is the optimal way to transfer the financial risk of death when you have exhausted the previous risk management measures.

Like all of financial planning, there is both a science and an art to life insurance planning. While there is enough subjectivity in the thought processes surrounding life insurance to create an exception for nearly every rule, we will begin by separating the various reasons to purchase life insurance into concrete NEEDS and WANTS. Life insurance needs are those things that would allow the surviving family members to continue on, unencumbered by the financial loss of the deceased. If no one else is reliant on your financial wherewithal, you have no life insurance need. Life insurance wants, then, are anything else that would further improve your situation beyond what it is today. Let's look at the primary examples.

Life Insurance Needs:

> *Final Expenses*
> *Payment of Debts and Mortgages*
> *Education for Children*
> *Needed Income Replacement*

Life Insurance Wants:

> *Pre-insurance*
> *Build Cash Value*
> *Estate Creation*
> *Wealth Replacement*
> *Charitable Bequests*

Until you have addressed your life insurance needs and all other financial planning priorities, you need not be concerned with life insurance wants. The other financial planning priorities discussed throughout the book are: 1) mastery of the three personal financial statements and their perpetual implementation; 2) adequate emergency reserves specific to your situation;

3) ensuring that all of your insurance needs are met; 4) contributing the maximum to your 401k(s); 5) contributing the maximum to Roth IRA(s) or to an equivalent liquid savings account if you're over the Roth income limitations; 6) contributing enough to 529 plans or equivalent for education savings; and 7) contributing to a "Freedom" liquid investment savings account. In order to accomplish all of these, I estimate that it would have an annual cost in excess of $70,000![i] That means that until you have an annual household income of over $250,000, or you have otherwise been blessed to amass an estate in the millions, you need not worry yourself with life insurance wants.

Economic Bias Alert!

When I went through sales training to be a financial advisor with one of the best insurance companies in the world, I was told in no uncertain terms, "If anyone ever asks you the question, 'Do I need insurance?', no matter who they are or how old they are, the answer is always a resounding yes!" When your income is derived solely and directly from commissions made on the sale of insurance, it only makes sense that these types of tactics exist.

Let's examine how you can determine how much life insurance it will take to cover the basic needs listed previously.

Final expenses are the costs that one will incur to make viewing, funeral, and burial arrangements. This cost can be estimated between $15,000 and $25,000. We'll compromise at $20,000. Some families will be able to self-insure this expense, but many will need to account for it in their life insurance planning.

Payment of debts and mortgages sets the surviving spouse or other heirs free from his or her largest and most demanding bills. The amount of life insurance for debts and mortgages should correspond directly with their balances. While it may be optimal for some spouses to take these funds and pay off the mortgage, it may be appropriate for others to keep the cash, invest it, and use the income and gains to help make the mortgage payments. This is an individual decision and should not be made until after the first year has passed since the loss of the loved one. During that time, the life insurance proceeds should be kept in a liquid account with U.S. government protection. Certificates of Deposit (CDs) are a logical choice, but be aware that FDIC protection has its limits. In 2009, the FDIC limits were extended from $100,000 to $250,000, but that is set to revert back to $100,000 at the end of 2013.

Education for the children is for expected costs of private elementary or high school education and especially college. Throughout our life insurance planning, we're going to assume a "safe" rate of return of 5% for the invested life insurance benefit. The cost of education is also thought to rise at a rate of approximately 5%, so we'll want to have enough life insurance to cover the cost of every year of expected education in today's dollars. Therefore, if you have two children, ages nine and 11, who are attending public elementary and high school and then going on to an in-state, state university that currently costs $15,000 per year, you will want $120,000 of life insurance to cover the future costs of education. If you send the same two children to an expensive private school ($25,000 per child per year) and expect them to go to your alma mater, Harvard ($50,000 per child per year), then you'll need $800,000 of life insurance simply to cover future education costs. We address saving, planning, and paying for education in Chapter Fourteen.

Needed income replacement is going to be less than 100% of the spouse's income since our calculations have already pre-paid debts, mortgages, and education. With those major expenses covered, most people will only need to replace approximately 50% of the deceased spouse's income. (This multiple will vary depending on the income of the decedent and the lifestyle of the family.) So, if the primary wage earner in the single income household had an income of $100,000, you should use life insurance to recreate a $50,000 income going forward. We'll again use the 5% rate of return assumption, and seek to create a $50,000 income stream from the amount of cash that—earning 5%—would satisfy the income need. In order to determine what lump sum earning 5% would generate $50,000 of annual income, divide $50,000 by 5% (.05), and the answer is $1,000,000. Properly invested, this amount should take care of the income need and also most of the inflation to be expected into the future.

Timely Application
Life Insurance Audit

The first step in your personal insurance analysis is to figure out what you own or have currently by conducting a Life Insurance Audit. Yes, it's possible to have some even if you didn't buy any as most companies give you a relatively small group life insurance policy at no charge.

Collect ALL of your existing life insurance policies and the most recent annual statement corresponding with each. These documents are filled with legalese and jargon, but they also contain almost everything you need to know about your policies. Create a chart using the template provided on our website with the pertinent information from your policies, including the following: Inception Date, Type of Insurance (Term, Whole Life, Universal Life, or Variable Life), Length of Term, Death Benefit, Cash Value, and Surrender Value.

There are two additional documents associated with permanent life insurance policies (Whole Life, Universal Life, and Variable Life) for which you'll need to contact the insurance company. These are an In-force Illustration and a Cost Basis Report. I recommend calling the company's customer service number instead of calling your agent directly, because most agents know that the request for these two documents is often the indication that someone is investigating the viability of the policies they sold. At the least, their judgment is being called into question. At most, they may also be losing residual commissions.

The information you collect will be combined with your Timely Application in the following chapter to help you conclude which policies you should keep, what additional policies you may need to apply for and which policies you should surrender (however, you should NEVER surrender any existing life insurance policies until you have determined your needs and applied for any additional insurance needed).

Visit www.thefinancialcrossroads.com to find a template to use for your Life Insurance Audit.

Tim Maurer

Next we'll examine the most common scenarios and provide a framework you can use in making your life insurance decisions for both your needs and wants.

[i] Emergency Savings	$12,000/year ($1,000 per month)	
401ks for Husband & Wife	$33,000/year ($16,500 annual limit per person)	
Roth IRAs for Husband & Wife	$10,000/year ($ 5,000 annual limit per person)	
Education Savings	$ 4,800/year ($200 per child per month, 2 children)	
+ Liquid Investment Savings	$12,000/year ($1,000 per month)	
Optimal Household Savings	**$71,800/year ($5,983 per month)**	

Life Insurance Audit

Policy #	Inception Date	Insurance Type	Term Length	Death Benefit	Cash Value	Surrender Value	Cost Basis

seven

LIFE INSURANCE, PART II: HOW?

> Everything should be made as simple
> as possible, but not simpler.
> *Albert Einstein*

Life insurance should be simple, but it's typically not. Made complex by companies and agents with a powerful economic bias, it's very difficult to separate wheat from chaff and determine the difference between your life insurance needs and wants. Following is an analysis of the prospective needs of the four primary demographic households:

1) D.I.N.K. *(Dual Income/No Kids):*

DINK households have "the life"—financially speaking anyway. They have two incomes coming in and fewer variable expenses. Much beloved by retailers, they can afford all the iPhones, Playstations, flat screen TVs, and vacations that come their way. Their insurance needs are slim, and the primary objective of life insurance is to pay off the debts and mortgages for the surviving spouse. Their insurance needs break down the following way:

1. Final Expenses:

    $ 20,000 Final Expenses
    _____
    $ 20,000 Life Insurance

2. Debts & Mortgages:

    $ 255,000 Mortgage
    $ 43,000 School Loans
    $ 11,000 Auto Loan
    $ 2,000 Credit Card
    _____
    $ 311,000 Life Insurance

TOTAL D.I.N.K. INSURANCE EQUATION:

    $ 20,000 Final Expenses
+ $ 311,000 Debts & Mortgages
_____
    $ 331,000 Life Insurance

2) Leave It to Beaver:

This is the single-income, two-parent household with two children. With a growing number of men becoming stay-at-home dads, Ward may be the one with the apron, and June may bring home the bacon, but in either case, the insurance logic is the same. To plan for the unexpected death of the breadwinner and assume that the spouse working in the home is able to continue that course indefinitely, this scenario often results in a large amount of insurance on the income-earning spouse. Here is how we plan for their life insurance needs.

1. Final Expenses:

    $ 20,000 Final Expenses
    _____
    $ 20,000 Life Insurance

2. Debts & Mortgages:

   $ 325,000 Mortgage

   $ 36,000 School Loans

   $ 11,000 Auto Loan
   _____

   $ 372,000 Life Insurance

3. Education:

   Public Schools—Equation #1:

   (No cost for elementary, middle, or high school)

   $ 15,000/year

   X 8 years (2 kids X 4 years)
   _____

   $ 120,000 for state university
   _____

   $ 120,000 Life Insurance

   Private Schools—Equation #2:

   $ 25,000/year

   X 26 years
   (2 kids X 13 years for elementary, middle, and high school)
   _____

   $ 650,000 for Private School
   _____

   + $ 50,000/year

   X 8 years (2 kids X 4 years)
   _____

   = $ 400,000 for Harvard
   _____

   = $ 1,050,000 Life Insurance

   Income Replacement:

   $ 100,000 Income

   X 50%
   _____

   = $ 50,000 Income to be replaced

   / 5%
   _____

   = **$1,000,000 Life Insurance**

TOTAL LEAVE IT TO BEAVER INSURANCE EQUATION:

$ 20,000 Final Expenses
$ 372,000 Debts & Mortgages
$ 120,000 Public School OR
$ 1,050,000 Private School
+ $ 1,000,000 Income Replacement
_____
$ **1,512,000 Life Insurance** (public school)
OR
$ **2,442,000 Life Insurance** (private school)

    A common and excellent question regarding life insurance planning for the single income household is, "What about the stay-at-home spouse? Does he or she have a life insurance need?" This traces back to our discussion of what life insurance is—and isn't. It isn't an attempt to put a value on someone's life, but instead a hedge against the financial risk of the loss of someone's life. So, what about the stay-at-home mom who doesn't earn any income? The amount of work that Mom does on the home front might not earn her income, but it certainly is worth something! Without Mom, Dad is going to either work less (and earn less money) to spend more time at home trying to make up for Mom's absence; or he's going to need to hire a significant amount of help with childcare and the myriad other duties on the home front that Mom managed. Although it's not one-size-fits-all, a $250,000 life insurance policy on the life of the stay-at-home mom or dad should provide the surviving spouse with about $35,000 of additional annual liquidity for seven to ten years.

    Another great question for a single income household is, "Do we really need all that life insurance to perpetuate the lifestyle, when in actuality the surviving spouse who was staying at home would go back to work?" The answer here is no. If the surviving spouse would intend to go back to work, at least after the children are in school, you may assume a lesser amount of insurance need. This is when it becomes important to recognize the purpose of your insurance planning at the onset. If the objective is to allow the current lifestyle to go on unimpeded, you should err on the higher side of the calculation. If you'd prefer to calculate down to the month and year that a surviving spouse will go back to work, you can specifically tailor your insurance calculation to reflect that.

3) D.I.W.K. (Dual Income WITH Kids):

For the many families that have sources of income from both parents, the calculation for life insurance is very similar to the single income household. In this case, you simply have to run the calculation twice assuming that the household is reliant on both sources of income. In this example, let's assume that the wife earns $60,000 and the husband earns $40,000.

1) Final Expenses:

(Husband):	(Wife):
$ 20,000 Final Expenses	$ 20,000 Final Expenses
$ 20,000 Life Insurance	$ 20,000 Life Insurance

2) Debts and mortgages:

(Husband):	(Wife):
$ 328,000 Mortgage	$ 328,000 Mortgage
$ 68,000 School Loans	$ 68,000 School Loans
$ 396,000 Life Insurance	$ 396,000 Life Insurance

3) Education:

(Husband):		(Wife):	
$ 15,000/year		$	15,000/year
X 12 years		X	12 years (3 kids X 4 years)
= $ 180,000 Education cost		= $	180,000 Education cost
$ 180,000 Life Insurance		$	180,000 Life Insurance

Income Replacement:

(Husband):		(Wife):	
$ 40,000 Income		$	60,000 Income
X 50%		X	50%
= $ 20,000 to be replaced		= $	30,000 to be replaced
/ 5%		/	5%
= **$ 400,000 Life Insurance**		= **$	600,000 Life Insurance**

TOTAL D.I.W.K INSURANCE EQUATION:

(Husband):	(Wife):
$ 20,000 Final Expenses	$ 20,000 Final Expenses
$ 396,000 Debts & Mortgages	$ 396,000 Debts & Mortgages
$ 180,000 Education	$ 180,000 Education
$ 400,000 Income Replacement	$ 600,000 Income Replacement
$ 996,000 Life Insurance	**$1,196,000 Life Insurance**

4) Empty Nest:

As mentioned earlier, if someone has enough retirement income and assets to sustain their lifestyle indefinitely (regardless of whether or not they are working), there is no additional need for life insurance. But what about the many individuals and couples in this scenario who have made it past the child-rearing and college years but still aren't yet financially independent? They need a life insurance bridge to financial independence. The easiest way to calculate this is to determine what their prospective retirement income would be today, then calculate the assets that would need to be added to their holdings to get them to the point of financial independence. Let's assume in this scenario that the husband and wife both are old enough to be receiving Social Security.

Existing Income:

Husband's Social Security =	$ 18,000 per year
Wife's Social Security =	$ 21,000 per year
Husband's Pension =	$ 4,500 per year
Total Existing Income =	$ 43,500 per year

Existing Assets:

Husband's IRA =	$130,000
Wife's 403b =	$215,000
Total Retirement Assets =	$345,000
Assumed Rate of return =	X 5%
Assumed Income =	$ 17,250 per year

Income Replacement need:

Desired Retirement Income =	$ 80,000 per year
Prospective Annual Income =	- 60,750 per year
Income to Replace =	$ 19,250 per year
	/ 5%
Insurance Need	**$385,000**

Consideration should also be made for any income that would be lost per spouse if an Empty Nester leaves behind his or her spouse, and the above calculation should be tweaked to reflect this. One spouse may have a pension stream of income that will die with them, or be materially reduced. In this case, it may be necessary to include additional funds in this insurance bridge to replace that income. In the above calculation, the husband had a small pension of $4,500 per year. If you divide that number by .05 (5%), you'll find that $90,000 would be the lump sum expected to recreate that $4,500 annual income stream. Social Security income will also inevitably be impacted by a spouse's passing. The rule is that the surviving spouse would receive the higher of the two spouses' Social Security incomes. Therefore, in the above calculation, regardless of who passed away, it would be the husband's lower income benefit of $18,000 that may need to be replaced. Again divide $18,000 by 5%, and you'll find that $360,000 will be required to replace the surviving spouse's lost Social Security income. Remember, however, that life for one person will be less costly than for two. Since we're planning for life insurance needs, lost pension or Social Security income that would not be required after the passing of a spouse need not be replaced with life insurance.

Now that you have a better understanding of how to calculate your insurance needs, let's explore the most common life insurance wants to help you determine if any of them are appropriate for you.

Pre-insurance is when you don't need life insurance today, but you feel you may need it at some point in the future. The rationale with this line of thought is that, "You're likely to need it at some point in the future, so why not buy it while you're young and healthy?" This is a want, not a need. If you pre-insure everything in life, you won't have money for life.

Building Cash Value is also a life insurance want. Cash

value is a feature of whole life, universal life, and variable life insurance policies. The intricacies of these products will be discussed momentarily, but cash value is one of the "bells and whistles" that comes with life insurance policies. As in every case, those bells and whistles come with a price tag. An agent intent on making a nice life insurance sale may say, "Term is like renting. whole life is owning your life insurance." That's a sales pitch if I've ever heard one! Owning a house is typically one-and-one-half to two times the price of renting a comparable residence; whole life insurance can cost more than 20 times the price of comparable term! There are wise uses for permanent life insurance with cash value. For business owners and folks blessed with the problem of having an estate large enough to be diminished by federal estate tax when they pass on (in 2009, that is a married couple who has an estate valued at over $7 million), term insurance will likely not be sufficient to handle their desires. But, those are still wants, not needs.

Economic Bias Alert!

Because the premiums are so much higher for cash value life insurance policies, and the commissions for life insurance agents are based on the premiums, agents are actually incentivized to make poor recommendations to clients. I was conducting a comprehensive analysis for two different married couples with very young children. In both cases, the husband was almost solely responsible for the household income. I was astonished that in both cases, these couples were sold policies that would pay only $250,000 if the husband passed away although it was quite clear that in order to cover the mortgage, education for the kids, and income replacement, he needed at least $1,000,000 of life insurance. The $250,000 policies were cash value insurance policies with premiums up to the maximum that either of these young families could afford. They actually SAVED money by purchasing the $1,000,000 term policies that they needed and dumping the cash value policies that their agents wanted. You would think that the insurance agents making the recommendations to clients would have a legal obligation to act in the clients' best interest, but they don't. Insurance is regulated by each state, and in most states, the legal burden placed on a life insurance agent is caveat emptor—buyer beware. As long as the policy is approved in that state, the burden is on the consumer to make the right choice.

Estate Creation is the life insurance want for the individual with a strong desire to leave a financial legacy behind but doesn't yet have the estate in place. Picture the single mom or dad with adult children. The adult children don't rely on the parent financially and are living an independent life, but the parent daydreams about leaving behind a financial lump sum. This, by its very definition, is not a need but a want.

Charitable Bequests and the accompanying charitable inclination are honorable and virtuous, but to make a
charity or charities the beneficiary of a life insurance
policy is certainly a life insurance want.

Wealth Replacement is the final life insurance want we'll
discuss, and it will be discussed in greater detail in our
estate planning chapter. Many families have been
blessed financially to the point that they have estates
large enough that the federal government sees fit to tax
their money a third time. They do this through a federal
estate tax, or as it is known by its detractors, the Death
Tax. As it stands in 2009, federal estate tax is levied on
estates in excess of $3.5 million. In the context of a mar-
ried couple, each of them receives an exemption of $3.5
million, although it takes some fancy legal work to do
so. Everything over $7 million for a husband and wife or
$3.5 million for an individual will be taxed at a rate of up
to 45%—almost half! So, the couple with a $10 million
estate will have $3 million exposed to federal estate tax
and, therefore, may pay the feds $1,350,000 for the mere
privilege of dropping dead in their country.

To add insult to injury, many of our united states also
charge a state estate tax on top of the federal tax. You
may now see why some wealthy families find a benefit
in purchasing life insurance to be held in an irrevocable
life insurance trust to "pay the estate taxes" when they
die. Theirs is not complete satisfaction, however, because the tax is still being taken out of the estate. The
life insurance only seeks to make their heirs whole. This
is clearly a want for most families, but it almost reaches

the need status when the large estate is made up of extremely illiquid assets, like a business or farm. In many of those cases, the family business or farm would have to be liquidated in pieces to keep the operation going. I concede that as a justifiable exception in this case.

Timeless Truth

Life insurance exists to provide money that you or your family do not have. If you already have the money that will be needed, having insurance is like carrying two umbrellas on a sunny day. Never insure a risk you don't have. And remember, when you're paying someone else to cover your risk, it is more expensive than doing it yourself.

When you go out to eat dinner, the owner of the restaurant buys the food for far less than you or I can buy the same food. They prepare and serve it to you and then charge you far more than you would pay to cook the same meal at your home. This certainly does not mean we all shouldn't enjoy a nice dinner out. We should simply remember that we are paying for the privilege. In the same way, if an insurance company covers your risk, you are paying a "premium", literally and figuratively, for that safety net.

Conversely, if you are using insurance as an investment vehicle, you have invited a very expensive middleman into your world. Rarely, if ever, will you find a case where the investment portion of an insurance policy performs better than buying term insurance and investing the rest on your own. It's just like cooking a meal in your own kitchen. It will always save you money. While there are other benefits to eating out versus eating at home, when you're considering insurance to cover your risk or investments versus covering them yourself, there are no benefits to consider other than the dollars.

Jim Stovall

Life insurance can be split into two basic categories: term life insurance and permanent life insurance—term and perm. As is evidenced in their names, term life insurance is intended to exist for a stated term or time frame and permanent life insurance has features allowing it to exist into perpetuity. One of the sales ploys I've heard used to sell permanent insurance products when term is more appropriate is, "Only 2% of term life insurance policies pay out!" That statistic is true, and to that I say thank God! Much like we never hope to receive the benefit of our auto, home, liability, and disability insurance coverage, I very much hope that your term life insurance policies never pay out! A good risk manager is willing to temporarily transfer risk that she cannot bear until which time she has enough assets to self-insure.

Term life insurance is "pure insurance." It is a calculation on the part of the brilliant number crunchers called actuaries to determine the probability of your passing away in a set period of time. There is no cash value to the policy. It only pays out when you die in the vast majority of cases. (There is a relatively new term product now available called Return of Premium. It solves only an emotional need, not an economic one. You are likely better off buying straight term for less and putting the difference into your Roth IRA.) The most common term is a 20 year period. Twenty year term guarantees that as long as you make the level premium payments for the next 20 years, the insurance company will pay out to the beneficiaries if you croak. For the family that can reasonably assume that they would reach financial independence in the next 20 years, this is a very appropriate product. Term is also sold in many variations with lengths as short as one year, but also in just about every increment of five up through 30 year term. Virtually all of the life insurance needs can be adequately insured with term.

Permanent life insurance can be viewed as having a core of the pure insurance as discussed above with an additional layer around the core of a cash savings vehicle. This additional savings receives certain tax privileges and allows policy owners to take loans against or distributions from that cash value. The investment components also come in various forms. Whole life, the most costly of the varieties of permanent insurance, has a fixed income savings mechanism inside. It should function similarly to a conservative fixed income investment, like a CD. Variable life has an investment component that is more like the purchase of a mutual fund. It will have a range of investment options, known as sub-accounts, which are various types of mutual fund style stock, bond, and cash investment vehicles. Another form of permanent insurance is universal life. Universal life was designed to offer a less costly form of permanent life insurance. It is a hybrid between whole life and term life insurance. Several of the life insurance wants require the purchase of some form of permanent life insurance to be implemented properly, but remember, if you earn less than $250,000 per year and/or have an estate below $3 million, there is little chance that one of these products is appropriate for you.

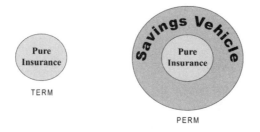

While the benefits of permanent life insurance exist, the cost must also be weighed. I recently replaced one of my term life insurance policies with a death benefit of $1 million and an annual premium of $465 per year, so in preparation for this chapter, I reached out to several life insurance agents to see what the cost would have been for permanent life insurance policies with the same death benefit. The answers? A comparable whole life policy was twenty times more costly—$10,380 per year! The universal or variable life policies would cost around ten times the amount that I am paying for my term policy. I'd rather control the fate of that extra money than trust a life insurance company to do it.

One additional type of insurance that we must mention is group life insurance. Group coverage is that which is attached to the company for which you work. In many instances, your company may provide a life insurance benefit based on a multiple of your salary or compensation. For example, your company might give you your salary multiplied by one or two ($60,000 salary X 2 = $120,000 benefit). These policies often then offer additional coverage to be purchased by the employee that will increase in multiples of your salary. Advantages of this type of insurance are that it may be free, and it requires little to no underwriting. Take the free insurance, but carefully weigh the benefits of purchasing additional coverage through your employer for the following two reasons:

1) *Unless subsidized by your employer* (and these subsidies have become few and far between in recent years), the cost for group life insurance is typically higher than insurance that you could purchase privately, especially if you are in reasonably good health and would garner a favorable report from a life insurance underwriter. The coverage is more expensive because it often is available with no underwriting. They assume something close to a standard (average) underwriting level because they recognize that in that group there are likely to be many who would meet higher underwriting guidelines and others who will meet lower guidelines. The insurance company reduces their risk by giving everyone standard pricing. This could result in a cost that is 50-100% higher for someone that would otherwise qualify for preferred or preferred best underwriting. However, for an employee who has a health condition that precludes him or her from being approved for a privately written life insurance policy, group life insurance presents a great opportunity for them to get coverage that they otherwise couldn't get.

2) *Most group life insurance is not portable*—you can not keep it after you leave the company through which you gained the policy—and, therefore, is significantly diminished in its value. Most of us will change companies seven to ten times in our careers, by choice or not, and if you are too reliant on your group life insurance to be there for you indefinitely, you may be in for a rude awakening if you change companies and find that the new company does not offer the same level of group life insurance.

There are several ways to purchase life insurance. Numerous online calculators are available, and while this is a good place to start your research, I don't suggest completing your process with an 800 number. Your rates will likely not be any lower if you apply online than if you go through a life insurance agent or broker. A life insurance agent represents a company to the consuming public while a life insurance broker represents you to a plethora of different insurance companies. When searching for term life insurance to cover your needs, an insurance broker is typically going to be the best bet; however, if you are shopping permanent insurance, you will need to include some insurance agents in your search. Some of the best insurance companies in the U.S. are captive agencies. This means that they do not make their products available to brokers. Only their company's agents can sell their products.

While there are many reputable, respectful, knowledgeable, helpful insurance specialists out there, most of whom, by the way, are very good dressers, there are also many who have helped solidify the stereotype. But, don't allow that stereotype—

or even a bad experience—to let you mistakenly assume that you don't need to worry about it. Instead of going directly to an insurance salesperson to buy life insurance, talk to a fee-only financial planner who has given up the ability to take commissions. Allow them to give you an unbiased, third-party recommendation on how much life insurance you should have and then go to an insurance salesperson with your "prescription" and place your order.

Timely Application
Life Insurance Needs Analysis

Using the demographic templates above and the calculator for Insurance Needs Analysis on our website, determine what your needs are for your final expenses, debts and mortgages, education, and income replacement.

Contrast what you found in your Insurance Audit and your Insurance Needs Analysis in order to get an idea for your next steps.

Remember that life insurance planning is an art and a science.

Your individual situation requires an individual analysis that would best be completed with the help of a knowledgeable financial planner who does not accept commissions on the sale of life insurance policies.

If you conclude that you have policies that you don't need or want, and you've confirmed your research with an independent planner who does not accept commissions on the sale of life insurance, then you have several options for terminating your policies. But don't make those decisions hastily. Even if you shouldn't have purchased the whole life insurance policy that you bought 15 years ago and don't have need or want for it now, in some instances it will make sense to keep it. Requesting an In-force Life Insurance Illustration and a Policy Cost Basis Report from your agent will help you and your independent planner determine whether the policy should be kept or surrendered.

Especially in these economic times, it is important to ensure that every dollar of yours is working hard for you, and that includes the dollars that you are channeling towards life insurance.

Visit www.thefinancialcrossroads.com to find a template to use for your Life Insurance Needs Analysis.

Tim Maurer

Now that you have an idea how much life insurance you need, you'll expect to have insurance companies falling over themselves to get you to take one of their policies, right? Yes and no. Sure, they want to sell you a policy, but they really don't want to lose money on you either, so once you've decided what kind and how much insurance you need or want, the prospective insurance company will turn you over to the underwriters. When I was going through life insurance training, underwriters were referred to as the company's Business Prevention Unit. You will fill out an application asking you a string of personal and financial questions deep and wide enough to make anyone blush. They will ask about a number of your personal habits and even delve into the health and welfare of your parents, grand-parents, brothers, and sisters. Beyond the application itself, you'll also have to have a nurse visit you to take blood and urine and ask you a bunch of the health questions again to ensure that you don't tell a different story than you did in the application. It is vitally important to remember these two underwriting tips when applying for life insurance:

1) *Tell the truth.* Beyond its being a generally good char-acter trait, honesty will allow you to keep your story straight. If an insurance company catches you in a lie, they can decline you completely, leaving a mark on your record for future business with insurance companies. And while it is difficult for them to catch a host of little white lies, if they catch one in the unfortunate instance that you die shortly after the policy was initiated, any fraud on your part, if exposed, could mean that your family is left with *nothing*.

2) *Don't answer questions that aren't asked!* I want you to be honest, but I also want your answers to be as concise as possible. If they ask if you are a mountain climber, and you're not but you enjoy doing hiking and bouldering with your kids on weekends, the concise answer to their questions is, "No." If they ask if you have plans to visit a host of nations that they deem politically or medically unstable and you don't have airline tickets and accom-modations for an upcoming visit, don't go into a diatribe about how you've yearned to go on a hunting expedition to Africa to hunt boar!

Isn't it amazing how complicated a simple financial product intended to care for one's family in the case of an untimely passing can be? At this point, if you are not thoroughly frustrated and confused, you should consider a career as an economist or insurance actuary. We are all baffled by the myriad of information thrust at us regarding life insurance. Unfortunately, we are using technical, mathematical, and legal jargon to try to make decisions about the most emotional eventualities that a family can face.

Our natural reaction may be to throw up our hands in frustration and do nothing, or turn the matter over to an insurance salesman and hope for the best. Either choice would be wrong. You must get the help you need to get the information you require to provide the protection that your family deserves.

Insurance presents some of the hardest decisions you will ever have to make, and unfortunately, you've got to get it right the first time. There are no spell checks, mulligans, or do-overs when dealing with life insurance after the fact. By the time your family figures out they don't have adequate insurance, it is too late to do anything about it.

In the next chapter, we'll continue to simplify insurance decisions involving products with even more moving pieces than life insurance.

Life Insurance
Needs Analysis

Input Area			
Debt		**Children**	
Mortgage	$293,000	Number of children	2
School loans	$26,000	Total number of years education remaining	12
Other debt	$5,000	Cost per year of education in today's dollars	$15,000
You		**Spouse**	
Final expenses	$20,000	Final expenses	$20,000
Income	$10,000	Income	$35,000

Insurance Needs Analysis			
You		**Spouse**	
1. Final Expenses			
Final expenses	$20,000	Final expenses	$20,000
Life Insurance Need	**$20,000**	*Life Insurance Need*	**$20,000**
2. Debts and Mortgages			
Mortgage	$293,000	Mortgage	$293,000
School loans	$26,000	School loans	$26,000
Other debt	$5,000	Other debt	$5,000
Life Insurance Need	**$324,000**	*Life Insurance Need*	**$324,000**
3. Education			
Cost per year	$15,000	Cost per year	$15,000
Total years remaining	12	Total years remaining	12
Life Insurance Need	**$180,000**	*Life Insurance Need*	**$180,000**
4. Income Replacement			
Income	$10,000	Income	$35,000
50% income replacement	50%	50% income replacement	50%
Amount to be replaced:	$5,000	Amount to be replaced:	$17,500
Estimated annual return	5%	Estimated annual return	5%
*Life Insurance Need**	**$250,000**	*Life Insurance Need**	**$350,000**
Total Insurance Need	**$774,000**	**Total Insurance Need**	**$874,000**

* If either spouse has income under $25,000 the calculator will automatically replace their "*Life Insurance Need*" with $250,000 to represent the cost of nonfinancial benefits they provide.

15 MINUTES COULD COST YOU A FORTUNE!

> "15 minutes could save you 15% or
> more on your car insurance."
> "Quote in 6 minutes. You could save
> $550 on car insurance."
> "Get more and pay less."
>
> *Various advertisements*

Y ou're involved in a car accident. It's your fault. The person driving the car you hit is injured. He visits with an attorney who runs late night commercials in between *People's Court* re-runs. They decide to sue you. They win and are awarded $950,000. Who pays that bill? The insurance company? Hopefully. You? Possibly. If insurance, which one of those different types of coverage tells you how much they'll pay? "Gee, I hope that when I saved 15% in 15 minutes I didn't reduce that particular coverage."

You've seen that commercial that claims to save you 15% on your auto insurance cost if you're willing to spend 15 minutes. I've talked to several people who liked that idea, spent their 15 minutes, and, indeed, saved 15% or more on the premiums that they paid for their car insurance. What is not promised by the unnamed insurance company, which incidentally is also represented by an over-sized lizard and a couple of prehistoric humans, is whether new converts could be guaranteed to maintain or improve upon their auto insurance pricing and still have good coverage. In other words, they may be spending less...for less.

It is not my intent to demonize the above-referenced company. You may very well have your auto insurance with them and be properly insured for a reasonable rate. But it is inside the insurance realm that economic bias is so ever present that we must be very careful to understand what coverage we own for the stated price. Too many have spent 15 to save 15, or followed through on some other tempting sales pitch, only to find that their auto coverage would leave them financially exposed in the case that it was needed. Another "forward thinking" company has recently invited television viewers to choose the price that they would like to pay for their car insurance and allow the company to build a customized policy around the spending restrictions. I'm going to make another suggestion specific to your home, auto, and liability insurance: determine the coverage that you need, and then shop around for apples-to-apples quotes to see who will offer you the best price.

Timeless Truth

My grandfather, who is the source of much of the wisdom I talk and write about, gave me a lesson and some words that apply to our exploration into the mysteries of insurance.

I was a small boy, and we were doing some type of woodworking project. I was rushing through one of the steps in the process, and he asked a question that remains with me today. "If you don't have time to do it right, when are you going to have time to do it over?"

The unfortunate thing about insurance coverage is that, by the time you find out you didn't do it right, you can't do it over. You are risking everything that you and your family have worked and sacrificed to create, on a moment-by-moment basis. If you're going to take the time to build and create wealth, it's worth a few minutes to make sure you protect your wealth.

When you look at the economics of insurance, your primary goal should be protection, not saving premium dollars. People will continue to advertise and push cheaper premiums at you, simply because it's hard for you and me to know when we think we're making a comparison, and we're really looking at apples and oranges.

All premiums are not created equal, because all coverage is not created equal.

Just as you invest your money, make a commitment to invest some time and acquire the expertise through your own knowledge or a financial planner so you and your family can truly be protected.

Jim Stovall

Home and auto insurance is often the most neglected risk management tool because it's so often commoditized. It is seen as insurance that we are legally required to own if we wish to drive a car or own a home, and so people spend 15 to 60 minutes calling a couple folks—or the guy at church who mailed them a fridge magnet—and not paying a second's notice to the details of the policy. Let me first show you why it's so important to understand your auto insurance.

Our at-fault driver mentioned previously, who is on the hook for $950,000, need look at his auto and liability insurance to see if he is covered for this loss. The vast majority of the hundreds of auto insurance declaration pages that I have reviewed did not provide adequate coverage to insure against a $950,000 loss.

If you shopped your car insurance recently, you may recall the agent mentioning something about "fifty, one-hundred," or "one-hundred, three-hundred," or "two-fifty, five-hundred." The type of coverage that would pick up the tab for the law suit would be bodily injury liability. Typically, that coverage is quoted listing two successive numbers. The first number is how much liability protection you have per person. The second is the amount that covers you per occurrence.

The chances are good that you have $100,000 of bodily injury liability coverage per person and $300,000 per occurrence. In our hypothetical accident and law suit, since there was only one person in the car you hit, your liability coverage is going to top out at $100,000. I hope you have an extra $850,000 lying around somewhere!

Many people intent on saving a few bucks on their premiums opted for a number even lower than that—maybe $50,000 and $100,000 or $25,000 and $50,000. Indeed the minimum insurance amount in most states is $25,000/$50,000. Save in the short term, you may, but it could cost you a fortune. Since we covered the Risk Manager's approach to an automobile accident in Chapter 5: Don't Be Sold Insurance! Manage Risk, we'll immediately delve into the various types of auto and home insurance coverage.

The primary types of coverage listed on most auto insurance declaration pages are the following, along with some suggestions for coverage limits; but since insurance is regulated by the state and every person's situation is different, it is important that you review these with an independent planner individually:

Bodily Injury Liability – This is the example we used above. The key word here is liability. You did something non-malicious that was nonetheless due to your own negligence, and you're now liable for the damage, pain, and suffering caused. Consider having minimum coverage of $250,000 or $500,000 per person and $500,000 per occurrence. (But, you say, even $500,000 isn't going to take care of that $950,000 bill. Read on.)

Property Damage – This coverage pays for damage done to another vehicle or other immovable object you "moved." Consider having minimum coverage of $100,000 per accident.

Medical Payments – Medical payments and its cousin, personal injury protection (PIP), help compensate an injured party for that which may not be otherwise covered by health insurance. For this reason, this limit can be lower. Consider having minimum coverage of $2,500 per person.

Uninsured/Underinsured Motorists Bodily Injury and

Property – Yes, it's true. You need to insure yourself for injury that may be caused to you or a passenger by a negligent driver who is uninsured or underinsured. As much as that may bother you, the risk is too significant. Statistics vary greatly by state, but states report anywhere from 4% to over 30% rates of uninsured drivers. Statistics for the underinsured in some states indicate that over half of insured drivers have less than adequate coverage. Consider having minimum coverage of $250,000 or $500,000 per person and $500,000 per accident, and $100,000 per accident for property damage. (And be careful. If you're in that category of premium savers who pay very little because you have $25,000/$50,000 for bodily injury liability, you're one of the underinsured!)

So if you can't skimp on these coverage amounts in order to get your premium down, what can you do? If you have sufficient emergency reserves, the prudent Risk Manager would utilize the Risk Assumption technique by having higher deductibles. The deductible is the amount that you are responsible to pay in the case that you suffer or inflict damage before the insurance company starts to pitch in. You will pay less in premium annually if you have a $1,000 deductible than you will with a deductible of $100. If you can only afford to pay $100 or $250 in the case of an accident, your deductible should be $100 or $250. But, if you have sufficient emergency reserves, increasing your deductible to $1,000 or $2,000 will save you money on your premiums. Prior to making a change to increase your deductible, however, ensure that the difference in premium is meaningful enough to make it worth the change.

The most common words denoting different deductibles on your auto insurance declaration pages are collision and comprehensive. The easiest way to remember the difference between the two is that collision coverage applies when you have one—a collision. Comprehensive is utilized when just about anything else happens. Your car was vandalized or caught in a hail storm—comprehensive. You have an accident—collision. You're driving down a nice country road and a deer leaps from the bushes and lands on your car while you are in your lane—comprehensive. You're driving down the same road and the same deer jumps out a bit sooner, giving you time to swerve, but you veer off the road and hit a tree—collision!

I still haven't told you how you're going to cover the rest of that law suit without digging into your personal savings, but that's because I must first tell you about homeowner's and renter's insurance. The primary homeowner's coverage varieties with which you must be aware are the following:

Dwelling – Dwelling coverage insures your home, not your homestead. If a tree in your yard falls on your family room, dwelling coverage will pay to fix your house. If that tree falls in the other direction and lands in the middle of your beautiful yard, your standard homeowner's policy will pay approximately zero dollars to help with the clean up. In most policies, your land is simply not covered.

What if the same tree falls, landing on your neighbor's house? She rings the doorbell to let you know that your tree fell on her house in the middle of the night. You suggest she inform her homeowners agent, as it is her policy that will handle this damage. What if the tree fell on your neighbor's car? You got it—her comprehensive auto coverage. Consider covering at least 80% of the cost to rebuild your house from scratch—not 80% of the value of your dwelling and land combined. In many policies, if your dwelling coverage represents a number that is less than 80% of the true replacement cost of your home, you may be required to pay a proportionate amount of any damages to your home, so it is important to regularly update your dwelling coverage to reflect changes in your home's value.

Other Structures – Since we've established that dwelling coverage only covers the dwelling, other structures will give you some coverage for a detached garage, shed or...outhouse (I guess). This coverage will usually be determined as a multiple of the dwelling coverage.

Personal Property – Dwelling covers the actual structure; other structures, the other structures. Personal property covers your stuff—everything *inside* of your house. This coverage is also usually determined as a multiple of your dwelling coverage, but be wary of the exclusions and caps in your policy. There are typically limits placed on the individual value of jewelry, collectibles, guns, and cash. An individual rider is necessary—and recommended—for articles in your house with individual values above the policy limits. Remember these two important things about your personal property coverage:

1) Actual cash value coverage of your personal property will only pay for the depreciated value of your home's contents. Consider requesting full replacement value coverage that will replace damaged or stolen items with a brand new comparable item.

2) You are responsible to inform the insurance company of your household inventory in the case of a loss. The last time you want to try to remember the details of your property and contents is right after your house burns to the ground. Consider conducting an inventory of your home's contents with a video camera or online software designed for that purpose. If you use a video camera, describe the contents audibly as you are taping, and then remember to store your tape outside of your home. Know Your Stuff™ Home Inventory is a free online software provided by the Insurance Information Institute. You can go room-by-room offering descriptions and including pictures, receipts and appraisals.

Personal Liability – This is the coverage that protects you financially if the neighbor's kid falls down your stairs and the neighbors sue you. Interestingly, personal liability coverage also follows you and your family outside of your house. If your son, visiting a friend, drops the ancient urn holding great-great-great-grandma's ashes, the personal liability coverage attached to your homeowner's policy may cover the resulting damages. Consider maintaining a minimum of $300,000 of personal liability insurance coverage.

Renter's insurance is very similar to homeowner's insurance with the obvious exception of the dwelling. You don't own it and are not required to insure it; however, it is very important that renters do not assume that they don't need coverage because they don't own the building. The property and liability insurance is still vital. Your clothing alone is something that most couldn't afford to replace, not to mention all of your other household items. And remember, the liability insurance follows you even when you're not in your own apartment or home.

So, I still haven't answered the $950,000 question. How do you cover the cost of the lost lawsuit in excess of your underlying liability coverage? The answer is supplemental liability or "umbrella" insurance. In addition to the liability provided by your home and auto insurance, we must recognize that, while living in the most litigious society on the planet, we may well be faced with a liability suit above the $300,000 or $500,000 policy limits, the balance of which we'd be responsible to pay. An umbrella policy guards you from those litigious clouds that may rain down on your home or auto worlds.

Supplemental liability is typically purchased in increments of $1,000,000. Therefore, if you had the car accident that was your fault and the law suit awarded to your victim was outside the parameters of your bodily injury liability protection with your auto policy, your supplemental liability policy would pick up the slack. So, in our story, if you only had $100,000 of bodily injury liability protection, the umbrella would cover the remaining $850,000. Know, however, that most insurers will require you to increase your underlying auto coverage to $250,000/$500,000 in order to give you umbrella protection.

The old rule of thumb was that you only needed an umbrella for up to the value of the assets that you own, but this is one instance where I recommend that virtually everyone purchase at least a $1 million umbrella policy because the cost is so low. The last time I looked into it, the premium quoted was under $250 per year. Remember that a law suit that you can't pay today may garnish your wages until it is paid off. If your net worth is in excess of a million, consider purchasing additional umbrella coverage in increments of $1,000,000.

Economic Bias Alert!

One of the most fascinating examples of Economic Bias in this book is that of the home and auto insurance agent. While most in sales are given an incentive to sell more, some home and auto agents have an economic bias to sell LESS!

An auto agent sells policies for which you and I pay premiums. Those premiums go into a virtual bucket, and throughout the course of the year, claims are paid out of that bucket. If the agency takes in more premiums than they pay out claims in a year, they have a profit; if the reverse, a loss. Most agencies are incentivized to keep that number in the black with the award of a persistency bonus—a cut of the profit.

This is the reason that I once had an insurance agent "advise" me NOT to purchase an umbrella policy that I wanted to buy. The agent would only take in $250 in premium for the year, but the claims risk potential was $1,000,000! Many insurance agencies, then, have an economic bias to sell you less than you actually need. Good agents do not engage in these practices, but you should be aware of the possibility to make certain that you're adequately insured.

Price is not the only factor in determining which insurer you use. The company with which you do business does matter. Do your homework to determine which companies in your area have the best service and claims records. Your geographic location will be a major factor in determining which company will offer the best coverage for the lowest price, but don't forget the importance of a good service and claims record as well.

Some companies will automatically cancel you after only a single claim, and it's not worth it to save money to get one of them, because once you've been cancelled, it's hard to find new coverage. Several highly-rated companies now offer First Time Accident Forgiveness, ensuring that you won't be cancelled or have a rate increase after one incident, and while that is in part a clever marketing campaign, it can also be a valuable benefit.

Consider quoting with the "15-in-15" company and the "forward thinking" bunch, but also quote other national and regional companies that may have more favorable rates in your area. Some companies offer participating policies. These companies may return some of the premium to their policyholders in profitable years, and mutual insurers will offer policyholders company stock if they ever go public. If you've ever been connected with the military, the organization that exclusively serves current and retired military is known for offering some of the lowest rates and best service.

Timely Application
Home & Auto Insurance Audit

In order to know if your home and auto insurance policies are providing you with the appropriate levels of coverage, you'll want to collect the Declaration Pages for all of your home, auto, condo, and renter policies. The Application Exercise online will provide a chart to fill in your various coverage limits next to our recommended minimum limits.

After you've tailored your desired limits with the help of an independent planner who does not accept commission or referral fees for the sale of insurance, you can use the Application Exercise to shop your coverage with several carriers.

Visit www.thefinancialcrossroads.com to find a template to use in creating your own Home & Auto Insurance Audit.

Tim Maurer

Building wealth and planning your financial future without protecting your family and your assets through appropriate insurance is like trying to fill up the bathtub with the drain open.

Bad things inevitably happen to good people. You want to take every step possible to make sure these bad things don't happen to those you care about, but if you do become one of those unfortunate statistics, proper insurance can be the difference between your dreams coming true and a nightmare.

Home & Auto
Insurance Audit

Auto Insurance

Insurance Company:

Category	Your Coverage	Recommended **Minimum** (Per Person/Per Occurrence)
Bodily Injury Liability		$250k/$500k or $500k/$500k
Property Damage		$100,000
Medical Payments		$2,500 per person
Un/Underinsured Motorist		$250k/$500k or $500k/$500k
Collision Deductible		What you can afford
Comprehensive Deductible		What you can afford
1st Time Accident Forgiveness		Yes

Auto Premium:

Home Owner's/Renter's Insurance

Insurance Company:

Dwelling Replacement Cost:		Other Structure Replacement Cost:	

Category	Your Coverage	Recommended **Minimum**
Dwelling		80% of Replacement
Other Structures		% of Dwelling Coverage
Personal Liability		$300K

Category	Insurance Value	Real Value	Category	Insurance Value	Real Value
Antiques			Firearms		
Art			Jewelry		
Collectibles			Sport. Goods		
Electronics			Other		

Home Owner's/Renter's Premium:

Umbrella Insurance

Insurance Company:

Category	Your Coverage	Recommended **Minimum**
Umbrella Coverage		$1,000,000

Umbrella Premium:

Disclaimer: Insurance is regulated by state, and every person's situation is different. It is important that you review these with an independent planner individually.

Chapter
nine

MONEY AND HEALTH

The poorest man would not part with health for money, but the richest would gladly part with all their money for health.

Charles Caleb Colton

Would you quit smoking if someone gave you $376,450 as an incentive to do so—today? Probably. You could take the money now, or if willing to wait 35 years from the quitting date, you could receive $1,059,279. Even 35 years from now, that would be a pretty decent addition to a retirement nest egg.

How did I come up with those numbers? I took the example of a reasonably healthy, self-employed 30-something male who is married and planning to start a family. Then, I assumed that the additional money he spends on smoking and smoking-related costs every year would be inflated and hypothetically invested, earning 7% per year. I'll prove it to you later in the chapter.

Fiscal and physical health are often seen as separate and distinct, but like most areas of our lives, money plays a significant role. This is also true in our pursuit of healthy living and the risk management of an unexpected health event. In this chapter, we'll discuss three types of insurance: Health Insurance, Disabiity Income Insurance, and Long Term Care Insurance. They are often lumped together, but there is virtually no overlap in the benefits they provide and the risk from which they shield us. Each of them could easily consume their own chapter, but those would be three fairly boring chapters, so we'll focus on the highlights and encourage you to go deeper in your personal analysis. We will examine each of them from our risk management perspective.

Timeless Truth

With rampant credit card overspending, the sub-prime housing crisis, and ridiculous long term automobile leases, most people assume poor spending habits cause personal bankruptcy. In reality, the number one cause of bankruptcy in our society today is medical bills.

For most people, it is not a matter of if but when you will need major medical coverage. And if you're one of the lucky ones who never uses your health insurance, HOORAY! I would be very pleased to pay the fire insurance premium on my house and never use it.

If you are earning part or all of the income for a young family dependent upon your ability to work, you need to realize that you're more likely to become disabled than to die. Most people understand life insurance is important, but they don't realize that disability insurance is critical.

Finally, there is a flaw in the way people look at long term care between them and their spouse. There is a serious danger I like to call the second spouse syndrome. People who fall victim to the second spouse syndrome assume they will be able to take care of each other in old age. In most cases, one spouse does not have the ability to take care of the other and, obviously, at some point one of you is going to pass away, leaving the other one alone.

The second danger in second spouse syndrome assumes that one nest egg will be adequate to take care of both spouses. Too often, a spouse dies at the end of a long debilitating illness. It is not unusual for that spouse to deplete a sizable nest egg in the last several months of life, leaving the second spouse destitute when it comes to their long term care needs.

None of us want to think about the issues represented by health, disability, and long term care insurance; however, if you don't face it as a statistical exercise now, you will face it as a daily reality later.

You will work very hard to earn, save, invest, and manage your resources. Make sure that one of life's inevitable bumps in the road doesn't derail you and your family financially.

Jim Stovall

Health insurance is the variety of insurance that we most often view as an entitlement—a gimme. It's pretty blah, right? Unless you are self-employed or the benefits coordinator of a company, you're not inundated with sales pitches for health insurance, as you are for life or auto insurance. This is because most health insurance is handled at the corporate level, and you often don't have much of a choice in what you get.

How does health insurance work? You, your employer, or some combination pays a monthly premium to the insurance company, and then they pay some or all of the cost of your medical care. The cost for a young, healthy, single individual with a bare bones plan can be under $100 per month, while the cost for a family or aging couple or individual can be in the thousands.

Most Americans receive their medical care through one of several managed care platforms, the most common of which are Health Maintenance Organizations (HMOs) and Preferred Provider Organizations (PPOs). HMOs are entities that employ a selection of doctors and health care providers with which insured patients can choose to work. There is a primary focus on preventative care in HMO platforms, and most require a patient to meet with a Primary Care Physician before being treated by a specialist.

PPOs are groupings of doctors and hospitals who band together to charge approved rates to an insurance company. The cost of a PPO is typically higher than the cost of an HMO, but they tend to offer greater flexibility in the number of doctors from which patients can choose, and they also allow patients to go directly to a specialist, without a referral from a Primary Care Physician. Another less common managed care variety is the Point Of Service (POS) option that acts as a hybrid between an HMO and a PPO.

If you have an HMO or PPO health insurance plan, you probably have a co-pay and possibly a deductible. The co-pay is the amount paid when you go to the appointment with your doctor or specialist. If you have a generous enough plan, you have no deductible and your only responsibility is the co-pay. If you have a deductible, you are responsible for a specified amount of out-of-pocket cost before the insurance plan will pitch in. Other plans have a cost sharing arrangement called coinsurance. Typical arrangements may require the patient to pay for 20% of a service or procedure while the insurance company covers the other 80%.

So in virtually every different kind of health plan, there are out-of-pocket medical costs for which you will be responsible. These costs can be handled in a tax privileged manner through the use of a Flexible Spending Account (FSA) or a Health Savings Account (HSA). Picture these accounts as buckets. You make a contribution into the bucket and you get a tax deduction for doing so. Then, when you buy Tylenol, aspirin, or pay for a doctor's appointment, you use the funds in your bucket and pay no taxes. The net effect is that most of the money you spend on medical expenses each year can now be tax deductible. That's the equivalent of getting a 15-35% discount (depending on your tax bracket) on those costs.

You would be interested to see what the IRS deems to be Qualified Medical Expenses, eligible for withdrawal from an HSA, and you can find a comprehensive list on the IRS website (www.irs.gov); search for Publication 502 which lists these expenses or Publication 969 for broader information about HSAs and FSAs. The following may be surprising allowable expenses per the IRS: acupuncture to treat a medical condition, smoking cessation programs, alcoholism treatment, chiropractic fees, psychiatric care, a host of over-the-counter medications, massage with a letter from your doctor, and even long term care insurance premiums. Specifically not allowed are the following: aromatherapy, deodorants, toothbrushes, breast enhancement, natural and herbal remedies and, of course, cigarettes and booze!

Flexible Spending Accounts can be used in conjunction with any health plan, but they also have two major pitfalls. First, most of them require you to purchase the goods and services yourself and wait for reimbursement, and second—and this is the real doozy—you must use 100% of your annual contributions or you lose them. They get swept into that dark financial black hole that no one can find (it's actually your employer that keeps the change). It is that use-it-or-lose-it feature that gives one pause before contributing to an FSA, but if you've done a great job budgeting, you can quantify a reasonable level of medical expenses to contribute to the FSA.

Health Savings Accounts are only allowable in conjunction with a high-deductible health plan, but unused portions of HSA contributions are yours to keep indefinitely. They can actually earn money over time and be used as a retirement account after you reach age 65 (unlike the 59½ rule applied to IRAs that we'll discuss in the retirement planning chapter). In order for your health plan to be deemed "high-deductible," you must have a minimum deductible of $1,150 for an individual or $2,300 for a family in 2009. That seems like a pretty penny to pay for the privilege of being able to contribute to this account, but you'll be paying less for this health insurance plan option, and your employer may even make a contribution to the plan for you. The result is often a surplus in your favor that accrues into the future.

Let's review this, because it gets pretty confusing. Instead of choosing the regular PPO plan with no deductible and a co-pay, you choose the high-deductible PPO plan and add an HSA to the mix. Since your employer is paying less for the high-deductible plan, they may very well make a monthly contribution to your HSA. If they contribute $200 per month and your family plan has a $2,400 deductible, then you've already covered your deductible. But for 2009, you can contribute up to the maximum of $5,950—an additional $3,550 for which you'll receive a tax deduction. Then, when you go to the doctor's office, you pay the full $175 for the visit and you pay for it with your HSA debit card, or you pay for it yourself and keep the receipt.

Here is where it gets interesting. You can reimburse yourself for all eligible medical expenses or you can allow them to accrue, even beyond the year in which they were paid. Then, at some later date when you've accrued a ton of receipts, you can write yourself a big check—tax free. But, there's no guarantee that the HSA will stick around or that health insurance, as we know it, will even survive.

Can our health insurance industry be saved? The answer lies in a very important question that I pose to you: How much does it cost to go to the doctor? If your answer was $20, $35, or $50, you answered like the majority of Americans, but those answers couldn't be more wrong. For most standard appointments with a family physician, the amount is probably closer to $200. For specialists, it's not uncommon for the price of a single appointment to be $600, $1,000, or more—all for the price of a nominal co-pay.

The problem with our health insurance does not lie with the medical system. It is the undisputed best in the world. The problem is with our payment system. The people providing the service (docs) aren't directly billing the people receiving the service (patients), and the people receiving the service aren't directly paying the service providers. A freshman economics major could tell you that's not going to work. Enter the all-too-late savior of the medical payment system—the Health Savings Account. When patients use a high deductible medical plan with an HSA, they actually see how much it costs for the doctor's visit, and they pay for it in full. They don't pay co-pays for prescriptions; they pay the full price. In the end, it doesn't cost them any more because of the employer contributions and lower cost for the plan, but the service provider and recipient are finally connected.

What the economists love most about the HSAs is that the prospective patient now has the proper incentive to avoid frivolous trips to the doctor. When I get common cold symptoms, I'm not going to pay $200 to have the doctor tell me I have a cold. I'm going to get plenty of sleep, drink a lot of water, and keep the two-hundo in my HSA.

Economic Bias Alert!

Every semester I teach The Fundamentals of Financial Planning, I give the students an Economic Bias assignment. They need to observe life throughout the course of their semester and present to the class an example of Economic Bias that they've found in life. One student presented a whopper related to the health care industry. This student had a close relative who worked for one of the big health insurance companies. The employee was a claims processor. That employee was given BONUSES to DENY claims. Did you catch that? The claims processor actually got cash bonuses in his paycheck for denying claims. The bigger the claim denied, the bigger the bonus!

This might be justified in some board room as a tool to keep the claims processors focused on the task at hand, but it also means that there's an Economic Bias—as big as an insurance company—that we need to know about. So next time you have a claim rejected, appeal it. I've talked to clients who appealed claims as many as three times and finally got the insurance company to accept the claim. Rejected claim? Appeal!

How then do we act as responsible risk managers of the personal and financial risk associated with health insurance?

Risk Avoidance: We can avoid the risk of getting sick by living in a bubble and eliminating all contact with the outside world. That's going to be tough.

Risk Reduction: There is a lot that we can do in this department. We can not smoke, wash our hands, take our vitamins, drink fish oil, sleep eight hours a night, don't oversleep, exercise at least three times per week, find time to relax, get outside to be exposed to sunlight, don't spend too much time in the sun, drink a glass of red wine each night, don't drink a bottle of wine every night.... The list of things that we can do to reduce our health risk is endless. You have to "listen to your body," and choose the right techniques for you.

Risk Assumption: There is no better example of assuming the financial risk of health care than the deductible. The higher your deductible, or the higher your co-pay, or the higher your coinsurance, the lower your health insurance premium. The optimal vehicle for risk assumption is combining a high-deductible health plan with a Health Savings Account.

Risk Transfer: We transfer the risk of a catastrophic health care event with health insurance. You remember my auto accident story? I didn't have a couple hundred thousand dollars as an eighteen-year-old punk who wouldn't have had insurance if I didn't automatically default onto my father's health insurance policy. And thank God I did, because otherwise, they'd probably still be garnishing my wages. Going without health insurance is simply...foolish (ever since I've had little kids running around my house, I've been trying not to use words like stupid; unless I'm talking to the dog, of course).

Of the three insurance varieties discussed in this chapter, that was the easiest. Disability income insurance and long term care insurance are the most complicated and complex personal insurance policies on the street, but they must not be ignored as a result. They could be two of the most important to consider.

Disability income insurance (DI) is just that. It insures your income in the case you are disabled. If you are disabled in a car accident, health insurance is going to cover the cost of your medical care. If you're out of work for a period of time, disability income insurance is going to replace a portion of your income. Short term disability income (STD) coverage will take care of the first few weeks or months. Long term disability income (LTD) coverage picks up the balance, possibly all the way through age 65 or beyond. Since your short term needs are probably covered by an STD policy through your employer, or otherwise should be covered by your emergency liquid reserves discussed earlier, we'll concentrate on LTD.

Most insurance companies will not insure anyone for LTD for over 60% of their pre-tax income because they don't want to offer them an incentive to be out of work, lest the incidence of disability oddly increase. You probably have a group DI policy through your work, and most of them cover up to the 60% rule. You may be thinking that it wouldn't be too bad because after taxes, you're not taking home a whole lot more than 60% of your paycheck anyway. The only problem is that if your company is paying the premium, and thereby gaining a corporate tax deduction, the IRS is going to require you to pay income tax on that benefit. If, on the other hand, you pay the premium with your own after-tax dollars, the benefit—in the case that you were disabled—would be tax free.

Therefore, if you find yourself in the situation of most Americans, where you work for a company that provides you an LTD benefit at no cost that will pay 60% of your income in the case of a disability, you'll really only be getting approximately 40% of your pre-tax income, with increased medical expenses on the home front, should you need the benefit. If your company gives you the option to pay for all or a portion of the taxes on your group LTD policy premium, strongly consider accepting the invitation, although this option is quite rare.

You may consider supplementing this gap—to get you back up to that approximate number of 60% of your pre-tax income—with a private LTD policy. While most insurance agents have a blatant economic bias to sell you more policy than you might need, this bias is restricted for sellers of LTD because the companies are scared to death of giving you too much, and therefore giving you that incentive to "become" disabled enough to stay home with pay; therefore, with LTD, you typically want whatever the company is willing to give you (seriously) because the company will never be willing to give you more than you'd want if you were to become disabled. This doesn't exempt LTD agents from economic bias entirely, though. Their bias can still bite you in the ridiculous number of details and moving pieces.

Following are the menagerie of moving pieces that I'm reading directly off of an LTD quote in my hands:

> base benefit, Social Security benefit, total benefit, elimination period, benefit period, renewability provision, own occupation provision, residual benefit, minimum residual benefit payable, recovery benefit, recurrent benefit, recurrent benefit paid from an unrelated cause, return of premium, COLA, future insurability options, age through which future insurability is exercisable, maximum presumptive disability paid, survivor benefit,

limitation on mental or nervous disorders, catastrophic benefit rider, company ratings.

Can you believe that? How is anybody supposed to know what to do with all that...stuff (remember my pledge about using child appropriate language)? You can't. As I mentioned earlier, if I go through all of it in this book, you'll stop reading out of sheer boredom, so I'll simply inform you that you must find an independent source who understands this stuff and doesn't have an axe to grind. And, I'll highlight the most important provisions to review:

Base Benefit is the amount you would receive monthly if you suffered a qualifying disability.

Residual Benefit gives you the option to go back to work part-time and receive part of your disability benefit. If you don't have residual, you'll be required to stay out of work entirely to receive any benefit.

Social Security Benefit provides a way to save some money on your LTD policy. Although it is notoriously difficult to qualify for, Social Security does offer a small disability benefit. If you opt for a Social Security offset provision, your disability benefit will be reduced by the proportionate amount that you receive from Social Security, if any.

Elimination Period is the time you would have to wait before the policy would pay a benefit. You can save money on your premium by having a longer elimination period if you have adequate liquid reserves.

Renewability Provision stipulates whether you have a policy that, at some point, the insurer could arbitrarily alter or cancel. A non-cancelable policy contractually binds the insurer to maintain the policy as-is. Guaranteed renewable is more of a pledge that they won't change the policy. A conditionally renewable policy can hang you out to dry.

COLA is a cost of living adjustment—sort of. In the LTD world, a COLA provision doesn't kick in until you begin to receive the benefit. So, if you buy a policy with a $2,000/month benefit when you're 35, and then you become disabled when you're 55, your benefit amount will begin at $2,000 per month—and then it will rise with the stipulated contract COLA. It's tricky, but you still want it.

Future Insurability Options are, for all intents and purposes, the pre-disability cost of living adjustment, but you have to pay for it. Every few years, as your income increases, an FIO option will allow you to buy more coverage without underwriting. (Only an insurance company could come up with this...stuff!)

Any or Own Occupation? That is the question. This may be the most important provision of all. If you have an "Own Occ" LTD policy, it will pay you if you become disabled enough that you cannot perform the material duties of your own occupation. This is what you want. "Any Occ" requires that you are unable to perform the material duties of any occupation in order to have your benefit paid. There is a genuine soft spot in my heart for the folks who work as "Greeters" at WalMart, so I want to be very sure this remark does not come across in a disparaging way, but if you can take a smiley face sticker and stick it on someone's shirt, you can perform "any" occupation and, therefore, would not be eligible to collect your LTD benefits. So, when you think of disability income insurance, remember this:

Your group LTD policy through your company is often a benefit for which you don't pay, and it's not worth a whole lot more than that. Most of the provisions that you'd ideally tailor above are less than ideal in the group policy. Most notably, most group LTD policies are "Own Occ" for the first two years and then convert to "Any Occ." Good LTD insurance is extremely expensive—much more expensive than your term life insurance—because actuarially, your chances of becoming disabled in your working years are far greater than your chances of suffering a life-ending disability in that phase of life. If you're supplementing a group policy, the cost will be manageable. Those who don't have group LTD coverage will be looking at a very steep premium in order to privately insure the desired amount, but it will be much better coverage. And don't assume that the companies with the best marketing for DI also have the best policies. That company well represented by an overly talkative duck—not necessarily the best policy.

Let's finish the disability income discussion as Risk Managers.

Risk Avoidance: Bubble.

Risk Reduction: Don't do anything fun—I mean, risky. This is a tough one for me because, as I said, I like playing sports, white water rafting, cycling, rock climbing, and motorcycling, so I can hardly lecture you. Let's just follow Mom's advice and, "Be careful!"

Risk Assumption: Maintain an adequate emergency liquid reserve.

Risk Transfer: Pick and choose your bells and whistles, but adequately insure with DI the catastrophic risk of doing serious damage to your family's money-making machine—YOU!

So, how do the government programs, Social Security, Medicaid, and Medicare fit into this picture? As we mentioned above, Social Security, which we'll be discussing in greater detail within the context of retirement planning, does offer a disability benefit (often referred to as SSDI) to those who qualify under age 65 (for those over age 65, the program is known as SSI or Supplemental Security Income). The benefit is notoriously difficult to receive and may be seen as an "any occupation" benefit. You can read more about these benefits at www.ssa.gov.

Medicaid is a federal program that is administered on the state level to provide care for the impoverished suffering from a disability at any age. While Medicare does not cover long term care costs for the elderly, Medicaid does offer assistance, to include nursing care, for those who have exhausted almost all of their assets. It had become big business for attorneys specializing in elder law to take people with money and make them appear to be people without, so that their assets would not be consumed by the costs associated with long term health care; however, Medicaid rules have been tightened in recent years, making that disappearing act more difficult to accomplish.

Medicare is a federal government health care plan for people over the age of 65. We pay into this system in our working years, and it is designed to reduce medical costs in our retirement years. Since it is a government program, it is naturally confusing and has many different elements. Medicare Part A is hospital insurance. Part B is medical insurance for physician care. While parts A and B are government run, Medicare Advantage, or Part C, is an A and B hybrid that is run through private insurance companies that are approved by Medicare. Medicare Part D is prescription coverage and if you're not satisfied with the care offered by Medicare Parts A and B, you're welcome to look into Medigap plans A through L. As you approach age 65, it is very important to do a thorough review of the plans available to you and balance your needs and wants with your cash flow requirements. For more information, visit the Medicare website at www.medicare.gov.

One very important thing to remember is that Medicare does not cover the costs of most long term care needs. Allen Hamm, in his book, *Long Term Care Planning*, quotes the following statistics:

71% of Medicare recipients mistakenly believe Medicare is a primary source for covering long-term care.

87% of people under the age of 65 mistakenly believe their private health insurance will cover the cost of long-term care.

In reality, Medicare will only pay for 100 days of skilled nursing care. Thereafter, the insured is responsible for 100% of the cost. But a risk manager does not automatically assume that the reflex response is to purchase a long term care insurance policy with all the bells and whistles. Every individual in their 50s or older should, however have a long term care plan in place. If you are younger than 50, you'll still want to read the next few paragraphs of this chapter for the bearing that it could have on your future life, or the life of a parent who should be going through this thought process.

Your long term care plan should incorporate the following:

Facts about you and your spouse, if applicable

Your age(s)

Your personal health

Longevity of lineage

Your retirement income and assets

Your tolerance for risk

The costs and demographics of long term care in your geographic area

Information about any long term care insurance that you own or have considered owning

What exactly is the financial risk of a long term health care incident? AARP breaks down the estimated cost by state on their website:

http://www.aarp.org/families/caregiving/state_ltc_costs.html

The annual cost of assisted living care in most states ranges from $30,000 to $50,000. The cost of full nursing care ranges from $50,000 to $100,000, with Alaska topping out at over $200,000 per year! States like New York, Connecticut, Maryland, and California are in the higher end of the ranges with states like Alabama, Louisiana, and South Dakota on the lower end. Regardless, you're talking about a significant amount of additional expense which most retirement plans are not prepared to support.

Long term care insurance is sold most often in daily increments, so you would purchase a policy that would pay $100, $150, or $200 per day for a stated number of years or your lifetime. LTC has almost as many moving parts as LTD; here are the most important to understand:

Facility Daily Benefit is the cost per day that the policy will cover. It is a good idea to ask for quotes based on a policy that would cover you for $100 per day, because then you can determine a higher or lower multiple of that policy rate easily based on the round number.

Facility Benefit Period is the length of time over which the policy will pay out. The average stay in a long term care facility is quite low—around 2 years—but most people utilize care for far less time. The numbers are skewed upward by the relative handful of folks who suffer from dementia or Alzheimer's for a particularly long stretch. If your tolerance for risk is very low, you may consider a lifetime benefit, but if you are focusing more on the probability, consider a five-year benefit.

Home Care Daily Benefit is the percentage of the policy benefit that could be applied to skilled care in your home. As the preferred method for most people, you will only want to consider plans that offer 100% of your benefit to be applied to home care.

Inflation Protection describes how the future inflation of health care costs will be factored into your benefit. With the future costs of health care expected to rise at a pace above the normal inflation rate, this should be a primary concern for the prospective insured. If you are in your 50s or 60s, strongly consider compound inflation protection. Unlike the quirky long term disability COLA factor, this feature does what you expect it to do—go up every year. If you are in your 70s or older and looking into a policy, the premiums are likely to be extremely costly, so you may consider a simple inflation protection calculation or no inflation protection to reduce the costs of the policy.

Facility Elimination Period is the initial time frame in which the policy will not pay. Since Medicare will typically pay for the first 100 days, consider an elimination period of 90 days or more.

Marital Discount is a significant discount for couples who are purchasing LTC together. Many insurance companies now offer "shared care" policies that offer less stringent underwriting and reduced costs; but be sure to conduct your LTC plan before choosing this insurance option. A spouse with a history of heart disease may have a higher probability of dying in an instant from a heart attack (and, therefore, may consider opting out of LTC), while a spouse with a family history of dementia or arthritis should strongly consider applying for LTC before major symptoms occur (because by then, you're likely to be turned down).

Economic Bias Alert!

One in two? A common statistic offered by agents who reap commissions from the sales of long term care insurance is that one in two of us will require some level of long term care services. I'm not suggesting that they're lying, but this statistic ignores a much more important statistic: How LONG does the average person require care? Certainly, you can think of many folks who received some form of long term health care towards the end of their life, but most of them only needed the care for a very short period of time—a risk that can be managed without insurance.

I've referred clients for whom I recommended the utilization of LTC to many intelligent and honorable insurance agents, but there is no denying the Economic Bias of an individual who WILL get paid if you buy and WON'T get paid if you don't. As we know, statistics can be made to say just about anything we want them to, so always temper the statistics presented to you with the recognition of the Economic Bias of the individual or company behind those statistics.

Your plan may very well include the purchase of long term care insurance, but it is simply one of the tools that you may use to neutralize a portion of the risk of a long term health care incident. Let's apply the Risk Manager criteria:

Risk Avoidance: You can't guarantee that you'll not suffer a long term health care incident, but you may be able to completely avoid the financial risk. There are now continuing care communities that offer every level of medical care from independent living to assisted living to nursing care and hospice care. Many of these facilities require higher payments for the more intensive levels of care, but some now offer residents the option of flat fee payments (usually in combination with a sizable down payment) that will not increase regardless of the level of care required. That is one way that you could virtually quash the financial risk of an extended long term health care incident (assuming the facility doesn't go bankrupt).

Risk Reduction: The risk reduction factors are similar to that of the disability and health insurance methods. Don't smoke, eat well, and exercise mentally, physically and spiritually.

Risk Assumption: The risk of a long term care incident could be reasonably self-insured if you have a liquid base of assets of $2 million and live off of no more than the growth and interest in the portfolio; but, there are no guarantees. If you have much less than $2 million, though, you can reasonably assume that you aren't a likely candidate for 100% self-insurance. Another way that you can assume risk in this case is by presuming that a family member or members will care for you. Before making this presumption, I'd recommend checking with them first!

Risk Transfer: The way you'd transfer the risk of a long term health care incident is with long term care insurance. But before you sign on the dotted line for the Rolls Royce of LTC policies because you conclude that you need and want coverage, first consider laying out your long term care plan and determining to what degree you can manage the risk with the other three methods. What may be appropriate for many is partially insuring this need.

A comprehensive risk management approach to health, disability income, and long term care insurance will help ensure that you insure the risks that you can't manage, and manage the ones that you can. The more that you can manage, the more dollars you'll have to apply to other valuable pursuits.

Timely Application
Disability and Long Term Care Plans

This Timely Application will help you complete your Health & Money Audit. This exercise is a three step process.

Step 1 is to determine what you need. This is accomplished by writing out a Disability Plan if you are in your 30s, 40s, or 50s. If in your 50s, 60s, or beyond, you need to articulate your Long Term Care Plan. Start the process by writing out a paragraph that begins with the following sentence: "If I became disabled (suffered a long term health care incident), here's how I would handle that financially..." We've provided space to do so in our online exercises for this chapter.

Step 2 is to establish what you already have. The online exercise includes a template with spaces to fill in for the primary features mentioned in this chapter. Once you have completed the template, you'll better understand the coverage you have.

Step 3 is to determine what you actually need and want, and quote to find the best coverage. You'll be better prepared for the engagement with the insurance agents because your template will ensure you're comparing apples-to-apples, a very difficult thing to do in DI and LTC.

Visit www.thefinancialcrossroads.com to find templates to use in creating your own Health & Money Audit.

Tim Maurer

I promised to back up my postulation that it could be worth up to a million bucks 35 years from now for the thirty-something smoker who's thinking about quitting. Here you go. The average cost for a pack of smokes these days is around $5.50 for Marlboros or Camels. You will pay more or less depending on the brand you smoke and the state in which you live. In some states, you can pay up to $10 or more for one pack of 20 cigarettes. Genuine smokers polish off about one pack per day, so the cigarettes alone will cost a smoker an additional $2,007.50 more per year than a comparable non-smoker.

This same guy would be able to buy $1,000,000 of 30 year term life insurance for $3,160 in the "Preferred Smoker" under-writing class, the best rating that a smoker can receive. If he didn't smoke, the best rates would be only $825, so the habit just cost him an additional $2,335 per year. This is the only cost described here that will not be expected to go up with inflation each year. The premiums are guaranteed for 30 years. Health insurance isn't quite as ugly. Here again, this will be state specific and company specific. Some states and companies gouge smokers while others allow the remainder of the risk pool to pick up the additional costs. We'll be conservative and say that the self-employed smoker who needs to get his own health insurance will pay $500 more per year for that coverage. Disability income insurance is another cost that the smoker will have to pick up and pay additional for the privilege to puff. This will cost him an additional $260 per year.

The aggregate of these costs amounts to $5,102 per year, so we assume that if that five grand wasn't going up in smoke, it could be invested to earn 7%. Then, if the increase in costs other than life insurance over each year (assumed to be 3%) were also invested, this would further compound the earning potential of the investment. When the ex-smoker is retired, he would have saved $1,059,279 just for having quit smoking. That's not a bad start to that retirement nest egg, eh? That $1,059,279 the smoker would have in 35 years could be discounted for inflation (using 3%) to be worth $376,450 in today's dollars.[i]

Yeah, money and health are connected.

---

[i] The future value of investing $2,767 in excess costs from smoking at 10% (7% investment return + 3% annual inflation of costs) 35 years from now is $749,924. The insurance costs would stay level for 30 years and then end, so the future value of $2,335 in excess premium in 30 years is $220,565 if it earns 7% annually. Then, no additional premiums would be paid, but the $220,565 would continue to compound earnings for another 5 years with an ultimate future value of $309,355. $749,924 plus $309,355 is $1,059,279 of additional savings from investing the excess costs of smoking. The present value of that amount—the amount of money that $1,059,279 in 35 years would be worth in today's dollars—accounting for 3% inflation, is $376,450.

Disability
Income Plan

Disability Income Insurance

Step 1

If I became disabled, here's how I would handle that financially:

Step 2

Current Disability Income Insurance

Insurance Company:

Policy Type:	☐ Long Term	☐ Short Term
Premiums Paid By:	☐ You	☐ Your Employer
Policy Benefit Is:	☐ Non-Taxable Income	☐ Taxable Income
Social Security Benefit:	☐ YES	☐ NO
Renewability Provision:	☐ YES	☐ NO
COLA Provision:	☐ YES	☐ NO
Occupation Provision:	☐ Own Occupation	☐ Any Occupation
Future Insurability:	☐ YES	☐ NO

Base Benefit:	
Residual Benefit:	
Social Security Benefit Premium Savings:	
Elimination Period:	

POLICY PREMIUM:	

Disability
Income Plan

Step 3

Disability Income Insurance Comparison

Insurance Company:

Policy Type:	☐ Long Term	☐ Short Term
Premiums Paid By:	☐ You	☐ Your Employer
Policy Benefit Is:	☐ Non-Taxable Income	☐ Taxable Income
Social Security Benefit:	☐ YES	☐ NO
Renewability Provision:	☐ YES	☐ NO
COLA Provision:	☐ YES	☐ NO
Occupation Provision:	☐ Own Occupation	☐ Any Occupation
Future Insurability:	☐ YES	☐ NO

Base Benefit:	
Residual Benefit:	
Social Security Benefit Premium Savings:	
Elimination Period:	
POLICY PREMIUM:	

Insurance Company:

Policy Type:	☐ Long Term	☐ Short Term
Premiums Paid By:	☐ You	☐ Your Employer
Policy Benefit Is:	☐ Non-Taxable Income	☐ Taxable Income
Social Security Benefit:	☐ YES	☐ NO
Renewability Provision:	☐ YES	☐ NO
COLA Provision:	☐ YES	☐ NO
Occupation Provision:	☐ Own Occupation	☐ Any Occupation
Future Insurability:	☐ YES	☐ NO

Base Benefit:	
Residual Benefit:	
Social Security Benefit Premium Savings:	
Elimination Period:	
POLICY PREMIUM:	

Long Term
Care Plan

Long Term Care Plan

Step 1

If I suffered a long term health care incident, here's how I would

handle that financially:

Step 2

Current Long Term Care Insurance

Insurance Company:

Marital Discount:	☐ YES	☐ No
Inflation Protection:	☐ None ☐ Simple	☐ Compound

Facility Daily Benefit:	
Facility Benefit Period:	
Home Care Daily Benefit:	
Facility Elimination Period:	

Facts For Consideration:	You	Your Spouse
Your age(s)		
Your personal health		
Longevity of lineage		
Ret. income & assets		
Tolerance for risk		
LTC cost in your area		
LTC insurance you own		
POLICY PREMIUM:		

Long Term
Care Plan

Step 3

Long Term Care Insurance Comparison

Insurance Company:

Marital Discount:	☐ YES	☐ NO
Inflation Protection:	☐ None ☐ Simple	☐ Compound

Facility Daily Benefit:	
Facility Benefit Period:	
Home Care Daily Benefit:	
Facility Elimination Period:	

Facts For Consideration:	You	Your Spouse
Your age(s)		
Your personal health		
Longevity of lineage		
Ret. income & assets		
Tolerance for risk		
LTC cost in your area		
Current LTC Insurance		
POLICY PREMIUM:		

Insurance Company:

Marital Discount:	☐ YES	☐ NO
Inflation Protection:	☐ None ☐ Simple	☐ Compound

Facility Daily Benefit:	
Facility Benefit Period:	
Home Care Daily Benefit:	
Facility Elimination Period:	

Facts For Consideration:	You	Your Spouse
Your age(s)		
Your personal health		
Longevity of lineage		
Ret. income & assets		
Tolerance for risk		
LTC cost in your area		
LTC insurance you own		
POLICY PREMIUM:		

Chapter
ten

RISK MANAGEMENT
INVESTING

> I am more concerned about the return of my money than the return on my money.
>
> *Mark Twain*

Mark Twain was the first to wittily claim that he was more concerned with capital preservation (the return of my money) than growth (the return on my money), but it is interesting to note that Twain passed away in 1910, prior to the Great Depression. Oklahoma's favorite son, Will Rogers (who died in 1935), also later made this a notable quote. I have another that I'd like you to chew on. "It is easier to lose money than it is to make it!"

That's not a catchy slogan or tagline. It's a mathematical fact. If you have $100 and you lose 10% of it, it will take an 11% rate of return to become whole. If you lose 20%, you'll need to make 25% to get your money back. What if you lose 50%? What rate of return would you need to make your money back? The answer is an astonishing 100%! I'm not being "tricksy" as Tolkien's character, Gollum, called the Hobbits in the *Lord of the Rings* trilogy. See for yourself:

$100 x 90% = $90; $90 x (100% + 11%)   = $100

$100 x 80% = $80; $80 x (100% + 25%)   = $100

$100 x 50% = $50; $50 x (100% + 100%)   = $100

Once you're down 50% and facing that big 100% hill, it will take you around seven years, if you're able to make an annualized rate of 10% per year, to get back where you started. If you're making closer to 7% each year, you'll be waiting a full decade to break even. If you earn 4% on your money, it will take you 18 years to recover from a 50% fall.

But you say, "I always learned that you need to buy and hold. The market will go up and down, and we can't time it, so we shouldn't try! It's not timing the market. It's time in the market!" It is true that market timing is a very dangerous business—betting, if you will; however, if and when you're able to see the bearish train coming down the tracks, would it not make sense to get out of its way? The price of staying in can be disastrous. From the day the market peaked on September 7, 1929, it would have taken until 1954 to break even if you bought, and held. That is a pretty long time to wait, especially if you were planning to retire in 1932.

And today? For the last decade, the market is down over 20% as of April 2009. You will find that the current logic that runs the financial services realm at the institutional level was developed in one of the best stretches the market's ever seen. From 1982 until March of 2000, the market ran upwards with little impedance. Objectively speaking, Buy-and-Hold and strict Asset Allocation concepts, born in that 18-year stretch, worked very well. But what about the stretch from 1964 up until 1982? Believe it or not, that span represented yet another 18-year stretch where the buy-and-holder would've made nothing—zip, zilch, nada. And we in the United States have it good! Japan's staring at their 20th year of an atrocious run that leaves the Nikkei still 70% south of its peak at 40,000. So, eight years into a rough losing streak for the U.S. market—and following a colossal financial demise brought on largely by ignorance and greed on the part of the U.S. government, corporations, and citizens—would you rather be buying-and-holding the Dow or the Nikkei?

It's not my intent to scare you, so let's go back, and I can try to give you some answers and some hope. The world's best investors are not buy-and-holders, asset allocators, or Modern Portfolio theorists. They're risk managers. These are folks like Sir John Templeton, Jean-Marie Eveillard, Jim Rogers and yes, Warren Buffett. They spend more time worrying about how not to lose money than they do trying to make it. I'm not talking about leaving all your money in T-Bills and CDs. I'm talking about resetting your brain to focus first on managing risk in your investments, then on your return.

Timeless Truth

The important thing to remember about investing is that all money is invested, but the majority of people today never become investors. Before you write me off as a total lunatic and my friend and colleague, Tim Maurer, banishes me from this project, please consider that the majority of people in our society today have consumer debt including credit cards, car loans, student loan payments, etc. that exceed their assets; therefore, these individuals have a negative net worth and cannot be considered investors.

To be an investor you must have an excess of money working for you. The majority of these indebted people have a deficit of money, so they are working to pay off their previous overspending plus interest.

For those of us who are investors who have amassed extra capital to put to work for us, we must recognize that all of this money is invested. Some people invest in the stock market, others invest in real estate and bonds, while still others choose to invest their money in a low-yield savings account or even in the form of cash under their mattress. But never forget all money is invested.

Since we never want to be in the category of debtors who make no investments, it behooves us to be wise investors. Wise investors understand that we cannot eliminate risk. We can only minimize our risk while selecting the type of risk we wish to take.

Poor investors assume that risk either guarantees high rates of return or, conversely, that risk guarantees loss of principal. The former automatically choose high risk investments assuming that their willingness to weather volatility will ultimately provide superior gains. The latter choose to invest entirely in low-return or even no-return investments. These individuals expose themselves to one of the most significant risks of all, the risk of inflation. At some point in the future when you liquidate a portion of your investment portfolio for retirement or for something you wish to purchase, it is not important how much money you have. It is important what your money will buy.

When I began my career as a young investment broker, I remember a seasoned veteran colleague of mine showing me a full page ad from a glossy magazine that had been published 30 years before, sometime in the mid-1950s. This colorful ad showed an attractive mature couple on the beach in front of their beautiful home getting ready to climb aboard their very expensive boat. The couple appeared to have achieved everything in life they ever wanted and were looking forward to a luxurious carefree retirement. The caption below this photo next to the logo for a fixed-rate investment company said, "Retire for life on 150 dollars per month." After I quit laughing, my experienced colleague informed me that many people bought into these types of investments 30 years before and had believed they could live that lifestyle. It's important to realize that those sad individuals invested consistently, never lost a dime, and enjoyed the exact investment performance that had been promised.

They had fallen victim to the unseen risk of inflation. Remember it's not the return on your money or even necessarily the return of your money. It is a question of your money being there in sufficient quantities at the right time to make all the dreams come true for you and your family.

Jim Stovall

I've had many discussions with my good friend and colleague, Drew Tignanelli, on the topic of investing. Drew is the architect of Risk/Opportunity investing and suggests that a good risk manager needs to have a solid grasp of each of the following: national and global economics, market valuation, and market cycles. Are national and global economics important? Unless you've been living under a rock for the last two years, don't need a place to live, and have no interest in a job, you know that national and global economics have a significant bearing on how the market operates. The Federal Reserve, Congress, and, only occasionally, the President, have a significant impact on what happens to our market and real estate investments. Let me support that hypothesis.

In advance of the widely-hyped computer meltdown that was supposed to happen when 1999 turned into 2000, then Federal Reserve Chairman, Alan Greenspan, began lowering interest rates to make liquid cash more available and, hopefully, prop up the markets. With the bursting of the tech bubble in early 2000, followed by the 9/11 terrorist attacks, rates went lower and stayed low. For years. This extended stretch made money cheap for banks, who in turn gave cheap money to consumers. As interest rates hovered, more homebuyers realized that they could now afford that bigger home or that huge addition, and before long, housing prices were jettisoned upward. All the while, the personal savings rate in the U.S. plummeted. No one needed to worry about saving when their house kept going up each year by double digits, and the bank kept handing out home equity lines of credit up to and occasionally over 100% to backfill the spending sprees of Americans.

The optimism carried over into the stock markets after a host of dot-coms were wiped off the investing landscape. After a three year slide in the stock markets ended with 2002, the real estate optimism spilled over into the markets and, with the exception of the horde of dot-com companies that were swallowed up or wiped out, markets went higher yet again. People figured the dot-com bubble was anomalous and that the ghosts of dot-this and dot-that had reincarnated themselves into brick and mortar in the form of beach front condos in Florida and McMansions dotting the suburbs. The banks sent out blank checks (literally) that were tied to the equity in houses, and real estate appraisers gave everyone something to talk about at neighborhood cocktail parties. "Yeah, I bought this house for $275,000 and now it's worth $550,000—in just 5 years!"

Low Federal Reserve interest rates, easy money and loosening lending standards by the banks, irresponsibility on the part of investment banks and product-pushing brokerage firms, and blindly-utopian outlooks and materially-hedonistic consumer spending on the part of virtually every American demographic boosted U.S. markets to new highs eclipsing 14,000 on the Dow, only to fall back under 7,000 in March of 2009. The impenetrable Wall Street establishment that survived the Great Depression was brought to its knees, and plenty of good companies were dragged down with it. Yeah, national and global economics matter to investors.

Market valuation, or fundamental investing, is fairly straightforward. You buy stock of good companies—companies that you'd be willing to buy completely. That is how Warren Buffett has become so successful, and it is also why it is so difficult to emulate his investing style in your 401k or your discount brokerage account. You and I can't afford to buy the whole company—Warren can and does. His company, Berkshire Hathaway (originally a textile company with roots as far back as 1839), is now a conglomerate holding company with holdings in insurance, utility, manufacturing, and retail companies among others. Famous for some of his long term holdings, Buffett is often mistaken as a buy-and-hold investor, but the record shows that he holds some companies for the long term, others for the mid term, and still more only for short holding periods. Buffett is a risk manager—not a blind buy-and-hold guy.

In addition to owning stock of good companies with a bright future, the best fundamental investors look not only at the ability of a company to outperform its rivals, but also at its share price. Depending on the type of company you analyze, you'll be examining everything from the cash and debt that a company has on their books to the earnings per share of stock and the ratio of the stock price to that company's earnings, called the P/E ratio. The higher the P/E ratio, the more that stock owners are paying for each unit of corporate income. Although they vary significantly over history, an average P/E ratio is thought to be around 15 times earnings. The P/E ratio for the S&P 500, a broader index than the Dow (which is only 30 stocks), was just shy of 35 in 1929 and fell down to around six in 1932. In 1982, it fell to seven. In the year 2000, it was close to 45, and in 2009, we're still hovering around 20 times earnings.

I want to avoid over-simplification on this point, but I'll let Bill Bonner and Addison Wiggin tell you in their words what they think about our current market valuations. They co-authored the international best-selling book, *Empire of Debt*, which was used as the basis for the award-winning movie, I.O.U.S.A.

> Based on past experience, the bear market that began in January 2000 will probably continue for another 10 years, taking prices down to six to eight times earnings. Then, their faith in stocks will finally be crushed out...at the very moment stocks are ready for another bull market.

The scariest part about that quote is that it was written in 2006—before 2008's collapse and subsequent record-setting stimulus package. Yeah, market valuations matter.

Market cycles, or technical investing, is the piece of the puzzle that is hardest to grasp. It gets extremely complex and sometimes even starts to sound like voodoo magic, but the cycles that run through the market tell us more about how to be the best risk manager. As mentioned in the opening of the chapter, the markets seem to run through long term cycles of ups and downs. The stretch from 1982 until 2000 is referred to as a "secular bull market." That means that there were plenty of ups and downs in that span, most notably the Crash of 1987, but on the whole, there was financial inertia pushing the market higher. It is also one of the reasons that the Crash of '87 was quickly recovered. In secular bull markets, buying-and-holding typically works.

In secular bear markets, however, buying-and-holding is often disastrous. If Messrs. Tignanelli, Bonner, and Wiggin are correct, we're only about half-way through a secular bear market right now. Inside a secular bear market, you must rely even more heavily on the other two previously mentioned forms of analysis:

economic and market valuation. And from there, the cycles get weirder and wackier.

Have you heard of any of the following theories? The January Effect? The October Effect? The Sell in May Then Go Away Theory? The Santa Claus Rally? If you are a doubter of their validity, you're not alone, but when the real estate bubble, the sub-prime crisis, and an over-valued stock market all started to collide—in September, historically the worst month for investments—was that just another reason for Tignanelli, the Risk/Opportunity investor, to further reduce equity exposure? Yes, and his clients are glad he did.

Did you wonder what the authors in the previous quote meant when they referred to the faith of investors being "crushed out"? They alluded to a concept that has bearing in both the valuation and cyclical mind sets called capitulation. This is a word that had not been used for decades when it reappeared in 2008. The term capitulation means surrender. It is the point at which most investors give up on the market, never to return. The notion suggests that when inside of a long secular bear market, in order to return again to a secular bull market, a genuine capitulation must take place. This cycle is a natural purging process that weeds out casual investors and returns overall valuations to a state of normalcy. Yeah, market cycles matter.

Economic Bias Alert!

I'm naturally skeptical, and if you are, too, you're starting to wonder, "Hey, if all this stuff about buy-and-hold and asset allocation isn't right, how did it become so popular?" The answer is that it IS very helpful...if you're a huge financial institution or mutual fund company that gets paid by inducing their clients to buy—and HOLD! They take fees and commissions off of assets that stay in their firms and funds. Their Economic Bias is to keep you holding.

The irony is that the brokerage world has taken the last 10 to 20 years to convince their stock brokers that they shouldn't be a bunch of cowboys individually picking stocks. They should, instead, sell this concept of asset allocation, and funnel clients' assets through proprietary mechanisms of the firms. That way brokers can spend less time trying to manage investments and more time pounding the pavement bringing in new clients.

The broker charges 1 to 2% per year and the proprietary firm managing the individual slices of the allocation pie chart charges another 1 to 2% on top of that. That's a pretty big hole that you're digging out of each year before you are actually making money. If your portfolio management is absent, other than an attractive, colorful pinwheel statement that reminds you that "we're staying the course" or simply rebalancing your positions regardless of the performance of the market, you may be the victim of the illogical logic that drives most of the investing world.

In the defense of your advisor, planner, banker, or broker, they didn't have much of a choice. Most of these platforms were sophisticatedly designed at the top of firms and pushed all the way down as a matter of policy. Remarkably, these strict allocation platforms were based on supposed market science that was probably intended to push investors away from salespeople. Have you ever heard of the Efficient Market Hypothesis (EMH) or Modern Portfolio Theory (MPT)? In summary, they claim that the markets are perfectly efficient, up to the second— meaning that stock prices represent every piece of available information there is in existence. In that imaginary world, there is no point in trying to do better than the market because over time, those trying to beat the market will inevitably end up falling short of their goal. Can you hear Warren Buffett laughing now at the notion that no one can beat the market?

Because this research was so hard to understand or contradict (it was done by brilliant academics, not experienced investors), the financial services institution decided that if we can't beat 'em, we'll join 'em. They fused the EMH and MPT together with another study done by the trio of Brinson, Hood, and Beebower which posited that 90% of an investor's return was simply based on maintaining the appropriate asset allocation mix according to the investor's risk tolerance. That other 10% or so, however, was reason enough to fill each of the pie slices with the company's own proprietary mutual fund managers, netting them even more fees.

Brilliant, really! Frankly, as a young broker, I bought it— hook, line and sinker. When these concepts are taught as absolutes and you're learning the ropes in the financial business, it's very difficult to question their validity. As I was told by more than one sales manager, "Stop asking questions! You don't need to know—you need to sell!"

Timely Application
Investment Audit, Part I

In order to be prepared for the next chapter, you'll want to conduct an Investment Audit. This information should already be together from the Personal Balance Sheet exercise, but if not, pull together the most recent holdings information that you have for your various investment accounts. If you have on-line access to these accounts, it will be as easy as printing out the page with your current holdings. If not, pull together each of the most recent statements for all of your investment accounts.

Then, aggregate your holdings on a legal pad, or using the form we've made available online. Segregate them between investments that are inside of retirement accounts (like your 401ks, 403bs, IRAs, etc.) and non-retirement accounts. For any mutual funds, you'll want to have the name AND the five letter symbol.

Visit www.thefinancialcrossroads.com to find a template to use in creating your own Investment Audit.

Tim Maurer

What good is all this information if you don't have the knowledge, experience, tools, or time to implement? In the next chapter, we'll examine how you can apply these principles in the selection of your investments and your investment advisors.

Chapter eleven

PORTFOLIO MANAGEMENT:
ALL THINGS CONSIDERED EQUAL

> The conventional wisdom is often wrong.
>
> *Steven Levitt & Stephen Dubner*
> *in Freakonomics*

Have you ever heard anyone say, "All things being considered equal..." and then follow it up with a statement? They may just be an economist. It's like saying, "If everything happens the way I expect it to, I'll be home on time for dinner." It's really an out. In economics, enormous models are created with assumptions too numerous to count, and the aforementioned phrase gives the economist an out when circumstances beyond his or her control change. This phrase is especially important in the management of investment portfolios.

All things being considered equal, stocks are more risky than bonds. Growth companies, more risky than value companies. Small companies, more risky than large companies. International countries and companies, more risky than the United States and companies domiciled here. In investing circles, each of these categories is called an asset class. If all things were equal, the above presumptions would hold true. But, especially in the world of investments, all things are never equal! They're in a constant state of flux, and as Mark Twain told us, "History doesn't repeat itself, but it does rhyme."

Departing momentarily from theory into reality, consider the notion that instead of risk being determined by asset class, risk is determined by the price of that asset. The risk of a particular asset is not correlated with its label, but instead, its price tag. Let's use an example that is "close to home":

Timeless Truth

You need to know what you're buying and why you're buying it.

Suppose you live in a neighborhood on a court with five other houses. Each of these houses is identical to the other and is presumed to have a market value of 350,000 dollars. Your next door neighbor comes to you with a request: He's been offered a job if he can relocate in under a month, and he'd like you to purchase his home, an exact replica of yours, for its current market value of 350,000 dollars. You'd like to help him out, but you think that in this current real estate market, you'd be taking on a lot of downside risk, with little to gain. Sorry, pal.

He comes back the next day and says that after talking to his wife, they understand your reasoning and would drop the price to 300,000 dollars. You remind him that marketing and transaction costs alone could easily cost 10% of the home's value, so you still stand to gain very little considering the deadlocked real estate market.

Each day, he offers to sell you the house for yet another lower price. Each day you decline until he gets all the way down to 225,000 dollars. You know it's a crazy real estate market, but you also know this particular investment very well, after all your house is an exact replica. Even if you spent 35,000 dollars in marketing and transaction costs, the house would have to drop in value an additional 90,000 dollars or 25% before you'd start losing money. We've got a deal!

Even though this is one of the toughest real estate markets for a seller that this country has ever seen, the primary determinant on the level of risk in the asset was not its asset class, but its price. This seems obvious, but it runs contrary to prevailing investment "logic."

Another important lesson to learn from this example is that your knowledge, or the knowledge of your advisor or mutual fund manager, also has a great deal of bearing on the confidence with which you should transact. If you don't know what you're buying, don't buy it.

Market investors can learn from this housing example, but the inverse is also true. Home buyers and sellers can learn from market investors. Even in a tough real estate market, a property cannot be judged only by "days on the market." Virtually any property in any location, no matter how long it's been on the market, can be sold today by adjusting only one factor: the price. A good deal can become a bad deal, and a bad deal can become the opportunity of a lifetime simply by adjusting what you paid. The pricing forces of supply and demand are more visible in market investing, but even though there is no visible ticker, the same forces exist in real estate.

The hardest mistake to overcome is that of paying too much for an investment; therefore, we learn there are no good investments or bad investments, but simply over-priced and under-priced investments. After all, the simplest and most timeless truth ever with respect to investing is "Buy low and sell high."

Jim Stovall

So what if we did live in a world where all things could be considered equal perpetually? In that case, the following list is ordered from the asset class with the least amount of risk to the most:

U.S. Treasury Bills (short-term debt vehicles that are directly backed by the United States Government)

Certificates of Deposit (CDs have indirect Federal protection through the Federal Deposit Insurance Corporation – FDIC)

U.S. Treasury Bonds (these are directly backed by the feds, but as their maturity stretches further out, they are accompanied by interest rate risk)

Municipal Bonds (bonds that states and municipalities issue to fund state and local projects)

Investment Grade Corporate Bonds (bonds issued by

companies in good credit standing)

High-Yield or "Junk" Bonds (bonds issued by companies in less-than-good credit standing)

International Bonds (bonds issued by everything from credit-worthy sovereign nations to risky emerging market companies)

U.S. Value Company Stock (stock issued by "Blue-Chip" companies at a latter stage of a company's life cycle)

U.S. Growth Company Stock (stock issued by companies earlier on in the corporate life cycle)

International Company Stock (stock issued by companies outside of the U.S., ranging from stable countries like Great Britain and Canada to emerging markets in Latin America, Eastern Europe, and Asia)

Commodities, Options, Futures, and other Derivatives (in this category would fall the notorious credit default swaps, but for sophisticated investors, alternative investments can be very helpful)

Purchasing a company's stock makes you a part owner of a company. When you own a share of stock, you're entitled to the privileges that come with that ownership, including dividends paid by the company, gains in the value of the company when you sell, and a seat at the table with the company decision-makers proportionate to the amount of stock that you own and the corresponding risk of loss of your investment.

Stocks are helpfully categorized as value or growth stocks. Value companies are the Blue Chip companies whose names have been on the ticker for generations. They are in a mature phase of the company life cycle. Typically, their stock price will be less volatile than a growth company and investors are also rewarded with a share of the company's profit in the form of dividends paid to shareholders. Growth companies are in the more formative stages of the company life cycle. They are still making their presence and purpose known in the world and rarely pay dividends, seeking instead to plough that money back into further growth opportunities for the company. The risk is perceived as greater than the Blue Chip companies, but the opportunity for growth is also expected to be greater.

Bond ownership positions you as the creditor of a company. If you are willing to loan the company $10,000, for instance, they will pledge to pay you a set interest rate over a stated period of time based on the prevailing interest rates and the credit worthiness of the company. The lesser the credit worthiness, the greater the interest the company is required to pay to get their loans. If you hold the bond until maturity, you'll get your initial principal investment along with your final interest payment. But, as interest rates rise and fall in the interim, the value of your bond in the open market will fluctuate.

Let me explain. You loan Company X $10,000, and they pledge to pay you 5% per year for the use of your cash for the next 10 years, at which time they promise to return your investment. A year later, Company X sees that, due to the increase in prevailing interest rates, they now have to give 6% to new lenders to attract capital infusions. Do you think your bond, paying 5%, is going to be worth more or less? Less, of course, and the reverse is also true. This is because bond prices and interest rates have an inverse relationship, and this phenomenon plays an important role in both stock and bond investing.

When the stock market is flying high, in order to attract new bond investors, companies are forced to pay higher rates of interest. When our current market collapse became most convincing in the latter part of 2008, the flight to safety from stocks to U.S. Treasuries was so fast and furious that the price of bonds jumped higher, bringing the yields on those debt instruments to almost zero! In times of economic and market turmoil, it is very important to keep your eye on prices and interest rates of treasuries and corporate debt instruments. When in a more normal economic environment, the spread between treasuries and corporates is miniscule, but when people are really scared, the spread between treasuries and corporates widens. In the direst days of our current crisis, that spread was three times wider than normal.

A mutual fund is a collection of securities—usually stocks and/or bonds and some amount of cash (although mutual funds can own actual commodities like gold bullion and all varieties of derivative contracts like options and futures). Since the vast majority of investing is done inside mutual funds or similar accounts managed by a third party, our discussion will center on those vehicles.

Mutual funds are sold as "load" and "no-load" mutual funds. Each variety has expenses that you must bear—some that are visible and others that are harder to find. What is known up-front is whether or not there is a commission to purchase the product and, if so, when the consumer must pay the commission. Additionally, there are management expenses and trading costs. Management expenses are quantified for investors, but their cost is not visible as a statement line item. They are consumed from the value of your shares throughout the year. Trading costs are the hardest of all costs to quantify, but mutual funds that buy and sell their inventory regularly may have high trading costs that are indirectly borne by the mutual fund investor.

Load funds are mutual funds purchased through a stock broker who is compensated by a commission. The three most common share classes are nicely alphabetized—A, B, and C *shares*. The original form of mutual fund shares was the A *share*. A *shares* have a front-end load or commission which is consumed from the investor's initial deposit. Subsequent deposits will also be charged this up-front commission. The amount of commission is typically between 3% (for some bond mutual funds) and up to 6% (for stock mutual funds). That means that if you put $10,000 into a mutual fund, $600 is initially taken off the top to feed the broker and brokerage firm while $9,400 goes to work inside of the fund. A *shares* will typically have the lowest ongoing management expenses of these three share classes, but they pay your broker the most up-front.

B *shares* have a back-end load structure. You invest your money, and it appears to have no up-front commission, but it has a higher management expense ratio and charges a "contingent deferred sales charge" of up to 7% if you leave the fund within the first several years. This share class appears to have little reason to exist for the benefit of investors, but it is the variety that may pay your advisor the most over time. A notable red flag for any investment product is any form of back-end load or surrender charge. The investments you choose should be good enough to keep your business without holding you hostage with a charge if you leave them in the first several years. While a typical *A share* pays the broker 5.75% up-front, a comparable *B share* may pay 4% up-front to the broker with an additional 1% each additional year, so if the broker can keep you in the fund, more commission will be received than with an *A share.*

C shares function the most like a fee-based account, but have no doubt that they are a commission-sold product. They have no front-end load and no back-end load (unless you sell within the first 12 months, in which case you are typically charged a 1% surrender charge), but they have the highest management expense ratio of the three load funds. *C shares* typically pay the broker 1% up-front and also in each successive year. See the below example of how a common mutual fund breaks down across the A, B, C spectrum:

Putnam Voyager					
Share Class	Front-end Load	Back-end Load	Expense Ratio	Yr 1 Commission	Annual Commission
A	5.75%*	0%*	1.20%*	5.75%**	0.25%**
B	0%*	5%*	1.95%*	4%**	1%**
C	0%*	1%*	1.95%*	1%**	1%**

*Information obtained from Morningstar.com on 7/30/09
**Information estimated based on past experience and may differ for broker or fund

No-load mutual funds should not be seen as no-cost mutual funds, but instead as no-commission mutual funds. The

Fidelity Contrafund and the Growth Fund of America are two of the largest mutual funds in existence, and are both considered large cap growth funds. The Growth Fund of America charges a commission of 5.75% up front and has annual expenses of .62%, while the Contrafund has no commission, and a higher expense ratio of .94%. In general, the more exotic an asset class, the higher the expense ratio will be. Matthews Asia Pacific is a fund doing research geographically in Asia and expectedly has a higher expense ratio (1.23%). The key in analyzing expense ratios—especially in no-load mutual funds—is not to allow your decision to be entirely led by the expense ratio. The objective is to understand what you are getting for the expenses paid. Phenomenal investment management is rare, and it is worth paying for, within reason.

Asset Allocation, as discussed in the previous chapter, is the term given to the investment portfolio management style that mandates that a portfolio contain a specified ration of several different asset classes. At the most elementary level, a split is made between those assets that are stock based and bond based. You've probably heard of the Rule of 100. This gross over-simplification postured that one should take the number 100 and subtract from it the number corresponding with your age. The resulting balance was the percentage amount of your investment portfolio that should be invested in stocks. So, if you were 70 years old, you should have 70% invested in bonds and 30% invested in stocks. There was a time in the 1990s when this rule got greedy and became the Rule of 120. After the tech boom busted, the rule and its supporters retreated back to the 100 mark. The rule of thumb that may actually serve you best regarding investing is:

Rules of thumb in a discipline as dynamic and volatile as investing are more dangerous than they are helpful.

As individual securities are filtered by mutual fund managers, they are categorized. Stocks are categorized as growth, blend, or value stocks, and then as large, medium, or small companies. For bonds, delineation is made between those that are short, intermediate, or long term in their maturity and high, mid, or low quality bonds according to their rating. Each mutual fund is a basket of filtered securities. Several companies offer services deconstructing this process to help investors better understand what exactly is inside of mutual funds, but the dominant company that made this analysis visual through their "Style Boxes" was Morningstar. Here's how they describe the concept in their own words:

> The Morningstar Style Box™ was introduced in 1992 to help investors and advisors determine the investment style of a fund. The equity Style Box is a nine-square grid that classifies securities by size along the vertical axis and by value and growth characteristics along the horizontal axis. Different investment styles often have different levels of risk and lead to differences in returns; therefore, it is crucial that investors understand style and have a tool to measure their style exposure.

Here's a visual example of a stock and bond Morningstar Style Box from their website:

Morningstar Style Box

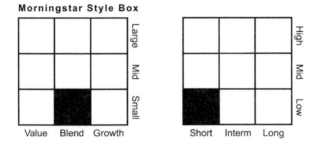

Morningstar's tools of analysis were and are helpful to consumers and advisors alike, but when they became the lens through which mutual fund portfolios were viewed, it helped create a shift in the industry for the worse. Since a growing number of investment portfolios were being designed with an unwavering amount of exposure to each of a predetermined basket of asset classes, individual mutual funds were encouraged to keep their exposure consistent in distinct asset classes. If a 401k plan, for example, offered one large cap growth mutual fund, and that fund started to increase their holdings in cash and small cap stocks, they no longer fit into their prescribed Style Box. Over time, mutual fund managers were derided for "style shift." If a mutual fund moved too far away from its mandatory Style Box, the fund might get kicked out of that and many other 401k plans, a staple client of many mutual funds.

The Style Box phenomenon has forced nearly every mutual fund investment manager to be tethered to the respective Style Box indices, quite possibly hampering them from doing the best job for investors. Even though most consumers rate the success of their investments the way Mark Twain did—the return of my money—those in the mainstream investment management realm are judged differently, on their performance relative to their comparable index. This means that the best interest of the consumer is often not in alignment with the best interest of the fund manager.

Doesn't it seem like we've been trained by an industry telling us what they want us to do instead of helping us achieve what we want? Are you more concerned with beating an index or making money? If you answered the index, you are placing your faith in the market to take care of you. Who is the market anyway? Bear Stearns? Lehman Brothers? Merrill Lynch? Bank of America? Citigroup? AIG??

Have you heard the terms relative return and absolute return? The success of a money manager attempting to gain a positive relative return is gauged by whether or not the manager beats the index to which the fund is compared. So a large cap blend mutual fund is most often compared to the S&P 500 index. The S&P 500 is the index containing the 500 most prominent company stocks trading on the two primary U.S. exchanges, the New York Stock Exchange (NYSE) and NASDAQ. That mutual fund management team has done its job in superlative fashion if the fund's return is above the S&P 500. Yes, that means if the S&P 500 is down by 22%, as it was in the year 2002, a mutual fund that loses 19% of investors' money would have achieved success. Success?!? That 22%/19% comparison is an actual example that took place in 2002, when the Legg Mason Value Trust lost 18.9%.

The Value Trust made headlines in 2002 when it continued its unparalleled streak of beating the S&P 500. While the champagne bottles were uncorked in downtown Baltimore at Legg headquarters, investors were choking on their dinner looking over statements that showed their fund down nearly 20% from the previous year, which had also been a negative return. All the blame can not fall on the shoulders of Bill Miller and the management team of the Legg Mason Value Trust. The Style Box backed them into a strategic corner. When Miller took some chances in 2006, the fund lost to the index for the first time, losing by 10% (the fund was actually up about 6%). Then, in 2007, to make up for the previous year's loss to the index, Miller had to take more chances and underperformed the index by an additional 12%. Finally, in 2008, it happened. The fund that put the Baltimore underdog on top cratered. It lost 55% (18% more than the benchmark)!

If you recall our discussion in the last chapter about how losing money is easier than making it, let's run the numbers on this one. After losing 55%, you need to make a 122% rate of return to get your money back. If you're able to make 7% per year, it will take you 12 years to get back where you started!

Economic Bias Alert!

The industry's obsession with Style Boxes and relative returns has set the managers at odds with the best interest of the mutual fund share holders. If managers don't outpace the index in a particularly big market up year, they are likely to be yanked from any number of the institutional retirement plans and investment platforms that make up the bulk of their managed assets; however, if they go too far outside of their prescribed Style Box to achieve that illusive outperformance, they could get yanked for style drifting from the same platform that promises to punish them if they don't beat the index.

So, much like politicians, the fund managers find themselves in a game of chance where their livelihood is at stake. Self-preservation becomes the primary objective and the result is an abundance of tepid mediocrity for the vast majority of mutual fund investors across the globe. In order to achieve that primary objective, most managers keep their funds looking almost identical to their respective index to keep from losing (relatively speaking); they then try to marginally outpace that index to keep their spot in the money management platform and/or retirement plan.

This Economic Bias leaves consumers paying the bill for sub-par investment management.

Absolute return is practically a dirty word (or phrase, really) in the industry. The goal of absolute return is easy to remember. It's to make money! I know it sounds crazy, but that is the objective of a relative few mutual fund managers who choose to spurn the Style Boxes and ignore indices seeking to make money in every year. These are not funds that guarantee that they'll accomplish that mission successfully. There will almost certainly be years in which even the best of absolute return managers will fail in that mission. But, when the primary objective of a fund is to keep from losing money for their clients, fascinating things can happen.

Let's compare another mutual fund with the Legg Mason Value Trust over the recent decade of market turbulence. The Value Trust's 10 year annualized return (the average that your money would have returned each year if you made a deposit into the fund 10 years ago) is -6.5% as of the end of April 2009. The cumulative loss (the total amount lost in that stretch) over the 10 years was -48.9%. A $10,000 investment would have been reduced in 10 years to $4,894. In that same stretch, First Eagle Global, a mutual fund that follows an absolute return discipline, had a positive annualized rate of return of 11.24%. In that fund, your $10,000 would have turned into $29,014, a cumulative rate of 190%! This illustration is not made to suggest that all—or even any—of your money should be put into the First Eagle Global mutual fund, but to illustrate how differently certain managers go about their business.

The irony here? You can actually make more money by making your primary objective not to lose. In the year 2003, a big up year for the market (when the market bounced back from three straight losing years), the Value Trust made 43.5%. First Eagle Global lagged behind with a respectable 37.6% return for the year; however, when it really mattered, in 2002, the worst year of the tech bust, First Eagle Global was up 10.2% while the Value Trust was soaking in the limelight of "beating the market" yet another year with a negative return of -18.9%. Even First Eagle Global suffered in 2008, with a return of -21%, but if you recall from our previous chapter, being down 20% requires a 25%

return to break even. That is much more manageable than the 100% return required to recover the 50% loss.

Opponents of absolute return will show charts that seem to prove that pure growth managers or market indices alone will outperform absolute return managers when viewed over a longer stretch of time. This may or may not be true, depending on the statistic, but what this theory does not take into account is that while rates of return are reported on a linear hypothetical basis, assuming that no distributions are taken, life is not linear. In reality, investors need to take distributions from investments, and if they do so in one of the years when the market is down significantly, the distribution magnifies the market loss. This is especially important for retirees who have begun to take distributions from their portfolios. The objective of investing is eventual distribution, and while long-term buying-and-holding appears to work in hypothetical linear projections, the impact of distributions in downward market cycles can devastate a portfolio in real life.

There are many different varieties of absolute return managers, and not all of them are good. They have notoriously high internal expenses and a great many of them were humbled as they failed to achieve their objective of positive gain in 2008; however, most of them are Risk Managers.

Risk Manager is one of three classifications into which most mutual funds fall: Index Huggers, Return Chasers, and Risk Managers. Index Huggers make up the vast majority of a largely mediocre array of mutual fund options. Most of the funds you hold—and, unfortunately, most of the fund options in 401ks and other retirement plans—are Index Huggers. If you look at a chart of the performance of the fund, you'll find that it seems to move in perfect correlation with the benchmark index to which it is compared. If you are going to own an index, the best way to do it is with a no-load index mutual fund or Exchange Traded Fund (ETF). An ETF is a mutual fund that trades like a stock on an exchange. Do not pay a mutual fund company or financial advisor to settle for Index Huggers.

Return Chasers are typically high flying mutual funds that seem hell bent on making it to the cover of a financial magazine for having a stratospherical up year. The problem is that when they bet wrong, you're likely to suffer greatly on the downside. Be careful!

Risk Managers are a small subset of mutual fund managers who spend most of their time avoiding losses instead of chasing returns. The vast majority of mutual funds, however, fit into that bloated category of those who daily seek to attain the daring heights of just-good-enough-to-keep-their-job. So, how can you determine what kind of mutual fund managers you have?

Timely Application
Investment Audit, Part II

Pull out your completed Investment Audit from the last chapter and point your web browser to www.morningstar.com. With the analysis here, you'll be able to use that final column of your Investment Audit to fill in the Manager Category column. You can examine your mutual fund managers with the tools on Morningstar using the basic service at no cost. Take the symbol of each of your mutual funds and plug it into the "Quotes" field. (Another good, free resource for the analysis of stocks, bonds, and mutual funds is Yahoo's Finance website http://finance.yahoo.com/.)

After you've poked around on the Snapshot page for each fund, select the Performance tab. Here, you'll be able to look at the last 10 years of year-by-year performance for your mutual funds.

You'll find your Risk Managers by examining years like 2001, 2002, and 2008. Those were years where the major market indices were down, along with most mutual funds. If you have a fund that was positive or only mildly down throughout the three year stretch from 2000 through 2002, that's a sign of a Risk Manager. In 2008, even most good Risk Managers were down by a decent margin. If your fund survived the 2000-2002 stretch, and was down by around 20% or better in 2008, you may have a capable Risk Manager at the helm.

In order to spot Return Chasers, take a look at years like 1999 and 2003. If your fund was up by a very significant amount in either or both of those years, even as high as 50% in 2003, you likely have a Return Chaser. You should certainly not be opposed to a fund that gives you a phenomenal return, but you'll probably notice that any fund that achieves single year returns in the 40%s or above will also have years where they bet big, and lose big. Return Chasers need not be eliminated from your portfolio altogether, but they must be very carefully monitored and avoided by novice investors when in the midst of a secular bear market (as described in the previous chapter).

Most of your funds probably fit into the final category, Index Huggers. Most managers, in the spirit of self-preservation, resort to plugging along with the index, playing it safe to keep their status in the big institutional programs that pay for the lifestyle perks to which they've become accustomed. Of course, playing it safe to an Index Hugger doesn't mean safe in the way that you or I tend to think. It's not safe like a T-Bill or CD at the bank. It's relatively safe, relative to their benchmark index. These funds are easily spotted because their chart on Morningstar will be almost indistinguishable from their benchmark index. What are supposed to be two separate lines (the performance line chart visually comparing the fund to its benchmark) look like no more than one.

In the Action column, on the right hand side of the worksheet, check any of the Return Chasers and Index Huggers for additional review. Again, Return Chasers should be well understood, carefully monitored and dumped if misunderstood. Index Huggers should be replaced.

Visit www.thefinancialcrossroads.com to find a template to use in creating your own Investment Audit and categorizing your mutual funds.

Tim Maurer

When determining what to replace Index Huggers with, there are two options to consider. If, based on your economic, valuation, and cyclical analysis, the hugged index is one that is desirable at this time, consider replacing the hugging fund with an index mutual fund (Vanguard is a mutual fund family with a number of good, low cost index funds) or an exchange traded fund. Although most ETFs are simple in their objective (they seek to track a specific index), they're quite complicated in design and require a level of sophistication on the part of the investor as they have virtually no professional management. There is no Risk Manager behind the wheel of an ETF. If you own the ETF that tracks Taiwan, for instance, and the Taiwan index takes a dive on rumors that North Korea is planning a full scale attack, your ETF is going to follow that index all the way down.

Exchange traded funds can be used by Risk Managers very effectively, though. When oil dropped from around $150 per barrel to around $35 per barrel, we could be quite sure of two things. First, oil was over-priced at $150 per barrel. Second, oil was under-priced at $35 per barrel. Commodities are quite a volatile asset class; however, at a price of $35 per barrel for oil, a compelling case could be made that the risk—especially with a multi-year time horizon—was quite reduced and the opportunity promising. But before you run out to buy an oil ETF, you must understand how they function. They are built upon futures contracts, one of the alternative investments mentioned previously, and will not always directly follow the price of oil.

Once great risk managers wring as much of the risk as possible out of their investments, all that should be left is the opportunity for returns. At times—especially times where the market is going through a bull cycle, lifting all boats with the tide—Risk Managers are looked at with condescension. Return Chasers scoff at their unwillingness to gorge on returns and even Index Huggers get a chance to breathe and wonder if the big salary will assuage their conscience. But I submit to you that the idea of risk management investing is not to settle for long-term lesser returns.

At this point, you may be suffering from information overload and pulling the white flag out of your pocket to negotiate terms of surrender. You don't know how to keep an eye on all of this stuff. You don't know what percentage you should put into this or that mutual fund, ETF, stock, or bond. If the discussions of the last two chapters are interesting, even compelling, but you have absolutely no idea how to integrate them into whatever practice you currently follow in managing your investments, you're most certainly a candidate for professional help.

Some very well-intended and gifted financial educators have attempted to minimize portfolio management to a newsletter, book, or chapter and have over-simplified it in doing so. Many who followed their advice saw their portfolios—made up of only a handful of prominent large-cap growth mutual funds—sawn in half over the last 12 months. It is not our objective that the chapters contained herein on investing would be an all-encompassing how-to. It is instead our desire to pull back the veil on the industry norms and invite you into further exploration.

Success is not found in learning a set of principles that you can use to create an impenetrable portfolio that you'll rarely have to adjust. Interesting theories, including strict asset allocation, have been developed over time and have even worked for a period of time; but one constant in free-market investing is that once any one theory becomes widely spread enough that every Tom, Dick, and Harry is using it, the laws of supply and demand wipe out the benefit.

If you followed the majority of investors downward through the financial crisis, you have also likely seen your accounts rebound if you left your depressed assets in the portfolio. Do not assume that on the basis of this or any subsequent boost, the ills of short-sightedness have been completely cured. We likely have a long way to go before we experience our next secular bull market, and if you don't know how you got where you are today, it's all too likely that you don't know how to get where you'd like to go. It's okay to get some help. You will see an entire chapter at the end of this book dedicated to how to interview and choose a financial planner or advisor. You've had a bad experience? We know. We know how this industry operates, who to steer you away from, and who to recommend.

Absolute or relative? The choice is yours, but remember what a wise man once said, "You can't eat relative return!" Index Hugger, Return Chaser or Risk Manager? If it seems too simple, hopeful, or too good to be true... You fill in the blank.

Investment
Audit

Non-Retirement Accounts						
Account Type	Symbol/ CUSIP	Name/ Description	Shares	Market Value	Manager Type	ACTION?
						☐
						☐
						☐
						☐
						☐
						☐
						☐
						☐
						☐
						☐
						☐
						☐
						☐
						☐
						☐
						☐
						☐
						☐
						☐
						☐
						☐
						☐
						☐
						☐
						☐
						☐
						☐
						☐
						☐
						☐
						☐
						☐

Investment
Audit

Retirement Accounts						
Account Type	Symbol/ CUSIP	Name/ Description	Shares	Market Value	Manager Type	ACTION?
						☐
						☐
						☐
						☐
						☐
						☐
						☐
						☐
						☐
						☐
						☐
						☐
						☐
						☐
						☐
						☐
						☐
						☐
						☐
						☐
						☐
						☐
						☐
						☐
						☐
						☐
						☐
						☐
						☐
						☐
						☐
						☐

Chapter twelve

THE "A" WORD

> Annuities are not bought—they're sold!
>
> *Unknown*

In the realm of personal finance, no word has been dragged through the mud more times than The "A" Word— Annuities. Yet, annuities still survive and even thrive. How they do is not a mystery.

There is not an outcry on the part of consumers demanding annuity products. The reason for the continued vibrancy of annuity products and sales is that they pay a big honkin' commission to the selling broker or agent. (There, I've said it.) And, as most of the financial sales tactics exposed in this book, I'm especially qualified to make such a statement, because I have sold them myself. I wasn't a bad person in those days, conniving to separate prospects from their hard-earned money for my own selfish benefit. Conversely, every time in years past when I sold an investment product to a client for a commission, I did so thinking it was best for the client. My recommendations met all the legal requirements of suitability that are required of a broker, but I declare to you now that in hindsight there is no question that my judgment was partly influenced by the amount of money that I could make (or not make) in the sale.

And how could it not be? Let's say you, as a salesperson, had three different products to sell with the following characteristics: one would pay you 1% for every year that the investment continued to be held by the client, one would pay you 5.75% up front followed by .25% each additional year, and another would pay you 12%—all up front. Which one would you be likely to pick, all things being considered equal? Hmmmm. Let's add to the scenario the assumption that you were selling in the midst of an economic downturn which had resulted in a significant loss of revenue for you and your family. Is it possible that in that circumstance you may be inclined to favor the product that pays 12% up front over the one that pays 5.75% up front? And forget about the one that pays 1%, because in tough times, that simply isn't going to butter the bread. These aren't imaginary numbers that I'm using. One percent is a slightly below average amount that a financial advisor may charge for discretionary management of your investment assets; 5.75% is the average commission paid to a broker who sells a mutual fund (A share); and annuity products pay up to—and in some cases over—12%!

The sale of annuities is justified entirely too often because of the massive commissions that go to the broker or agent selling the product. Powerful organizations have made it their lives' work to decry this very notion and have built elaborate systems designed to convince themselves, their brokers and agents, and the consuming public to believe in the justness of their actions. I was a part of one such group and was encouraged—along with a room full of other financial folks who had been invited to San Diego for an all-expense paid trip to hear what this organization had to say—to join the ranks of the "Safe Money Specialists." Other people were selling products. We were selling peace of mind and getting paid 10 times as much!

I repeat: people who sell annuities aren't bad people. But, they are sales people. You expect timeshare salespeople to have an economic bias to sell you a timeshare. You expect a phone solicitor who interrupts your dinner to keep you on the phone to convince you to buy something before you hang up the phone. You don't, however, expect someone who refers to themselves as a financial planner or advisor or professional to have the primary aim to sell you something. Unfortunately, many of them do. Your broker or agent may have drank the company Kool-Aid and genuinely believe that he or she is doing the best thing for you, so treat them with respect when you tell them you'll be moving your business. As I learned growing up in the Baptist church, we should, "Hate the sin, not the sinner." We will be discussing in much greater detail the ways that financial services employees and financial advisors are compensated and what you should look for in Chapter Seventeen.

Timeless Truth

There is a continuum on which products and services are rendered based on the level of care provided by the product or service provider to their prospect or client.

At the far left of that continuum is LYING. While it is illegal, people do it every day on eBay, in newspaper advertisements, and in email solicitations. Regardless of the many benefits that the Internet revolution has brought us, there is little doubt that it has also given outright thieves a far vaster medium in which to carry out their trade.

Next on the continuum is DECEPTION. Deception is rampant in all too many forms of advertising and packaging, especially in the sale of products. How is it that every single bottle of shampoo at the grocery store is offering "25% more!"? 25% more of what? Deception is found in the fine print and disclaimers. It comes after someone has already given you their pitch. "Oh, by the way, there is this to consider," once your heart has already embraced the product or service.

Next comes FULL DISCLOSURE. Full disclosure is when all the information that is legally required to pass from the seller to the buyer is disclosed. In many states, a disclosure form is required of a home seller listing anything that the seller knowingly recognizes as broken. That doesn't mean that you should count on the seller to tell you what they know is likely to break in the next few months.

Finally, we reach the highest form of business practice: FIDUCIARY. A fiduciary is legally obligated to act in the best interest of the client they serve. The client's interest must rise above that of their own. Doctors, lawyers, psychologists, pastors, priests and a small subset of financial advisors are a handful of professionals who are required to act as a fiduciary

```
+-----------------------------------+--------------------------+----------------------------------+
LYING                              DECEPTION              FULL DISCLOSURE                      FIDUCIARY
```

Going through life as a skeptic, distrusting
everyone, is no way to live; but you should know that
in virtually every product sold or service rendered,
YOU are your own best fiduciary. Having a better understanding of the economic bias of the seller will
make you a better, more informed consumer.

Jim Stovall

Before we go off the deep end and give you the impression that there is never a valuable use for an annuity, let me assure you that there is. And we'll be getting to that soon, but know that the criteria for appropriate annuity sales are quite narrow. Most of the time that an annuity is sold, there's probably a better option. To understand their use, we must give you a fuller explanation of the types of annuities in existence and how they function.

The best definition for the word annuity is an investment product sold by an insurance company. While many equate the term annuity with a different definition—a perpetual stream of income—this definition is too tapered for the broader class of investment products known as annuities. The four broad types of annuities are Immediate Annuities, Fixed Annuities, Variable Annuities, and Equity Indexed Annuities.

The first type of annuity, immediate annuities, are those that meet the short-sighted definition for annuities mentioned previously. Immediate annuities are those in which a consumer gives an insurance company a set number of dollars. In return, the insurance company provides a stream of income to the annuity owner, the person making the monetary investment. The annuitant is the person on whose life the stream of income is based. (In most cases, the owner and annuitant are one and the same.) It is the annuitant's life expectancy that is used for the insurance company's actuarial calculations in order to determine how much money they will send out to the annuity owner on a periodic basis.

In a life-only annuity, the agreed-upon stream of income will be paid to the owner as long as the annuitant is alive. When the annuitant dies, the stream of income ends. If someone receives their very first periodic payment and then dies, the income stream ends. The longer the annuitant lives, the better the investment the life-only annuity becomes. It's really a bet between an insurance company and a person on when that person is going to kick the proverbial bucket. In some cases, the annuitant will actually present medical information and submit to a physical examination—much as they would with life insurance—to determine the expected periodic payout.

A period certain annuity will change the time frame from one that is tied to the life expectancy of the annuitant to a set period of time. For example, someone could give an insurance company a lump sum of money that would pay out over the next 10, 15, or 20 years. In the case of the death of the annuitant, the annuity beneficiary would continue to receive the periodic payments until the end of the stated term.

Pension recipients will be familiar with the terminology used above because a pension annuity recipient will often be presented a combination of annuity payout options based on the life expectancy of the employee, the employee's spouse's life expectancy, or a specified period. Lottery winners, or the far more common lottery daydreamers, are familiar with the decisions between receiving a lump sum or some form of periodic annuity.

Immediate annuities are not registered products that require a securities license to sell them. They are sold by insurance agents with a caveat emptor standard—buyer beware. They can be purchased with cash or converted from an existing fixed or variable annuity. The sale of insurance and insurance products is regulated by states, and in most states, if the insurance commissioner has permitted the product in that state, it is the responsibility of the buyer—not the seller—to ensure the suitability of the product.

Fixed annuities closely resemble Certificates of Deposit (CDs). They offer a set or variable rate of interest for a specified period of time. While CDs pay interest that is taxed in the year in which it is received, the interest in fixed annuities is tax deferred until the owner takes a distribution from the annuity. That tax deferral is, for some investors, an advantage of the fixed annuity over the CD, but the two major disadvantages are the lesser degree of principal protection and the surrender charges of annuities.

Certificates of Deposit can be purchased with FDIC insurance. The FDIC has federal backing. Annuities are backed only by the full faith and credit of the insurance company, a promise that seems worth less today than in January of 2008. CDs purchased through a bank often do assess charges to owners who take distribution of the funds prior to the maturity of the instrument, but that charge is typically not in excess of the expected interest of the CD. Fixed annuity surrender charges, however, are often onerous. It would not be uncommon to purchase a fixed annuity with a maturity of seven years and find that if you tried to get your money back in the first year, you would pay 7% or more, resulting in a net loss in the product. Surrender charges that are long and painful are the answer to the question, "How can these companies afford to pay commissions that are that high to brokers and agents?"

One of the many deceptive tools of annuity products is the fixed annuity "teaser rate." Many fixed annuities will offer a low annual flat rate of, say 3%, but offer a 2% bonus in the first year. This enables salespeople to position the annuity as having a 5% rate of return with the fine print that reads, "in year one." Fixed annuities, like immediate annuities, are sold on a caveat emptor basis and regulated in each state.

Variable annuities are the insurance industry's answer to mutual funds. A variable annuity is an investment product with multiple investment options inside of it. These options, called sub-accounts, function very much like mutual funds. Like fixed annuities, variable annuities offer tax-deferral on growth inside of the product until the investor takes distributions from the annuity. Mutual fund owners must pay tax on the capital gains taken by the fund managers and any of the dividend and interest income produced by the fund. A major disadvantage of the annuity, however, is that when distributions are taken, all of the income is taxed at ordinary income tax rates. Today, taxes on stock capital gains and dividends are taxed at a rate no higher than 15%. Ordinary income taxes can be more than twice as much at 35%. The "good news" is that you can be quite sure that both of those tax rates will be on the rise in the future. These concepts, among others, will be discussed in greater detail in Chapter Thirteen on taxes.

What further differentiates variable annuities from mutual funds is that annuities, as insurance products, come with various types of benefits attached to them, some that offer guarantees. In the world of investing in stocks, bonds, and mutual funds, the word guarantee is expressly forbidden; however, annuities offer pseudo-guarantees on the return of principal as well as some gains in accounts. Most variable annuities have a guarantee on the return of principal; the bad news is that you typically have to die to get it! The death benefit guarantee pledges return of your invested principal to your beneficiary—even if the market has gone down. Some products now also offer a "Living Benefit" guarantee, pledging a chance to reap the benefit of that principal protection during your own lifetime. That sounds like a benefit that could come in handy after the market crash of 2008-09, but these benefits are shrouded in mystery and fine print.

In the June 1, 2009 edition of *The Wall Street Journal*, the title of an article discussing annuity guarantees read, "Annuity Fine Print: Guarantees Aren't Always Guaranteed." The article opens as follows:

> For many years, variable annuities with guaranteed minimum returns had a bad reputation for being loaded with fees and traps. And besides, why pay anything for a guarantee against investment losses when stocks

inevitably marched upward?

Those guarantees looked a lot better after last year's market slide. Then investors started checking the fine print—and learned their guarantees might not be as secure as they thought. Under some provisions, the insurance company that issued the guarantee can cancel it, or sharply reduce its annual payout.

In many cases, the guarantees appear less valuable than consumers were led to believe. One of the ways that living benefit guarantees are made less beneficial is that they are paid out over a long stretch of time. So, if you invested $100,000 in the annuity in 2007 and the market dragged it down to $50,000, you'd think the purchaser of a living benefit would be able to call up the company and ask for their full $100,000 back. No, on at least two counts. First, like all annuities, there is going to be a surrender charge in place, so if you want to take distribution of your money, you'll have to pay a hefty surrender charge to get it back. Second, you don't normally get your money back in a lump sum when you call in a living benefit; they can take many years to pay it back to you, further diminishing their risk and your benefit.

Think of it this way: An insurance company would never create an annuity benefit that they didn't think would actually benefit them. It would be suicidal! They offer benefits, at a cost, that they think (or at least hope) they'll never need to pay. If there was a widespread, systemic failure in the actuarial composition of the benefits of a particular product, it could put the company at enough risk to make the guarantees difficult to live up to.

The thing that initially got annuities in hot water with educators and the financial press were the expenses, and while the competitive forces have driven costs for consumers down some, they're still a problem. I pulled the following from a website that is actually promoting the sale of annuities:

Death Benefit Expenses: The mortality cost is in your contract and is subtracted from your account. Depending on the variable annuity you own or are considering, these fees could be as high as 1.25% of your total account value.

Other Fees and Expenses: Variable annuities can charge fees for added riders and benefits. Each benefit can have a cost associated with it that is subtracted from your total account value. It could be possible that these fees and expenses could be as high as 1% to 2% and these fees are on top of the death benefit fees discussed in number 2 above. (Please read the prospectus, which by law must reveal fees and expenses.)

Loads and Acquisition Expenses: Some variable annuities have a front end or a back end load that can have an effect on the overall performance of your variable annuity. (Please read the prospectus, which by law must reveal fees and expenses.)

Administration fees and distribution costs: Many variable annuities charge a fee for administration expenses. These fees can range from .15% to .40% of your total account value and these fees are in addition to other fees in your contract.[i]

Variable annuities are registered products, which means that they do require at least a Series 6 License (the license to sell mutual funds); however, this license does not require the selling broker to act as a fiduciary. They are held to a lesser standard known as suitability that only sanctions the transaction and does not include advice from the broker. If you thought that immediate, fixed, and variable annuities were confusing, wait 'til you get a load of the next example.

Equity Indexed Annuities (EIAs), according to a commentary in the *Barron's* April 13, 2009 edition, are *Designed to Deceive*. Even though they have the word equity—a synonym for stock—in their title, as of this date, the seller of an EIA is not required to have an investment license, although that is scheduled to change in 2010. These products are relatively new and took off following the tech bust of 2000-2002 because they offer "equity style returns with protection from the downside" in stocks. Well, sign me up, right!?

Who wouldn't want the upside of stocks with no downside? It is true that these products offer annual returns that are attached to stock market indices, like the Dow Jones 30, the S&P 500, or the NASDAQ 100. If the market goes into the tank, you earn zero percent that year. The catch here is that they cap your upside earning potential; some offer a 5-8% annual cap on earnings while others offer a much lower monthly cap. In addition, many products also have an asset fee (a flat percentage fee assessed in any positive earning years), a participation rate (allowing you to participate only in, say, 80% of the market upside), and index terms (which restrict your liquidity for anywhere from five to over 17 years with surrender charges in the teens!). And, by the way, the upside attributed to the respective market indices does not include the gains from dividends.

Frederic Marks, the co-founder and co-chief investment officer of Cheviot Value Management in Santa Monica, California, in analyzing an EIA that was pitched to one of his clients, determined that while the S&P 500 annualized rate of return, including the reinvestment of dividends from 1975 through 2004 had been 13.87%, the monthly averaging S&P 500 Equity Indexed Annuity would have returned 5.81%.[ii] That's 58% less than the market in that stretch—hardly equity style upside—and even less than the Lehman Intermediate Government/Credit Bond Index, which earned an annualized return of 8.6% from '75 through '04. Every great lie is surrounded by a cushion of truth.

Economic Bias Alert!

Do you remember when I said I sat under the tutelage of one of these monster annuity sales companies for a short time? They gave me tapes to listen to in my car (I told you it was a while ago) to beat my skeptical brain into submission. They flew me to San Diego and sent me to five star hotels in Vegas—twice—with top notch speakers like Walter Cronkite and political duo Mary Matalin and James Carville. Unfortunately, due to my wife's pregnancy (the pregnancy wasn't unfortunate!), I had to miss the cruise with George and Barbara Bush! Where'd they get the money to do all this? They got a cut of all the annuity business that we sold. Just a little bit of Economic Bias there.

They also disseminated the "Sales Process" of the top sales person in their organization. Here are a couple of his tips if you wanted to be a top producer like him:

"The key to closing your client is positioning that client. The first step in the process is to get people to accept the idea of an indexed annuity without really knowing. The quality of the close is dependent upon the fact that the client doesn't know where you are taking them until the very end.

"The objective is to take away the surrender period argument against annuities. Hammer them on that and repeat it....

"Most senior clients, because they are savers, like to have a bit of extra cash on hand.... The goal is to make the client comfortable. They don't want to think you are coming after their cash. Many other financial advisors will come after their cash first. Get the cash later rather than up front, if you don't need to."

Can you believe that someone actually put that in writing!? This shows how rampant the

Economic Bias is in the sales of annuities and especially EIAs. The reward for the selling broker
or agent is so substantial that all common sense
and decency is thrown out the window and people are taught "by the best" how to con seniors
into parting with their money. If you get one of
these canned sales pitches, run for the hills!

Believe it or not, we've not yet touched the primary
disadvantages of owning annuities. These traits are common
among all the varieties mentioned above. Tax detriment is one
of the problems, and it's ironic, because for many years, annuities were sold on the basis of their tax privilege. That is because
annuities are tax-deferred investment products. So if you put
after-tax dollars into an annuity investment, any of the
earnings, interest, or gains in the product will be deferred until
you take a distribution from the annuity. But then you get
hammered, because as mentioned before, even if the gains in
your annuity are derived from stock based investments, you will
not get preferential capital gain tax treatment. You'll be paying
ordinary income tax on those gains. I mentioned that initially annuities were sold on the basis of that tax-deferral, which is a good
thing, but that was when capital gain tax rates were much higher.
At 15% currently, that is a far cry from the top bracket of 35%.

This tax-deferral allowance has another catch. The IRS
allowed the preferential tax-deferral to take place under the
pretense that these investments were intended specifically for
retirement use. So in granting the tax-deferred treatment, they
also imposed an age 59½ rule to annuity distributions. If you
take a distribution prior to age 59½, any gains in the policy will

be taxed at ordinary income rates and assessed a 10% early withdrawal penalty. This is the quirky age rule accompanying Traditional and Roth IRAs that will be discussed in our chapter on retirement planning. If you own an annuity inside of a Traditional or Roth IRA, the distribution rules will not change; they are a mirror of each other.

Additionally, the taxes are handled on a Last In First Out (LIFO) basis in annuities. Therefore, if you put $100,000 of after-tax money into an annuity and it grows to $120,000, and then you choose to take a distribution of $20,000 from the annuity, you'll be paying tax on 100% of that $20,000 distribution because the gains were the last thing in...and the first thing out. This can be especially painful for the many annuity owners who are in a very low tax bracket. An additional tax disadvantage of annuities is that when an annuity owner dies and passes the annuity to his or her heirs through the beneficiary designation, the heirs receive no step-up in cost basis. An annuity owner who intends to pass a nice inheritance to heirs may actually be creating a tax time bomb for them.

Cost basis is the amount of a given investment that has already been taxed once and is pledged not to be taxed again. For example, if you purchased $5,000 worth of Microsoft stock and it grew to $15,000, you would have a cost basis of $5,000. The additional $10,000 would be considered a capital gain. If, during your lifetime, the stock is sold, you'll pay capital gains tax on the $10,000 of your $15,000 stock position. If, however, you pass the stock to your heirs through your will, they would receive a step-up in cost basis to the price of the stock on the date of your death; therefore, the cost basis they would inherit, if the stock position was worth $15,000 on the date of your death, would be

$15,000. If they sold it the next day at the same price, they'd pay no tax whatsoever. If you invested $5,000 in the annuity and it grew to $15,000, and you passed it to them at your death, they would have to pay tax on the entire $10,000 gain—and they'd be paying at their ordinary income tax rate to boot.

We're coming down the home stretch on disadvantages of annuities. The last we'll discuss is an investment option disadvantage. Because of the painful surrender charges, changes to an annuity investment are naturally penalized. In markets such as these, where extreme volatility and rapid change are the norm, annuities do not offer the flexibility that you want and need. If you buy a five-year fixed annuity at 3% because it's paying you 1% more than the 2%, one-year CD at the bank, you may think you've made an advantageous investment move. But, if interest rates jump up to 6%, as is perfectly possible after the biggest stimulus package in the history of the universe, you've now locked in a guaranteed loser because you're afraid to break the chains of the annuity and lose your surrender charge. Variable annuities were supposed to be the answer to that problem, but while they have more choices, it is still a limited number from which to choose. The fewer the choices, the greater the risk. The less liquidity, the greater the risk.

Now, at long last, the good news about annuities: If you just bought an annuity because you were at the bank moaning about the putrid rate of interest you are earning on your savings account and CDs, and the teller said, "Why don't you talk to our financial specialist who can tell you about investment options that may result in a higher rate of return?" and you signed on the dotted line, most states offer a "free-look" of 10-30 days in which the buyer of an annuity can get out of their contractual obligation without any financial pain. Use this free-look and look hard, because annuities are contractual obligations that are very hard to separate from after the free-look period.

"Is that it?" you say. "Is that the only good thing you can say about them?" No, I'm holding out on you, but only a little bit. If interest rates do what they're likely to do at some point and go higher—a lot higher—you may consider locking in a rate of 8% or higher in a fixed annuity for a minimal slice of your investment nest egg. CDs will typically not offer as long a maturity as a fixed annuity and if you see signs of the '70s and '80s, with double digit interest rates, you may consider locking in some of your money into a fixed annuity at that point; however, if it was my money, I'd probably find some top quality bonds to reap that reward. Because of the inverse relationship of bonds' interest rates and prices, if you buy a couple of new issue bonds at 10% and 12% and you wait until interest rates drop back down to normal, you'll likely have a handsome capital gain on those bonds if you should choose to sell them.

When I recommend an annuity, it is usually to someone who already owns one. While I almost never recommend an annuity for someone at the onset because of my obvious opinion on their lack of benefit to clients, I am cautious to recommend that a client get out of one. Because of the surrender charges, tax treatment, and age limitations, a decision to take a distribution must be well thought out. When dealing with an annuity that you've had for many years in which your cost basis is very low compared to the current value, I may recommend "annuitizing" the product. Let's go back to the example where $5,000 went into an annuity and it's now worth $15,000. If you take a partial or total distribution, you'll have to pay all the taxes first. By annuitizing, you create a de facto immediate annuity and create a stream of income. In this annuitization (a word that only exists in the insurance realm), the IRS allows the taxes to be paid on a pro-rata basis, which means that each of the payments will be partly taxable and partly tax-free return of contributions. I recommend doing this not as a "life only" payout, but the shortest "period certain" payout available (usually 10 years).

And if you do decide to invest at all with annuities, look for no- or low-load annuities that pay little or no commission and have little or no surrender charge if you should choose to change your strategy. Admittedly, the options for no-load annuities are miniscule in comparison to the offerings with commissions, but while liquidity is not a tangible benefit, it is a very important benefit nonetheless. If an investment requires that you be held hostage to keep your money there, there's a better place for your money.

Timely Application
Annuity Audit

It is my hope that this is an extremely brief exercise for you, but many people who have long term relationships with folks in the insurance, brokerage, or banking industries, have a lifetime of annuities built up. If that is your scenario, it is very important that you do this exercise to get a handle on where your money is and what it is doing (or not doing).

When you did your Personal Balance Sheet, you probably pulled together the statements for any annuities that you own. These statements are often lacking in the information that you'll need for this exercise, so I also want you to pull together each of the contracts that you received at the inception of your annuity policy. Then, using the worksheet on our website listed below, you'll fill in the information cataloging the following: owner, annuitant, beneficiary, contract value, surrender value, cost basis (the sum of your contributions), and the surrender schedule. Some of this will be on your statement, but the remainder will be in your policy contract. You may have to do some digging.

Once you've collected the information, the analysis should start with a diagnosis of the investment value. If it is a fixed annuity, you'll know very quickly if the rate is competitive with today's rates. If it is a variable annuity, examine how it has performed versus the various benchmark indices. If it is an Equity Indexed Annuity, the chances are very good that it is not a phenomenal investment, but it also probably has a very long and steep surrender charge.

If you determine that you'd prefer to be OUT of an annuity contract, here are the questions to ask: 1) What, if any, surrender charge exists? 2) Is the surrender charge prohibitive? 3) How much longer will the surrender charge exist? 4) How much have you contributed (what is your cost basis)? 5) How substantial would the tax impact be (would you have to pay a lot in taxes)? 6) Is there a gain on which you would have to pay a penalty if you are UNDER age 59½?

Again, remember to make these decisions slowly because there are many moving pieces with annuities.

Visit www.thefinancialcrossroads.com to find a template to use for your Annuity Audit.

Tim Maurer

I had been in the financial services industry for over four years before I started to sell products directly to consumers. I went from having a salary and bonuses to strictly commission. At that point in time, I was married and we were planning to start a family, and after the birth of our first son, my wife made the decision that she wanted to stay home with him. Our mortgage and other living expenses were now to be fully on the shoulders of what business I could sell. I chose to start a fee-based business, not even knowing of the fee-only option. This meant that I would be recommending financial products and investments that would predominantly create a small income up front, but one that would be a recurring income that would build with my clients.

My sales manager knew my story. He suggested that we all buy expensive cars with high monthly payments that would force us to keep up by selling more, also increasing the amount in his pocket. I didn't bite. But then, I was counseled in private that if I didn't start selling products with big up-front commissions, I simply wouldn't survive in the business, and that "If you don't survive in the business, you won't be doing your clients or your family any good." He advised, "Once you get successful enough, you can run your business however you want, but until then..." Yeah, I got it. I've got to sell.

Some of the new sales trainees in the financial services world enter the business without a care for their future clients and are concerned only with their own financial well being; but most of them are good men and women who'd prefer to do right by their clients. Many of them have their idealistic visions dashed by an industry that plasters their weekly income on a screen in front of all of their peers in sales meetings. Most of them do as compelled and start selling. Once they're making good money, it's very difficult to return to any idealistic vision, if they can even remember it. It is my sincere hope that as a result of the financial crisis, these techniques will be exposed and become a thing of antiquity.

[i] I found this on www.annuity.com on June 9, 2009

[ii] Frederic G. Marks was the author of *Designed to Deceive* in the *Barron's* Monday, April 13, 2009 issue

Annuity
Audit

Annuity Information	
Company:	
Owner:	
Annuitant:	
Beneficiary:	

Contract Value:		Surrender Value:	
Cost Basis:		Surrender Period:	

Surrender Decision Questions

1) What, if any, surrender charge exists?

2) Is the surrender charge prohibitive?

3) How much longer will the surrender charge exist?

4) How much have you contributed (what is your cost basis)?

5) How substantial would the tax impact be (would you have to pay a lot in taxes)?

6) Are you under age 59½?

Chapter thirteen

WAG THE DOG

An unlimited power to tax involves, necessarily, a power to destroy; because there is a limit beyond which no institution and no property can bear taxation.

John Marshall, McCulloch v. Maryland, 1819

There is an alien in our house. Even though we willingly invited this being into our midst when it was very young, it's become abundantly clear that it does not fully understand the cultural norms of the human realm. For example, when left to its own devices, it will pillage our human food stores even though it subsists on its own specialized alien food. It seeks to re-create the style and substance of our outdoor landscaping by relocating the dirt and mulch of our purposefully designed flower beds onto our sidewalks, and creating anew trenches and holes in parts of our yard that were previously flat and covered with grass. And despite our munificent creation of an alien habitat inside of our home, it seeks to live in, and often bring destruction to, our human habitat, furniture, and creature comforts. It's...a dog.

She is, as much as it pains me to say it, our dog, and unless she hears Jack London's *Call of the Wild*, she will be for quite some time because she's still only a puppy. She was a shelter puppy—an adorable, lovable mix between a German Shorthaired Pointer and a Labrador Retriever (at best guess). An especially strong case can be made for the pointer, because as she grew, she became so tall and lanky that her youthful coordination simply couldn't keep up with her growth. The result was an hysterical few months of physical comedy.

After a February winter storm, she looked like Bambi scrambling to find her footing on the ice-covered snow. If she made it up a flight of stairs, she'd have to be carried down to avoid tumbling over her stilt-like legs. And her tail grew to a point where it seemed to double her overall length. That tail is a weapon capable of clearing off an entire coffee table. And she's so annoyingly happy that her tail is always in motion. I have, on more than one occasion, seen her lose control of her overjoyed tail, collapsing her entire awkward frame into a heap on the floor.

"Don't let the tax tail wag the dog." In college, I heard that quote for the first time from the professor that made the greatest impact on me in those years, Dr. Daniel Singer. He was—and is—that professor that unnerves students because he's not predictable. One semester, he'd teach a class with three tests and two quizzes in between; the next semester, your entire grade was based on only one presentation. But it was his unpredictability, his passion, and his depth of conviction that drew me to him, and I aimed to take as many of his classes as possible. It is now my privilege to teach alongside Dr. Singer as an adjunct faculty member at the university from which I graduated.

Dr. Singer would not claim to have been the first ever to say, "Don't let the tax tail wag the dog," but to me, in my junior year of college, it was groundbreaking, and it still is. Too many people, too often, make poor economic decisions because their judgment is clouded by tax concerns. In most financial decisions, the tax consequences are a secondary or tertiary—at best—consideration. Drew Tignanelli, a Certified Public Accountant and Certified Financial Planner™ practitioner with 30 years of experience balancing tax planning within the framework of good financial planning put it to me this way: "First, forget about taxes!"

How could he make such a claim? It's not because he sees taxes or tax planning as irrelevant or unimportant. He simply recognizes that in the realm of personal financial planning, you should make decisions first based on the wisdom of the investment, insurance, retirement, or estate planning strategy, and then take a look at the taxes.

Timeless Truth

You've probably heard it said that the only two things that are certain are death and taxes. With advances in medical science, we are gaining longevity with each passing year. In this way, we can, at least, prolong our life, therefore delaying death. But taxes, on the other hand, are an ever-growing certainty.

Given the exploding government deficits, it is not only certain we will pay taxes, but we will pay more taxes in the future.

If you were to ask random pedestrians on the street about the largest expenditures they are making in their financial lives, many of them would say they have spent more money on the purchase of their home than anything else. Some younger passersby might tell you all of their money has gone toward student loans or even an automobile. Business owners and self-employed entrepreneurs might describe how the majority of their money has been reinvested in their business.

If the truth be known, virtually all of these people will have overlooked the largest expenditure we all make, which is paying our taxes.

When you consider federal taxes, state taxes, city taxes, property taxes, sales taxes, and a myriad of other taxes too numerous to list, most of us approach or exceed paying 50% of our earnings in taxes. This is not only certain to continue but certain to increase.

It is very difficult to legitimately alter the amount of taxes we pay. Beyond the sensible strategies outlined in this chapter, the vast majority of investment strategies designed to create tax deductions should be avoided. Investments should match the return, safety, and liquidity goals that mirror the short- and long-term needs of your family.

It is far better to get a high return on an investment and pay the appropriate tax than to lose money through some exotic strategy for the purpose of creating a tax deduction.

Certainly you should employ every legitimate tax strategy but beyond those mentioned here in this chapter, one of the best tax savings strategies is to simply donate your money to a charity, church, or worthwhile cause. This creates a 100% tax deduction and makes the world a better place.

Taxes are a lot like the weather. We all experience it. There's not a whole lot we can do about it. And the best plan is to prepare ourselves as much as possible and simply get on with our lives.

I spent more money last year in taxes than I have ever paid before. While this is not fun, I hope I pay more in the future than I do now, because this means my income has increased.

Use the best professional advice you can get to plan your tax strategy and to file your taxes. These professionals will inevitably save you more money than they cost, and they will help you avoid the stress and hassle of costly mistakes.

Jim Stovall

In the remainder of this chapter, we will address the most common myths in personal financial planning regarding taxes and also share the tax strategies of which you should be taking advantage.

Myth #1: "I need a mortgage for the tax deduction."

It is not a myth that most homeowners are able to deduct all or most of the interest that they pay on a mortgage. That is true, and the deduction has the impact of reducing our taxable income each year, and that is a good thing. But, it is the pursuit of indebtedness for the primary purpose of having a tax deduction that is financial foolishness.

For example, when you have a mortgage at 7%, any interest that you pay will be deductible. If you're in a 25% tax bracket, that means that your effective interest rate—after taking the deduction into account—would be 5.25%. But you're still paying 5.25%! It's as if you're paying the bank one dollar to save 25 cents. Many have made the mistake of purchasing a car with home equity because of the income tax deduction. You may be paying less interest per year, but when you take 15 years to pay off a car, you'd be much better off to take an auto loan with your credit union, or better yet, buy with cash.

Further complicating matters with deducting mortgage interest, is that your mortgage comes with an amortization schedule that front-end loads the interest portion of your payment. So when you have just taken out a 30 year mortgage, almost 100% of your mortgage payment in that first year will be interest. By the time you have only 10 years left, most of your payment will be going towards principal repayment.

Remember, you don't get a deduction for your entire mortgage payment; it's only the interest part of your payment. So if you're about to retire and you only have 10 years left on your mortgage—and you have the money to pay the mortgage off—and someone advises you to keep the mortgage because you'll keep the deduction, recognize that you're not even getting much of a deduction at that point anyway. You would be better served to pay the mortgage off and be free from the payment in retirement.

The Truth: You should never carry a mortgage for the primary purpose of having a tax deduction.

Myth #2: "I can't sell this stock—I'll have to pay the capital gains tax!"

From Thanksgiving in 1999 through the Super Bowl in 2000, the above quote was mentioned at festive gatherings as much as lines from the Chevy Chase movie, *Christmas Vacation*, along with this other holiday favorite, "Oh, I think I ate too much." Cisco, the beloved darling of the technology stock boom of the late 1990s, tells an interesting capital gain story.

In October of 1998, you purchased 1,000 shares of Cisco for around $12,000. You bragged over eggnog in December of 1999 how much of a stock trading genius you were sitting pretty with a Cisco position worth over $50,000, and your crotchety Uncle Pervis said, "That stock's way overvalued! You'd be stupid not to sell at least half of that stock now." You retorted, "That's crazy! I read in a magazine that it's different this time, and besides, I'd have a huge capital gain tax bill if I sold now." You called Uncle Pervis to rub it in his face in March of 2000 as you were sitting on an $80,000 position, but Uncle Pervis would have the last laugh. By September of 2001, your position was back where you started; down from $80,000 back to $12,000. You no longer had to worry about capital gains tax because your gain had evaporated.

In this example, you had gained 566% or $68,000 on a $12,000 investment. The federal capital gain tax required, had you sold the stock in March of 2000, would have been $13,600. That's a lot of money, but it's not nearly as much as the $54,400 of pure, after-tax gains that you left on the table by holding the stock even after the economic, valuation, and cyclical factors all pointed towards a red neon SELL sign. Certainly, with the benefit of hindsight, it's easy to say you should have sold, but it was the tax consequences that made it hard to sell. The best investment decision was to take your gain and pay the tax.

The Truth: You should never hold an investment with the avoidance of taxes being the primary determinant.

Myth #3: "I'm buying this investment to lower my taxes."

In the 1980s, Limited Partnerships were a red hot investment. While they did have a bona fide investment component to them, they were sold largely on their seemingly magical ability to create a tax loss—and accompanying deduction—while the investment somehow made money. A change for the worst regarding tax preference and the incredible illiquidity of these vehicles resulted in painful losses for investors who had been sold shares in Limited Partnerships.

Annuities, also, have been touted by salesmen for many years with the primary pitch that they defer the taxation of gains. As discussed in Chapter Twelve on annuities, many annuities have high expenses, sub-par or limited investment choices, and look less attractive from a tax perspective as laws and times change.

Another investment often sold primarily on the basis of tax privilege is municipal bonds. Income from the bonds of a state or local municipality is exempt from federal income tax (and state tax, if you purchase bonds of a municipality in the state in which you live). While carefully purchased municipal bonds can be a wise investment for an individual in a high tax bracket, they make very little sense for individuals in lower brackets.

Let's assume an investor is faced with a decision to invest in either a highly rated corporate bond yielding 5.5% or a highly rated municipal bond yielding 4%. The corporate bond interest will be taxable and the municipal bond interest would be tax free. Which is the best investment? It depends on the prospective owner's tax rate. If the buyer is in a high income tax bracket, like 35%, the 4% taxfree municipal bond gives the buyer an equivalent taxable yield of 6.15%. Since that 6.15% equivalent taxable yield on the muni is higher than the corporate taxable yield of 5.5%, the municipal bond appears to be the wise decision. If, however, the owner of the bond is in a lower tax bracket—let's say 15%—the tax equivalent yield is only 4.7%, making the 5.5% corporate bond more attractive.

The Truth: You should never purchase an investment for the primary reason that it will benefit you from a tax perspective.

Myth #4: "The bigger the tax refund, the better!"

When winter begins to turn into spring, we all start thinking about taxes—or, at least, we should. It is that time of year when we'd rather be receiving a check instead of writing one, but we are missing the point. The point isn't to give Uncle Sam a free loan so that we can feel an imaginary sense of surplus when we receive a refund; nor is the point to be so aggressive in our tax planning that we end up having to write a big check, or paying a penalty for having held on to too much of the U.S. Government's income. Neither should we judge our accountant on his or her performance by how much of a refund we receive.

An objective of an informed taxpayer should be to regulate your withholding exemptions—the amount of tax that you pay the government throughout the year—such that you're not writing or receiving a huge check come tax time. Taxpayers must also be aware that it is you, not your accountant alone, who is responsible for the accuracy and fidelity of your return. You are signing on the dotted line, and the Internal Revenue Service is not a forgiving creditor.

One of the more painful examples that I've seen is that of an individual who changed tax preparers several years ago. The year of the change, he received a dramatically higher tax refund than he was accustomed to. It wasn't until I reviewed three years of his tax returns that I realized the accountant had fashioned fraudulent deductions in an effort to boost the refund. The taxpayer, originally referred to the accountant by a family member, was so pleased that he had referred friends and family himself. Now that he had realized that the accountant had materialized $15,000 in fraudulent refunds, he'd have to report the news to friends and family, and their lives would be negatively impacted as well.

The Truth: The amount of a tax refund has absolutely no bearing on whether or not the taxes were optimally computed. Take full advantage of the tax law and adjust your withholdings so that you neither write nor receive a huge check at tax time.

Myth #5: "This stuff is easy; anyone can do it!"

Helpful software tools and low-cost tax preparation

services leave the impression that tax planning can be done in a matter of minutes by people who have little or no training. There is a major difference between tax preparation and tax planning. The former can be done by a computer program or tax preparer, but the latter requires the help of a professional Certified Public Accountant working in tandem with you.

Your tax preparation software is only as good as the preparer, and don't forget that our own Secretary of the Treasury, Tim Geithner, couldn't get Turbo Tax to work properly! Even if you think yours is a situation that is easy enough to be handled on your own, you should visit with a CPA every few years to ensure you're not missing something significant.

The Truth: Most people would be best served by having a professional Certified Public Accountant prepare their taxes.

Economic Bias Alert!

Many new stock brokers and financial advisors learn the ropes of the business by cold calling and prospecting with little more than a couple weeks of education under their belt and a sales "hook." A hook is the line that is intended to grab the attention of someone on the other end of the phone line who certainly has something better to do. One of the first hooks I learned was to facilitate the sale of municipal bonds. As mentioned above, muni bonds have many valuable uses in financial planning and investing, but the hook that I was taught to use was the "tax free" hook.

The tax free hook is specifically designed to appeal to seniors, because most long term retirees have very little control over their taxes. Many live on a fixed income from Social Security, a modest pension, and the interest and dividends from their investments. They can't control the taxation of their Social Security and pension benefits, but they can control the taxable portion of their investments; therefore, when an opportunistic sales person says, "Good evening, sir. I'd like to offer you an investment product offering 4% TAX FREE," that salesperson is likely to get the investor's attention. Sadly, most of those being pitched to are not in a high enough tax bracket to even make the municipal bond purchase a wise one, but that hook gets the salesperson in the door, allowing them to sell other products.

The tax deferral of annuities is the most common hook that is used to draw investors into products that, oftentimes, do not help meet their goals and objectives. If someone tries to sell you an investment product with the primary benefit related to taxes, be very wary of the looming Economic Bias.

Now that we have tackled the major tax myths of which you should be wary, we'll provide some beneficial tax rules to consider implementing in your financial life.

Rule #1: *Take advantage of a 401k or other retirement plan.*

The most effective way for most people to minimize taxes is through the use of a pension plan, such as a 401k, 403b, or Simple IRA. These are corporate retirement plans that allow you to make pre-tax contributions to an account that will grow tax-deferred until you take distributions in retirement. In 2009, an individual can contribute $16,500 to a 401k; if over age 50, an additional $5,500 "catch-up" contribution is allowed. If you make $66,000 per year and contribute $16,000 to your 401k, your taxable income is reduced to $50,000, and you keep the investment. After someone has parted service from a company and reached age 55, distributions can be taken from a 401k without penalty, but the distribution will be treated as taxable income in the year in which it was taken.

Rule #2: *Take advantage of a Roth IRA.*

A Traditional IRA functions similarly to a 401k or other corporate retirement plan. Contributions up to $5,000, for those with income under $55,000 for a single individual or $89,000 for a married couple, are deductible and will reduce taxable income. As it is in a 401k, the growth in a Traditional IRA will also be tax-deferred, but distributions—in this case, after age 59½—are subject to full taxation. For individuals age 50 and over, an additional $1,000 "catch-up" contribution is allowed.

A Roth IRA, however, is a different animal. With a Roth, you do not receive a tax deduction on the front end, but the money grows and is distributed tax-free. You don't need to get your eyes checked; I did say tax-free, and those opportunities are few. The limitations are that you may only contribute $5,000—if 50 or over, $6,000—and make less than $105,000 for an individual or $166,000 as a married couple to be able to contribute the full $5,000 in 2009.

The argument historically has been that if you are young and in a low tax bracket, you should contribute to a Roth; if you're older and in a high tax bracket, contribute to a Traditional IRA because by the time you take distributions from your Roth IRA, your bracket will likely be lower. But, I suggest that anyone who is eligible to contribute to a Roth should do so. The reason my suggestion can be so broad is that almost all of us will have the bulk of our retirement savings in vehicles like a 401k—all of which will be taxed upon distribution. In retirement, if we need income, we'll be forced to take it from our 401k or Traditional IRA "buckets" and thereby be forced to pay tax on it.

It is beneficial for anyone planning for retirement or financial independence to have at least one bucket from which they can take distributions without paying any tax. Oh, and by the way, with Social Security, Medicare, and Medicaid in troublesome financial shape; global, perpetual military activity on the part of the U.S.; trillions (with a "t") in "Great Recession" stimulus packages; and over one trillion planned for a healthcare overhaul, the chances are good that we are all seeing the lowest tax rates that we'll see in our lifetimes. That makes for an even stronger case for the Roth.

Rule #3: Create a liquid investment account

A liquid investment account is just a regular individual or joint investment account in which you pay typical taxes. In this account, if you own income producing bonds, you'll pay ordinary income tax (which means the interest will be treated as taxable income) in the year in which income is produced. If you own stocks, you don't pay any taxes on the growth until you sell the stocks, and when you do, you'll pay capital gains tax (on any stock held over one year), which is currently 15% (with very few exceptions). If you lose money on stocks, when you sell them you can take a "tax loss." When you do your taxes, tax losses can be set against gains, neutralizing the taxable event. Dividends that come from stocks are taxed in the year in which they are received at the dividend rate, which is also currently 15%—but probably not for long. Mutual funds, which own stocks and bonds inside of them, pass on the taxable impact of capital gains and income to the mutual fund shareholders.

With all this taxation to keep track of, why would I suggest that you maintain a liquid investment account as a tax strategy? If a portion of your portfolio is focused on investing in stocks, long-term capital gains taxation is preferable to ordinary income tax treatment. If you invest in a stock in your IRA, it will grow tax-deferred, and if you sell it in the future and take a distribution from the IRA, you'll pay ordinary income tax rates, the highest of which is 35% (and climbing) in 2009.

If you bought the same stock in a taxable, liquid investment account, your gains would be deferred until you sell the stock in the future. When you sell the stock years later, it will be considered a capital gain and, based on today's rate, you'd pay 15% on the gain. If you are in a high tax bracket, the difference between that 35% tax in the IRA and 15% tax in the liquid investment account is significant. Some even orchestrate a strategy where they do their fixed income investing inside of their IRA and their growth investing in their taxable account, but remember, too much time focused on a strategy of this nature begins to look like the tax tail wagging the dog. The primary focus in investing should be making wise investment decisions.

Rule #4: Do long term investing for college in a 529 plan.

The 529 college savings plans offer a tax-privileged way to save for college, but this rule comes with a caveat. From a tax perspective, the 529 functions much like a Roth IRA. Dollars invested in the plan receive no special tax treatment initially, but they grow tax-deferred and are distributed—if used for qualifying education expenses—tax free. The caveat is that one's time horizon must be fairly long to withstand the volatility of the investment vehicles that are likely to net a meaningful gain. Our next chapter will discuss in greater detail the benefits and drawbacks to 529 education plans.

Rule #5 Utilize a Health Savings Account.

You heard us sing the praises of the Health Savings Account in Chapter Nine, but we need to mention it here again, because the HSA may be the multi-use investment vehicle with the most tax privilege allowed by the IRS. Whether you're talking about a 401k, a Traditional IRA, or a Roth IRA, the IRS only allows you to get a tax break on one side of the timeline—either your contribution is tax privileged or your distributions, but not both. The HSA, however, allows both the front and the back end tax break. Every dollar contributed to an HSA is a deduction. If your employer contributes, they get the deduction; if you contribute, you get it. The money grows tax-deferred, and if you take a distribution to pay for qualified health expenses, the distribution is tax-free! That's the best deal on the street.

Timely Application
Tax Myths & Rules

Put your own tax acumen to the test by reviewing each of the Tax Myths and Rules to see how they apply to your financial life.

With the aid of a chart provided on our website, you'll be able to examine your own posture towards each of the five tax myths and rules. You can then determine what actions you can take to avoid letting tax implications lead instead of follow in your financial planning.

Visit www.thefinancialcrossroads.com to find a template to use for your Tax Myths & Rules worksheet.

Tim Maurer

Have you heard the joke about the rocket scientist and the accountant? Most of us would imagine that it takes a lot more raw intelligence to be a rocket scientist, right? But as the joke goes, the rocket scientists have it easy because their practice is based on immovable scientific fact while accountants are working with a tax code as deep and wide as Lake Michigan that is manipulated by thousands of politicians, attorneys, and special interest groups on an annual basis. Okay, so accountants aren't known for their sense of humor.

It is because of the level of flux and complexity in the tax code—and the reality that there are too many forces at work in taxation outside our control—that we must not pin our investment, insurance, education, retirement, and estate plans on any particular tax structure. These decisions and plans should be made based on their own viability first and the tax impact later. Don't let the tax tail wag the dog.

Tax Myths
& Rules

	Have you ever thought?	Y/N
Myth 1	"I need a mortgage for the tax deduction."	
	Why?	
Myth 2	"I can't sell this stock. I'll have to pay the capital gains tax!"	
	Why?	
Myth 3	"I'm buying this investment to lower my taxes."	
	Why?	
Myth 4	"The bigger the tax refund, the better!"	
	Why?	
Myth 5	"This income tax stuff is easy. Anyone can do it!"	
	Why?	

	Do you take advantage of?	Y/N
Rule 1	A 401k or other corporate retirement plan	
	Why not?	
Rule 2	A Roth IRA	
	Why not?	
Rule 3	A liquid investment account	
	Why not?	
Rule 4	Long term investing for college in a 529 plan	
	Why not?	
Rule 5	A Health Savings Account	
	Why not?	

Chapter
fourteen

IF COST WERE NO OBJECT

> You don't have to go to college. This isn't Russia. Is this Russia? This isn't Russia.
>
> *Ty Webb, Chevy Chase's character in*
> *Caddyshack*

Amy Skogstrom, Managing Editor at Automobile Magazine said, "When someone asks me what car I'd buy if cost were no object, I pretty much always say the 911." Ms. Skogstrom is referring to the Porsche 911, the iconic sports car to best all sports cars. The magazine was reviewing Porsche's newest creation, the 2009 911 Carrera 4S. I can remember as a boy, too young to even drive, having one of those hypothetical daydreams as I thumbed through a magazine of sports cars, picturing a wealthy philanthropist walking up to me and saying, "Hey kid, I'll buy you any car in that magazine—the cost is no object." In that recurring daydream, I too have always answered, "The 911." There's just something about it. But alas, when it comes to automobiles, cost is an issue, so I'll not be parting with the $109,000 that would be required to buy the 2009 Carrera 4S, "as tested."

There are very few things in life for which we could actually say money is no object. The health and welfare of my family is the first that comes to my mind. But even then, I confess that I certainly have allowed money into my decision-making process. I have, for instance, chosen a pediatrician who is in my health insurance network. Is there a better pediatrician that may offer a concierge medical service independent of insurance hassles? Possibly, but I haven't explored those options because I know the cost is quite high. For most decisions in life, money may not be the primary driving force in our decision, but we delude ourselves if we claim that it is a forgotten non-factor.

This is no more evident than in the realm of education. Does education have a price? As parents, do we owe our children a particular educational path? Is a college education an entitlement or a privilege? Before we jump headlong into this debate, let me clarify a few things. Learning has inherent value that is incalculable. Education is one of the primary ways that we learn. I don't, even for a second, want you to receive a message suggesting that education is overrated. I teach on the college level and believe that it is one of the more important things that I do in life, but I don't believe that any and all education is priceless.

Timeless Truth

Learning is a lifelong pursuit that costs you nothing more than a library card or Internet access. Education can be one of the most costly endeavors that you and your children may ever face. It's critical that you keep this in perspective.

The great Warren Buffett often says, "People know the cost of everything and the value of nothing."

In 1980, I was in college at a private university. The cost seemed staggering at that time and miniscule as I look back on it today in light of current tuition rates.

I met many lifelong friends during my college years. One night, we were sitting around the dormitory at approximately 3:00 a.m. pursuing some scholarly activity. I believe we were bouncing a golf ball off of the wall as we discussed the fact that none of us had any money. We didn't even know anyone that had any money.

As the dialogue continued, we determined that if we ever got out of that institution (which was somewhat doubtful at that point) and if we ever had financial success in our lives (which was even more doubtful at that point) we would make it possible for talented and deserving students such as ourselves to receive scholarships to college.

Nine years later, we were all together again attending the wedding of one of my classmates. The night before the ceremony, we were sitting around a hotel room in the middle of the night discussing the good old days in college. Then someone remembered that long-ago commitment to do something for young people who wanted to go to college. That night, five of us started a private scholarship fund that, over the last 20 years, has provided 400 scholarships for students attending that private university.

The semi-annual process of reviewing scholarship applications and the accompanying financial forms has made me uncomfortably aware of the staggering cost of a college education today. Twenty years ago, we occasionally saw a student leaving the university with eight or ten thousand dollars in student loan debt. At that time, student loans were at a ridiculously low interest rate and did not even begin accruing interest until after graduation. Today, it is not unusual to see a financial aid form on a scholarship application where a student has racked up six figures of student loan debt for an undergraduate degree with interest accruing while they are still in the university.

People make financial mistakes because they make emotional decisions. A college education for your children is one of the hardest areas to not make an emotional decision, but it is critical for you and your child that you develop your education funding plan within the context of a sound financial plan.

Jim Stovall

This chapter is for students, prospective students, parents of students, grandparents of students, aunts and uncles of students, mentors of students...okay, just about everyone. We will regularly address parents, since this is a major concern of so many, but we fully recognize that many students are on their own financially, and we have specific counsel for you as well. The bulk of this chapter's content regards planning and saving for college expenses, not because there aren't financial considerations to be made for pre-school, elementary, and secondary education, but because the cost of college is large enough and far enough into the future (if you start early enough) that saving is a viable strategy.

The decisions you make about education for you and your children are informed by your Personal Principles and Goals, the topic of our discussion in Chapter Two and indirectly throughout the book. Please reference those as we propose a framework to answer the whether and the why before you invest a dime saving for education. Before you can enter into an education savings plan, you need to articulate your Family Education Policy using the following three steps:

Step #1: Can I?

Can you afford to pay for your children's college education? Some of the more interesting and inspiring folks that I have met are taxi cab and executive drivers in and around New York City. On most occasions, I hop in the car and exchange greetings and then say, "That doesn't sound like a New York accent. Where are you from?" The answers are like the roll call of the United Nations. And I've never tired of listening to the answer of my typical second question, "What was it like to pick up and move to a place so different from your homeland?"

Just think of the courage it takes to do that. In several cases, it was a personal aspiration that brought someone to the States—a young, single person who thought that America would offer unlimited opportunity. But many times, the answer has more to do with the hopes and dreams that the drivers have for their children. They want to give them greater opportunity, and they're working tirelessly to do so.

Many of them are working more than one job just to pay the rent, keep the lights on, and put food on the table. They have done everything imaginable to give their children the opportunity to go to college and succeed in the world, but they simply don't have the money to pay their children's way through higher education. Possibly their children will have the opportunity to provide that benefit to their grandchildren. It's hard as a parent to face this question—Can I?—but you know the answer, and you and your children will be better served if you answer it honestly.

One of the more financially selfish things you could do is to set aside your personal plan for financial independence in favor of paying for your children's education.

You don't have to be a first generation American cab driver to qualify for "I can't," even if due to your own ignorance or negligence. If you analyze your financial posture and you're not adequately funding your retirement or financial independence plan, you can't afford to sacrifice that plan to fully fund your children's college education. I know you have friends who've told their stories of financial martyrdom for the benefit of their children at cookouts and cocktail parties, but they're not actually doing their children any favors. Here's why: *It's easier to pay off a student loan than it is to bail out your parents when they've fallen short on liquidity in retirement.*

Step #2: Will I?

Will you apply the resources that you possess to pay for, or to help pay for, your children's higher education expenses? Even if you can afford it, this is a personal decision, and just because a mutual fund commercial, your stock broker or the manager at the bank told you that you should be paying (and saving in their investment vehicle of choice) for your children's education doesn't mean that you should. It may even be a parenting strategy of yours to allow your kids to fully or partially feel the pain of paying for their own college education.

It is not my intent to strip you of a healthy desire to pay for your child's education but to give you the freedom to recognize that it is a choice of yours. Remember to be impelled, not compelled, to find your own path in your financial endeavors.

Consider the example of Daniel, a young father of five children who makes close to $1 million annually. His is not old, but new, wealth, and he's made it his life's mission to ensure that his children do not become apathetic to the financial realities of this life due to his and his wife's new-found affluence. Certainly, in answer to Step #1, he certainly can afford to pay for his children's college educations. But he has strategically chosen to fund his children's higher education pursuits with a creative strategy that is designed to teach his children the lessons that he and his wife want their kids to learn.

Step #3: Develop your Family Education Policy

Whether your family is awaiting the birth of your first child or getting ready to send your first child off to college, you must craft an education policy for your family. Daniel and his wife decided that their education policy would be to fund two years of education for each of their children, but not the two you might expect.

They're putting the financial burden of college on their kids for the first two years. If their performance in those two years meets certain requirements, they'll fund the second two years. If their kids want to go to the out-of-state university in Miami or San Diego because they can wear shorts and flip-flops to class all year round, that's no problem; but they'll be the ones paying twice as much as they would for the comparable in-state university. If one of their children is showing signs of being more interested in partying than learning, then the pleasure-seeking youth can do that on his or her own dime initially. If the grades are there, Mom and Dad will pick up the rest. Their family education policy is not anti-education; it's pro-learning.

Our family plan is pretty plain vanilla. Assuming our boys meet a couple minimum requirements in their high school years, they'll be supported financially for the equivalent cost of an in-state, state university. If they choose to go to an out-of-state, state university or a private college or university, they'll be responsible for the balance. That could be made up by scholarships or loans for which they are responsible. I don't want to limit them only to in-state, state universities, but that sets a benchmark for their financial support.

Your plan shouldn't be mine or Daniel's—it should be your plan. Use creativity to craft a plan that suits Mom, Dad, and your unique children. As we absolve those who may be driven by guilt to do something that isn't consistent with their own Personal Principles and Goals, let me also clarify that there is nothing wrong with choosing to pay top dollar for your sons and daughters to go to an elite school. If you come from a long line of Harvard grads and you can't imagine seeing your children in anything other than crimson, that should be reflected in your family education policy. But before you commit, know what you're getting into financially.

Today, the average cost of tuition, room, and board at an in-state, state university is about $15,000. In order to go to an out-of-state, state university, you can reasonably expect that cost to double to $30,000. The top private and Ivy League schools cost upwards to $50,000 per year. So, if you committed to sending your newborn to college and intended to save 100% of the total cost by the time the expense is borne, how much would you actually have to save each month from the day Junior is born? The answers are $350, $700 and $1,200, respectively.

Type of School	Cost Today (Annual)	Cost in 18 years* (Annual)	Savings Required** (Monthly)
In-state State U	$15,000	$42,815	$357
Out-of-state State U	$30,000	$85,630	$713
Elite Private & Ivy League	$50,000	$142,716	$1,189

*Assuming 6% cost inflation per year
**Assuming an 8% rate of return

Am I telling you that if you wanted to save 100% of the expected cost of sending one child to Harvard you'd have to save $1,189 per month from the day that child was born until he or she started college? Yes. So if you had three children, all of whom you intended to send to Harvard, you'd need to save $3,567 per month? Yes. In fact, the assumptions I used in the above chart were 6% for the inflation of college costs and 8% for the earnings on your savings. Some estimates would suggest that the inflation expectation is too low and the rate of return too high. So, can you afford to send your children to the school of their—or your—choice?

I don't want to scare you to the point that you decide to give up on saving to send your kids to college. That would be a mistake. We haven't even gotten to the Education Savings Plan yet; we're still working on the Family Education Policy at this point. But these numbers speak volumes to support the notion that you must take your personal finances into account before you pledge to do this or that for your children or yourself regarding education.

Choosing the right school for you or your children can be incredibly expensive or surprisingly inexpensive.

As an optimistic benefactor, if you fall into the trap of, "I'll pay for whatever school you can get into," you are very likely to pay a fortune. Imagine the wide-eyed high school senior who received acceptance letters from three schools: the state university, a private school offering a one-half scholarship, and another private school offering no scholarship. The student just found out that two friends are going to the latter. How do you think that decision's going to go? If, however, you offer parameters to guide the prospective collegiate, you may be surprised at how economical the college experience can be.

For the budget conscious, consider attending a community college for the first two years of a four year degree. This was my path, and it served two purposes. First, it saved some money. Second, it allowed my educational maturation process to continue to develop (that's putting it nicely). I transferred those credits to the four year university from which I received my Bachelor of Science degree. The cost of tuition for the commuter community college student is still around $2,500—per year! Then, if you can commute to the state university as an in-state student, your cost would rise to approximately $7,500 per year. This means that you could get an entire four year undergraduate degree using this method for $20,000...less than your first semester at Harvard!

An enjoyable part of the process—for students and parents—is the exploration of the student's own Personal Principles and Goals. If you're a parent reading this, set aside a weekend to take your student away and walk them through the Personal Principles and Goals discussion. A high school student isn't likely to have well-stated goals and might not even be overjoyed with a discussion designed to articulate them, but the discussion of, "What is it in life that you want to be about?" can be affirming and encouraging. The results of this exploration can be very helpful in determining what schools would be ideal for a prospective student.

If you're just beginning this search, do not rule out the private institutions based on the quoted numbers for tuition, room, and board. Many times it is private colleges that have strong endowments and foundations designed to help students financially. The aid from private colleges may not even be contingent on the financial wellbeing of the parents or the students. Oftentimes, a smaller, more selective college may be looking for a diverse population and offer a financial incentive for you or your student based on a unique proclivity, passion, or hobby.

I know that virtue underlies the "wherever you want to go" family education policy, but it ignores the reality that the college of your children's choice might not be worth what they ask you to pay them, and (make sure that you've put away any weapons within reach before you read this next statement) the aspirations of your child may not be worth the price of admission (and tuition, room, and board). If your child shows an incredible aptitude for math and science, and specifically wants to become an engineer, then paying the price for MIT may be worth it for them. And since it is your child that would benefit financially from the additional clout that would come with an MIT diploma, he or she should see the logic of sharing in the additional cost. If your child has no direction (and there's nothing wrong with that at the age of 18), but he is quite sure that he needs to go to Penn State to experience tailgating in Happy Valley, that may not be a good value if you are a Montana resident.

Once your children reach high school, this is probably a good time to share the education plan with them, but remember, don't make any promises that you might not be able to keep. If there is ambiguity over your ability to follow through on a plan, be honest with your children. We parents have a tendency to have a fatal flaw when it comes to acknowledging our own shortcomings to our children. It's a defense mechanism. We've answered so many questions with an air of certainty as our kids grow up physically, mentally, and spiritually that we often subconsciously (or consciously) sweep any signs of our own personal failure under the carpet. But we don't serve our children well in this regard. Our kids have already learned that they are not perfect, and we can teach them a more realistic, useful lesson by acknowledging our own miscalculations and showing them how to navigate them.

If you are developing your own education policy without the aid of benefactors, take into account the probability of your being able to pay your loans back with the education you receive. The income that you will make after school does have some bearing on what you should be willing to pay for that schooling. If you're planning to be in international banking, getting an MBA from the Wharton School of Business at the University of Pennsylvania is going to be expensive, but you'll likely be making enough after graduation to pay those loans back, making the learning experience both priceless and valuable.

If instead you're planning to give your professional life to social work or the pastorate, two of the more noble paths that you can choose in life but that are known for underpaying, it may not make sense to get your undergraduate degree at Yale if you're not receiving any subsidy from the university. It will cost a fortune, and the debt will saddle you for years to come without the substantial discretionary income to pay it back. You may more ably meet your goals by choosing the community you'd like to serve and going to the local college or university connected to that community.

As the undergraduate degree has become more of a minimum requirement than a resume builder in the last couple of generations, the cache to be derived from the institution's name on that undergraduate diploma has decreased. It is now the graduate degree that has become more of a differentiating factor. This would suggest that if you are going to get the best value out of your education, you'll be better rewarded to pay-up for the elite name on your graduate school diploma than on your undergraduate.

U.S. News & World Report publishes a detailed list of the "Best Graduate Schools" on an annual basis, segregating among the best business, education, engineering, law, and medical graduate schools. Included in their ranking criteria is the anticipated increase in pay. You can view their annual findings on the following website:

http://grad-schools.usnews.rankingsandreviews.com/best-graduate-schools/

Once you have your Family Education Policy established, it's finally time to determine an Education Savings Plan. The number that most often arises in conversations of this type is 529. 529 plans, named after the IRS proclamation bearing the same number, are tax privileged education savings vehicles. They are plans that are administered by states, but you are not necessarily restricted to using only those available in your state. There are two types of 529 plans: pre-paid tuition plans and college savings plans.

Pre-paid tuition plans are designed to shelter education savers from future increases of the cost of tuition. With the cost of education rising at a rate faster than inflation in many instances, the benefit of a pre-paid plan is that you can lock in today's cost for future education. But pre-paid plans are typically tied to the state in which you live and pledge only to shelter you from the increase in costs in your state.

College investment plans are those to which you contribute funds that are invested in options like mutual funds or age-based "target-date" portfolios that grow increasingly more conservative as the time draws nearer for the student to use the funds for qualified education expenses. The good news with the investment plans is that they are more flexible; you can use the funds for a wide array of education expenses (including room and board) and tuition at schools outside of your state. The bad news is that the investment choices inside of 529 savings plans have inherent risk, a lesson that many investors learned the hard way in late 2008 and early 2009. Several mutual fund managers are now under scrutiny for having delivered big losses in target-date portfolios designed for capital preservation towards the end of the saving cycle.

The primary benefit to be derived from 529 education savings plans is tax-free growth on the dollars invested in the plan. As we mentioned in the last chapter, 529s work most similarly to a Roth IRA. You put after-tax dollars in the 529; the investments inside presumably grow in value over many years; the distributions that you take for qualified education expenses (even including expenses for a computer and internet service in 2009 and 2010) are tax-free distributions.

As a parent, you can set one such account up with your spouse as a joint owner (in some plans) or as a successor owner (in other plans). Your child would be the beneficiary. There is a profound difference in the way that these accounts function versus their education savings predecessors, the UTMA (Uniform Transfers to Minors Act) and UGMA (Uniform Gifts to Minors Act) accounts. When you use a UTMA or UGMA account, you are the custodian, not the owner; the child is the owner. You, as the custodian, are only watching over the money for the child, and if the child chooses to take that money and run when he or she reaches the age of majority, that is the child's prerogative.

With a 529, you, as the parent (or grandparent, aunt, or uncle), are the owner—it's your money—and the child is the beneficiary. If Johnny decides to ply his trade outside of the classroom, you can simply change the beneficiary to another child. You are in control, and that is one of the primary benefits of a

529 savings plan. Even if all of your children decide not to go to school, you could change the beneficiary to yourself and use the funds for an accredited golf school or basket weaving academy.

Contribution limits are quite liberal. An individual is able to contribute up to $13,000 per year (in 2009) and joint gifts of $26,000 are allowed. Additionally, lump sum contributions are allowed equaling the aggregate of five years' worth of contributions. In 2009, an individual can pre-fund five years of 529 savings plan contributions up to $65,000, or $130,000 for a joint gift. Most young parents don't have that kind of money to contribute to a 529 plan, but this is a strategy that works very well for wealthy grandparents who are attempting to reduce their estate's size to avoid federal or state estate tax. After a maxed-out lump-sum contribution is made, no additional contributions can be made for five years.

There are savings plans which are sold by brokers who receive commissions and plans which are no-load that are directly handled by the state and the mutual fund company sponsor. Since none of the plans have an ideal list of investments from which to choose, it will rarely make sense for a saver to give up 3% to 6% in sales commission for every dollar invested. Even the best investment manager will simply not have the tools available to create a truly optimal portfolio mix. Most savers will be best served with a no-commission 529 plan. Additionally, many states offer a state tax deduction for contributions made to a 529. Many of those require you to contribute to your state's plan in order to receive the deduction, but some will allow you to deduct contributions (up to certain limits) for contributions made to any plan.

Two valuable resources in hunting for the right 529 savings plan for you are www.Morningstar.com and www.savingforcollege.com. Morningstar puts out a report on "The Best and Worst 529 College-Savings Plans" each year. Savingforcollege.com is a website dedicated wholly to college savings plan information. Their content is useful, but be careful—they show a blatant economic bias exhibited front and center on their website.

Economic Bias Alert!

The website www.savingforcollege.com is a valuable resource for those researching the broad spectrum of available plans. But their reputation in my eyes is significantly diminished because of a little box that rests in the center of the website home page. It invites the user to "Find A Professional." "Use our directory to find a 529 professional near you." Curious, I put my zipcode in and hit the "Go" button. What came up was a list of "529 Pros," including even "PLATINUM 529 Pros," who sell 529 plans for commissions. Not even mentioned was my state's no-commission plan that is listed as one of the best in the country. It would appear that Savingforcollege.com is accepting advertising revenue from parties who stand to reap a commission from a 529 sale, therefore elevating them to some form of "Pro" status on their website. A representation such as this diminishes the credibility of the organization and the information they pass on to consumers.

Your broker or financial advisor also has an Economic Bias regarding his or her recommendations for the right 529 plan. In my state, for example, the highly rated, low cost, no-load 529 savings plan option is the only state sponsored 529 savings plan. State residents receive a state tax deduction for the first $2,500 per plan contributed each year; however, that means that financial advisors cannot be compensated for recommending the state's 529 plan. I'm sure you find this shocking, but as a result, most advisors in my state tend to find fault with our state's plan that has been heralded in third party analysis. Many advisors have found plans in several other states that would appear to be "better." Not surprisingly, those plans all DO offer a commission. As we've said many times, this doesn't make your broker or advisor a bad person, but it helps color your thoughts when you're analyzing the plan you own or are considering owning so that you can make a more informed decision.

Consider utilizing investment savings plans if you're saving for younger children. When your children are younger, you have absolutely no idea where they're going to go to college, if at all, and so you certainly don't want to hem them into only the state schools with the pre-paid tuition plan. A 529 savings plan is also a great way to set up a receptacle into which grandparents, aunts, and uncles can make gifts when the time comes for birthdays and holidays. I even recommend that you inform them of the plan's existence. Besides, how many race cars, superheroes, and dolls do your kids need anyway?

If you're starting out later in the game, and you have a better handle on what your and your child's expectations might be for a collegiate endeavor, the pre-paid tuition plan can be a wise place to put some of your college savings. The shorter the time horizon, the less the benefit of the savings plan (because you need to take an adequate amount of risk to outpace inflation anyway). The ideal for many savers is a combination of the two 529 plans, but again, the pre-paid tuition plan is primarily geared towards students intending to go to in-state schools.

Another consideration that has become even more apparent in the wake of the financial crisis is that with pre-paid tuition plans, you are purchasing a promise from your state that they will cover your education bills in the future. Due to market losses, a growing number of states are now underfunded, like most corporate and state pensions. They owe more in the future than they could currently pay. As reported in NPR's *All Things Considered*, "Alabama has one of the largest shortfalls, but other states with deficits in their prepaid tuition funds include Tennessee, South Carolina, West Virginia and Washington."[i] You should research your state's plan to determine its solvency and also establish what the state's obligation is to keep their word. Some plans are absolutely guaranteed by their state while others require state legislative and executive collaboration to guarantee your future college funding in the case of a shortfall.

Do you recall when I mentioned earlier how much you'd have to save if you wanted to cover 100% of the educational costs for your youth? Those are true numbers, but I don't actually want you to plan to save 100% of your expected college supplement in 529 plans.

I want you to save 50%. Call it *The 50% Rule*.

The benefits of 529 plans are many, but their faults mount up as well. For every inch of tax privilege received, you give away freedom, flexibility, and excellence. Like corporate sponsored retirement plans, 529 plans have a limited pool of investment options, and especially in difficult investing environments, the limited options may not give you the best chance to shelter your money from losses and take advantage of gains.

Where is the other 50% going to come from if you're only saving half of your goal in 529s? Cash flow at that time, scholarships, loans, and the missing ingredient in most people's balance sheet, the liquid investment account. You'll recall discussing this in our investment chapters. The liquid investment account is that in which you pay taxes when interest is earned and when capital gains are taken, but you have no restrictions on what that money can be used for and when you can use it. This account could be used for a home addition, a pool, a down payment on a second home, supplemental retirement savings, or if need be, your or your children's education.

Timely Application
Family Education Policy and Savings Plan

If you're starting from scratch, the following application steps will provide a great starting point; if you're re-evaluating, this will be a great opportunity to hone your approach.

Create your Family Education Policy. If you

are one of two parents, put your minds together. If you're a single parent or loner in your educational quest, your policy may be even more important. It may be helpful to pull out your Personal Money Story exercise, which likely includes some good or bad experiences that you've had surrounding the cost of your own education. Then, review your Personal Principles before articulating your educational savings goals. Utilize the Family Education Policy worksheet to concrete your family's plan, and then, at the appropriate time, share it with your children.

From that policy should spring your Education Savings Plan. Use the calculator we provide to help you determine what your monthly savings should be and how much of that should be going into a 529.

Visit www.thefinancialcrossroads.com to find templates to use for your Family Education Policy and Savings Plan worksheets.

Tim Maurer

A great college education is not priceless, but it is invaluable.

It is difficult to keep this in perspective, because we are dealing with our children, their lives, and their futures. While I realize you would give up virtually anything in order to create a benefit for your child, it is important that educational expense fit into your overall plan proportionately.

You have probably heard countless times the flight attendant's speech involving the loss of oxygen in the aircraft. In that case, the oxygen masks will drop down from the panel above you, and those of you traveling with children should "put your mask on first, and then help your child with their mask." This is not because you need oxygen more or sooner than your child. It is because, unless you take care of yourself, you won't be there to help them.

Whether you are a student or a supportive family member or friend of a student, the logic is the same. Enlightenment and learning are incredibly satisfying ends. Traditional education is a means toward those ends and must fit within realistic financial parameters lest it become a liability.

---

[i] This was reported on NPR's *All Things Considered* on May 18, 2009 in a segment by Debbie Elliott, *Market Slide Snags Alabama Tuition Program.* You can read or hear the report by following this link:

http://www.npr.org/templates/story/story.php?storyId=104268001

Family
Education Plan

Family Education Policy

Can I/we pay for the children's education? Yes ☐   No ☐

Will I/we pay for the children's education? Yes ☐   No ☐

What will I/we pay for?

☐ In-State   ☐ Out-State   ☐ Private   ☐ Public

For how long (# of semesters) will I/we pay?

_____
_____

Will there be performance requirements and, if so, what?

_____
_____
_____
_____

How can they pay for the rest?

Loans ☐   Scholarships ☐   Grants ☐   Part time job ☐

Other Family ☐   Other_____ ☐   Other_____ ☐   Other_____ ☐

How will I/we pay for it?

Education Savings Plan			
Child Age	Current Annual Cost	Current Savings	Number of School Years
1			
2			
3			

1 Future Cost is: $0 Monthly Savings: $0
2 Future Cost is: $0 Monthly Savings: $0
3 Future Cost is: $0 Monthly Savings: $0

Chapter
fifteen

~~RETIREMENT~~
FULFILLMENT PLANNING

> Twenty years from now, you will be
> more disappointed by the things you
> didn't do than by the ones you did do.
> *Mark Twain*

Please grab a pen or pencil. I don't want you to take the time to think about this, but instead, I want you to complete this sentence with the first thing that comes to mind. "RETIREMENT IS _____

_____

_____

_____

_____

This is an exercise that I've done in retirement seminars, but it's also one that I use in my Fundamentals of Financial Planning class with college juniors and seniors. The range in answers is astounding, and I'll share later in the chapter what I think a college student at the beginning of his or her financial journey has to teach an experienced adult contemplating retirement.

But first, what picture comes to mind when you read the word, RETIREMENT?

Is it Picture #1? A handsome, gray haired couple manning the helm of a restored, vintage sailboat in excess of 35 feet that had to cost them at least half-a-million dollars. Strangely, the sailing seems to take little to no effort, and all they do is smile lovingly at each other.

Or perhaps, Picture #2? A similar couple, equally as abnormally thrilled about their surroundings, playing their third round of golf—that day.

Or finally, Picture #3? The slacker couple, who have made it their lives' work to simply sit on the beach in khaki pants and brilliant white shirts toasting Pinot Noir looking over their shoulders at their modest, 5,000 square foot, right on the beach, second home.

Those pictures, or some very close variant, are what we're fed by the banks, brokerage firms, and insurance companies daily in the advertisements flooding the screens, pages, and airwaves. But it is not just the advertisements that promote the non-stop pursuit of seemingly unreachable financial goals. It is also the way that most financial plans are developed—especially by the majority of planners who work for one of "The Big 3" proprietary product producers. In those plans, the pinnacle moment of the presentation is when the retirement projections are revealed.

The retirement plan becomes the central point from which all other recommendations are made. Cash flow should be strictly monitored to ensure that you're amply filling the retirement coffers that will serve you at some hopeful point in the future. Insurance is purchased so that the retirement plan can be protected under any number of unexpected circumstances. Estate planning is making sure that your retirement plan continues on even if you don't. Education planning is making sure that you save enough for your children's college so that you don't have to impinge on your retirement savings.

What is the downside of retirement centric financial planning? For most people, it creates a goal that feels out of reach for the majority of their lives. You stress to hide away all that you can in your early working years before you have kids. You stress to keep your savings objectives on track through the expensive years of child rearing. You stress to save anything at all during your peak expense years of having children in college. You stress to get caught up on your savings objectives after your kids have passed through college. And then, if you're privileged enough to reach some seemingly arbitrary number that should produce enough income to live off of without working another day, you stress because—for the first time in your life—you no longer have any power over your income and you're forced to subsist off of what your aggregate savings can spin off in growth and income. If it sounds like a lot of stress, it is.

For the last 6,000 or so years of humanity, retirement was a relative non-issue. Even up through the so-called Depression Baby generation, those not born into wealth worked until they could no longer do so. Then they enjoyed a relatively short period of time when the company they worked for (all their life) continued their salary for five to 15 years in the form of a pension. But starting with their children—the Baby-Boomer generation—financial institutions have been training our minds that life doesn't really begin until you're completely retired from all productive activity. They want you to stay focused on the pictures on the commercials, requiring millions saved for an early retirement. As long as you keep striving for the 365 vacation days per year, your money stays with the institutions, and commissions, expenses, fees, and interest continue to build.

The biggest problem with our current view of retirement planning is that it rarely brings a level of satisfaction and fulfillment into the present. It's always about the future. It rarely helps serve the dreams and goals that you have in life, but instead becomes the goal in life; the goal around which everything else revolves. It discourages independence and creativity and seeks to bring people to the conclusion that their financial goals in life should be dictated to them by an "expert," as opposed to drawn from them by a professional. Is it possible that this modern day notion of retirement and retirement planning is prescribed more for the benefit of those who are writing the prescription than for the patient?

Timeless Truth

To the vast majority of people who populate this planet today and to virtually everyone who has populated this planet since the beginning of time, the concept of retirement would be unknown.

Retirement is not an age. It is, instead, an amount of money. It is important to realize that retirement funds do not exist so you can afford to do nothing. Retirement funds exist so you can afford to do anything and everything you want to do with your life.

Money only exists to give us choices. This does not change because you have crossed some imaginary age barrier at 65, 67, or 70.

Before you contemplate your future, which is uncertain at best, please first contemplate today. All of us have one important day that we deal with. It is not the day we retire. It is the day we're living right now. If you do not enjoy your life, your career, your leisure time, and every other aspect of your existence, you need to start making some changes now. Don't become a part of the growing herd of people who are willing to trade quiet desperation today for a fairytale existence somewhere in the nebulous future.

My father runs one of the larger retirement homes in the city where I live. He and my mother work very hard to help people adjust to their retirement years. It is interesting to note, as my father approaches his 78th birthday, that while being around retired people all day every day, he chooses to continue to work. He does not work because he needs the money, as my mother and father could have retired decades ago with more than enough money to live their lives as they choose. The irony is that they continue to work, because they are living their lives the way they choose.

Obviously, I echo the planning thoughts and logic of my coauthor, friend, and colleague Tim Maurer that proper financial planning for retirement is essential. This planning should never be undertaken with the thought that, with enough money, you could buy your way out of servitude in a job or career you hate.

Retirement financial planning should be looked upon as a way to continue to live your life the

way you have always lived your life as a happy, fulfilled, contented person, making a difference in the
world around you.

Several years ago, I became aware of a husband and
wife who had diligently worked for decades, scrimping and
hoarding enough money so they could retire in their mid
50s. As the magic date approached for their retirement, they
were like long-term prison inmates with a parole date ap-
proaching. They gleefully planned their retirement party
that would be followed by a luxury cruise for which they
had saved for many years.

Tragically, just a few months before the
retirement party and the luxury cruise into their sunset years of retirement, the wife died of cancer, leaving the husband to face an unknown future with
non-existent hopes and dreams for which he had sacrificed throughout his most productive years.

As you plan for tomorrow, be sure you don't forget to live for today. Your past is a cancelled check
that you can do nothing about. Your future is a prom-
issory note filled with doubt and mystery. Your present life that you are living today is cash. Spend it
wisely, and don't miss the boat.

Jim Stovall

What would a financial plan look like if a higher priority
was placed on fulfillment and satisfaction today? Is it possible
to reduce the financial noise and confusion that clutters our
present and still plan responsibly for the future? Would it be
wrong to intentionally decrease your savings for retirement,

take a lesser paying job that is also less burdensome on your time and stress level, or reduce the combined hours that a husband and wife work during their children's formative years to enjoy those years of rapid development with them?

If so, this could change everything about the way you'd approach your financial planning. Instead of just "buying insurance," you would manage risk—sometimes with insurance, but many times with good contingency planning or self-insuring when possible. Instead of being "guilted" into it, estate planning could be a healthful discussion about who you would trust to nurture the character of your children in their formative years and what legacy you'd like to pass on to your heirs later in life.

Instead of submitting to a pie chart of investments that has been "scientifically" designed to work if you can only "hold on for the long term," you could find a strategy that would be designed for each year of your life instead of only the last 15 or 20. Instead of stockpiling all of your investing dollars into accounts or investment products with locks and chains (in the form of penalties and taxes), you could concentrate more on short term investments that provide you with emergency liquidity and mid term investments that could be used for unexpected opportunities that may arise before your retirement party. Instead of existing solely of directives, charts, and graphs, financial planning could be an exploration of your Personal Principles and Goals and a living, breathing plan to help achieve them.

RETIREMENT PAST...

A convenient metaphor that has been used for many years in the financial planning community to describe planning for retirement is the *Three-Legged Stool*. This analogy is used to describe the sources from which retirement income will flow. The three legs are 1) Social Security, 2) Pension, and 3) Personal Savings. Social Security is the federal program initiated in the 1930s to help provide a base level of income for retirees to help them avoid complete financial deprivation. Pension is a word that actually encompasses much more than is intended in this illustration, but the corporate pension is an annuity stream of income that is provided to an employee by the company for which the employee worked. Personal savings is the remainder that pre-retirees can muster in cash, certificates of deposit, money market funds, stocks, bonds, mutual funds, and in more recent generations, retirement savings plans like 401ks and IRAs. My, how times have changed.

For the Greatest Generation, Social Security and Pensions made up the bulk of their retirement income. Any savings was typically in cash and CDs because most of the retirement savings vehicles weren't yet in existence, mutual funds weren't yet common, and this generation's connection to the Great Depression made them very skeptical of stock investing.

RETIREMENT PRESENT...

As Boomers sought greater freedom and flexibility in the work place, employers became less willing and able to provide their workers an income in retirement. As things stand in 2009, most companies have halted, clipped, or dumped their pension offerings, and of those that still exist, most of them are under-funded (they have less in the central pension fund than they are obligated to pay out). Workers have made better use of savings vehicles—like 401ks and IRAs—but largely not to the degree that it will make up for the pensions lost. The Three-Legged Stool is now a Two-Legged Stool—or stilts, if you will. Without that third leg, and after a decade of losses in retirement savings plans, the Boomers are grasping for a new financial identity in retirement.

RETIREMENT FUTURE...

Especially having just ended a huge political campaign, there is much talk of the future. Regarding the retirement stool, we're down to only one leg! Pensions are history, and there is much talk about the insolvency of Social Security as well.

Now, let's clear something up once and for all regarding Social Security. It is in trouble, but it's not going to vanish into thin air, because the entity writing the checks also has the ability to print the money, and more importantly, raise the taxes. Yes, Social Security is projected to struggle, and yes, Social Security will likely be worth less to future generations; but the United States is not likely to default entirely on this massive obligation to its citizens.

This doesn't mean that the financial problems of the U.S. aren't going to affect current and future retirees. The financial mishandling of our country's finances is likely to be made most evident in the form of future tax increases. Just recently, I read that the House of Representatives was working on legislation that could raise the highest marginal income tax bracket from 35% to 50% for the top earners in the country. In addition to the increasing costs of health care, these expected tax increases will make all of the legs of the retirement stool less effective.

The personal savings leg of our stool is broken down into several different components. Even though we've discussed them in the tax chapter, we're going to reiterate some of that information and go into further depth. The most common for working Americans is the 401k plan. 401k plans are the most common employer-sponsored retirement plans. They allow contributions on the part of the employee—in 2009, the employee contribution limit is $16,500, with an additional $5,500 "catch-up" contribution allowed for employees age 50 or older—as well as matching contributions and/or profit sharing contributions on the part of the employer. Contributions to a 401k plan are "pre-tax"—taken out of an employee's paycheck prior to any federal or state income tax being paid—and grow tax-deferred until distributions are taken.

Although their number was reduced throughout the 2008-2009 recession, many employers do offer a matching contribution to their employees' 401k plans. A common matching contribution is "100% up to 3%" or "50% up to 6%." This means that if the employee contributes 3% of his or her compensation to the plan, in the first example, the employer would match the employee's contribution 100% up to 3%. For any employee contribution over 3%, the employer would match nothing. Or, in the other example, if the employee contributes 6% of his or her income to the 401k plan, the employer would contribute 50% of that, up to 6%—effectively, 3% of the employee's compensation.

In addition to the match, or on its own entirely, a company may also make a profit-sharing contribution to the employee's 401k plan. The total "annual addition limit" per plan participant is $49,000 in 2009. That means that between an employee's contribution, an employer match, and an employer profit-sharing contribution, the maximum allowable contribution in any one year is $49,000 for any single employee.

In addition to corporate 401k plans, 403b plans function very similarly for not-for-profit companies. Non-profit retirement plans are also often referred to as TSAs (Tax Sheltered Annuities) and federal employees' contributory retirement plan is called the TSP, or Thrift Savings Plan. Deferred compensation plans, known as 457 plans, exist for some government employees. Appropriate for smaller employers are Simple IRAs and Simple 401ks, and for the self employed, SEP IRAs. Like 401ks, these plans allow employees and employers to receive a tax deduction for contributions and tax-deferral on the growth until distribution. These plans typically have much lower cost associated with the establishment and administration of the plans, an important feature for small business owners.

Distributions from 401k plans are taxed as ordinary income, but if taken before certain ages, early distributions may also be penalized at a rate of 10%. The common age at which distributions can be taken from most retirement vehicles is 59½, but for 401ks, as long as the participant has parted service, distributions can be taken free of penalty at age 55. Then, the IRS requires 401k owners to take Mandatory Required Distributions (MRDs) at age 70½. 401k plans also offer participants the opportunity to take loans from their plans in the case of financial hardship. While this feature can help in a pinch, you should be very wary to take a loan from your 401k, because if you leave that job for any reason in the midst of the payback period, you'll either be responsible to pay the loan back in full at that time or the outstanding loan balance will be taxed and penalized immediately.

To roll or not to roll—that is the question. When you leave a company, you have the following options facing you:

- If the plan allows, you may be able to leave your 401k in the existing plan

- You may do a direct transfer from the existing 401k to your new 401k

- You can conduct a "direct rollover" from the 401k to an IRA

The financial services world has long relied on old 401ks (most of which, an advisor cannot manage or receive fees or commissions from) rolling into IRAs (that they can manage) as a steady stream of new business as prospects and clients move from one job to another. While a direct rollover may be the best move for most people, there are a couple of reasons why someone may want to consider options one or two.

While an IRA requires that an owner reach the age of 59½ prior to taking distributions without a penalty, the owner of a 401k who has reached the age of 55 and has parted service from the company may take withdrawals with no penalty. So, if you're leaving your company between age 55 and 59½ and would like to retire, it may be in your best interest to keep your 401k where it is. Additionally, 401ks are thought to offer a higher level of protection from creditors than do IRAs. 401ks offer creditor protection—period—while IRAs may only be protected if the owner claims bankruptcy, so an individual in a particularly visible position professionally or in the community may find that additional protection comforting. Finally, you may take a loan from a 401k, while you may not from an IRA. As mentioned, taking a loan from your 401k is not normally advisable, but for those in a unique situation, it could be necessary; however, you can't take a loan from a 401k without working for the company sponsoring the plan, so you'll need to transfer that 401k balance into your new 401k to be able to take a loan.

These contingencies will not apply to the majority of workers who will benefit from the strengths offered in completing a direct rollover to their IRA. First, it is a benefit to be able to consolidate old 401k and other corporate retirement plans in one place. Often times, workers have a trail of old 401ks following their professional path. These older plans have a tendency to be forgotten and mismanaged. 401ks also have a limited number of investment options; it could be argued that to keep plan fiduciaries out of legal hot water, 401k plans are designed for mediocrity. While your 401k may have five to fifty (occasionally more) different options, the virtual investment universe is open to you in your IRA. This is the primary reason that an old 401k is typically best rolled into an IRA. Many plans even allow workers over the age of 59½ to conduct "in-service direct rollovers." While most must wait to conduct a direct rollover until they part service with a company, the IRS—and many company plans—allows a worker to periodically roll out their balance in their existing company 401k once they pass the age of 59½.

The Individual Retirement Account (IRA) came into existence in 1974. The plan was and is to give American workers the opportunity to save for retirement with tax privilege. The incentives offered with an IRA are that an individual with earned income may take a tax deduction for dollars contributed (if income falls below a certain threshold), and the growth in the account is tax-deferred. In order to take the deduction in 2009, an employee who is covered by an employer sponsored retirement plan (a 401k or equivalent plan) must make less than $55,000-

$65,000 as an individual or $89,000-$109,000 as a married household. The ranges given represent a middle ground where savers are phased-out of the ability to contribute. Above those upper limits, a saver is still able to contribute to an IRA, but no deduction is allowed. Non-deductible IRA contributions can make for a record-keeping nightmare because it is the taxpayer who is responsible to keep track of the contributions and growth in the account (that may also have deductible contributions in it). If one of two spouses is covered by an employer sponsored plan, the income limits for the household are increased to $166,000-$176,000, and if no one in a household is covered by a plan, there is no income limitation in order to deduct contributions to a Traditional IRA.

When distributions are taken from an IRA, they are taxed as ordinary income. If one chooses not to take distributions from an IRA after reaching age 59½, the IRS will force you to take them at age 70½. These are known as Required Minimum Distributions (RMDs) or sometimes Minimum Required Distributions (MRDs)—and no, I don't know who comes up with all the goofy names or half numbers—and are taken based on the presumable retiree's life expectancy. Each year, a higher percentage of the IRA is mandated to satisfy the RMD; those who forget are charged a 50% excise tax on the amount that was to be withdrawn! By the way, if you're gifted to be retiring prior to age 59½, but it really grates on your nerves that you can't touch your IRAs without penalty until you're 59½, I have a deal for you. The IRS allows an individual of any age to take distributions without penalty prior to age 59 ½ if you can prove that you're gainfully retired, as evidenced by your taking out "substantially equal periodic payments" as outlined in IRS Code Section 72(t). (That's not supposed to make sense; it just is.)

If you don't like paying taxes on your investments or having to remember the age 70½, consider using a Roth IRA as an investment vehicle. Named after a Senator from Delaware, a state recognized nationally for its favorable tax treatment of individuals and corporations, the Roth IRA was established by the Taxpayer Relief Act of 1997 as an account into which after-tax dollars are invested. While the Roth allows for no tax deduction on the front end, the growth—and eventual distribution—is TAX-FREE.

While the tax-free growth and distribution is my favorite reason to like the Roth, a close second is the liquidity factor. *The Roth IRA allows you to take out 100% of your contributions at any time for any reason with no taxes or penalties.* It is only the growth on which you must wait until age 59½ to draw penalty-free.

As mentioned, once you make a contribution to a 401k or Traditional IRA, your money should be seen as virtually being held ransom until you reach age 59½. For many people, this is a welcomed disincentive, helping them to maintain their discipline in the area of saving. But, unless you have three to twelve months of your living expenses in cash or a liquid investment account—which most people don't—you're bound to be faced with some sort of financial emergency that will require you to find some cash. In that case, you'll either have to pay taxes and a penalty or support the primary enemy of wealth accumulation by grabbing your credit card to cover the expense.

This access to unencumbered withdrawals of Roth IRA principal contributions allows someone who has not yet met their emergency savings goal to take advantage of the most potentially tax-privileged investment vehicle, knowing that they can get the money they contributed if they absolutely need it. If you make less than $105,000 for a single individual or $166,000 for a married couple, you can contribute $5,000 per person ($6,000 for individuals age 50 or older). Between $105,000 and $120,000 for an individual or $166,000 and $176,000 for a married couple, your allowable Roth contribution is phased out, and if you make over those top thresholds, you're not able to contribute a dime to a Roth IRA.

For those unable to contribute to a Roth IRA because they are blessed as a high income earner, check with your human resources department or retirement plan administrator at work to see if your employer sponsored plan offers a Roth 401k (or Roth 403b) option. This is a relatively new vehicle allowed by the IRS that enables an employee to contribute to his or her 401k with after-tax dollars and receive the tax-free growth and distribution of a Roth IRA *with no maximum income cap.* For plans that have a Roth 401k option, you can contribute any portion of your allowable $16,500 annual contribution to your Roth bucket. You may also parcel out your contribution so that 50% of it could go into the Traditional 401k and 50% into your Roth 401k. For anyone who has been making a substantial contribution to their 401k each year, it is recommended that you phase-in the use of an available Roth 401k so that you can weigh the impact it will have on your taxes. Remember, the pre-tax contribution to a Traditional 401k is the equivalent of a tax deduction; this won't happen in the case of a Roth 401k contribution.

So now the stage is set for the epic battle—Traditional IRA versus Roth IRA! This contrast is argued by many sides for various reasons. Most have focused on the difference between the two regarding taxation. It is suggested that for folks who would anticipate a higher rate of tax in the future, the Roth is the best option. For those, however, who are in their peak income earning years now and expect a lower tax rate in retirement, the Traditional IRA is best. Both of these arguments rely heavily on a static income tax code. Most indications would point towards higher taxes in the future, for the reasons outlined in the tax chapter. Advantage Roth.

But there is another reason that I recommend to those young and old, in almost any tax bracket, that they contribute to a Roth IRA—income tax levelization in the future. (Yes, I'm fully aware that "levelization" is not a word recognized in any dictionary, but you'll know what I mean in a second.) Most of the income generated by those in retirement is taxable. Even though at its inception Social Security income was not taxed, now up to 85% of one's Social Security retirement benefit is taxed. Pension income is taxed, although some states do not tax recipients of some pension income to draw retirees to their state. Every single cent of your tax-deductible contributions to 401ks and IRAs are going to be taxed in the year in which you take a distribution. Everyone would be better off in retirement with a healthy bucket of tax-free cash. With that bucket, you have the control to levelize your tax bracket by drawing from your Roth IRA after you've reached a certain level of income. Advantage Roth.

There is, however, reason to fear that the tax utopia of the Roth IRA will not go on forever. Especially in an environment where our government is spending more and taking in less, the Roth IRA looks more and more attractive to us, as investors, and less and less attractive to politicians who need us to pay their bills. The majority opinion is that if the Roth IRA train is halted, the ability of retirement savers to make new contributions would cease, but the existing contributions and future growth of existing contributions would be "grandfathered" to provide the tax treatment that was promised. If the risk of the Roth IRA becoming extinct is high, the response on most of our parts should be to take full advantage of it while we can.

The more skeptical view is that the situation could get bad enough that politicians hunting for tax revenue may even go back on their promise, making all future distributions from Roth IRAs taxable—just like Traditional IRAs and 401ks. However unlikely, that is a contingency that deserves a hearing. A Traditional IRA is "a bird in the hand," and the Roth IRA is "two in the bush."

The debate over the Roth's future is even more heightened as the year 2010 arrives. The income cap—currently set at $100,000—on Roth IRA *conversions*, goes away. In a Roth conversion, a retirement saver takes what is currently in a Traditional IRA or 401k and transforms (or, in IRS vernacular, converts) it into a Roth IRA. That sounds like a great deal—take money that will currently be taxed when it's taken out and turn it into money that will never be taxed! But did you really think that the IRS was going to let us get away with that? No, a converter will be asked to pay tax on every Traditional IRA dollar that is turned into a Roth IRA dollar. So, if you convert a $50,000 IRA into a Roth IRA, the year in which you perform the conversion, you'll pay tax on an additional $50,000 of income.

So why then is 2010 important? Currently, you are not allowed to conduct a Roth conversion if your income (your Modified Adjusted Gross Income, or MAGI, to be exact) is over $100,000 (single or married). The many who would find this tactic so appealing are not able to accomplish it because they make too much money. But in 2010, that income cap is lifted indefinitely. Then, even if you make a billion dollars a year, you can convert as much Traditional IRA savings into Roth IRAs as you'd like. Additionally, those who take advantage of this in 2010 are allowed to wait until tax years 2011 and 2012 to report the income. Is this made available because the Federal government is feeling generous? No, in fact, it's quite the opposite. This will be a problem for future congressmen and women to figure out. For the current, it will be a tax bonanza.

Is a Roth conversion right for you? Possibly. For those who have lost a great deal of the value in their investments in recent years, it would seem to make sense to convert depressed IRA dollars into Roth IRA dollars that will hopefully benefit from a tax-free market upturn, but there are a couple of other criteria you should meet before considering making a Roth conversion.

First, you cannot make a Roth conversion work unless you pay the taxes with cash *outside* of the Traditional IRA. If you used the funds in the IRA, you'd end up paying taxes on the dollars you'd raise to pay taxes (sounds confusing, I know) and make it very hard for this conversion to benefit you numerically.

Second, you must have a long time horizon. It will take around a decade for you to pass the break-even on this maneuver, so if you may possibly need the money prior to then, it's probably not a good idea.

Finally, the Roth conversion really works best for those who would like to leave their children an inheritance and have the money to do so. There is no better gift to inherit than a tax-free Roth bucket. Unlike you, your heirs will be forced to take distributions from the inherited Roth on an annual basis (based on their life expectancy), but they will still pay no tax. Like Cousin Eddie, in *Christmas Vacation*, said when Clark learned that he received as a Christmas bonus a subscription to the Jelly of the Month Club, "Clark, that's the gift that keeps on giving the whole year." The Roth is a gift that keeps on giving their whole life!

You see, it's very difficult to talk about retirement as a concept or stage of life without getting stuck in the minutia and legalese. The minutia will be much easier to tackle if you've put the entire notion of retirement in perspective. You may recall from the second chapter when we discussed putting the "cart before the horse." Retirement is one of those goals that is thrown out for some random date in the future without respect to the Personal Principles—*your* Personal Principles.

I encourage you to take the word retirement off of the table. What are the things in life that fulfill you? It's likely that a financially comfortable future for you and your family is one of them. That is going to require long term planning and a concerted and consistent effort now that we're down to a single leg on the retirement stool, but your fulfillment plan isn't complete if you're only focusing on the long term. The short and mid term are also part of your retirement plan.

A good friend and associate of mine has a unique posture towards retirement planning in the short, mid, and long term. Marcus Harris is a Certified Financial Planner™ practitioner in my firm and a board member of the Cystic Fibrosis Foundation. At the age of 35, he is a husband, father, financial planner, and one who suffers from Cystic Fibrosis, a life-threatening genetic disease that at this time has no cure. I asked Marcus how the knowledge of this disease has altered his view of retirement.

He told me that his personal financial planning philosophy took a serious turn about a decade ago. Up to that point, Marcus assumed that his life would be dramatically shortened—"in 2008, the median predicted age of survival rose to 37.4 years, up from 32 in 2000," according to the Cystic Fibrosis Foundation website—and, therefore, he had little need for saving for the long and even the mid term. He was a spender. But in his mid-twenties, Marcus made a conscious decision that he wasn't going to live life in the shadow of this disease; that he was going to continue to enjoy life, but he was going to approach it as though the cure was imminent. And it may be. This realization opened the door to Marcus entering into serious relationships, and in 2003, he got married. Now, he and his wife have four-year-old twins, and Marcus is a saver.

I think that his is a situation that offers us all a profound lesson in financial planning. Especially because of Marcus's condition, he is very motivated to plan for his family's future so that it is secure even if Marcus is unable to enjoy it with them. At the same time, Marcus is reminded daily, with a host of medications that follow him, that he has a disease that could have already taken his life. You might not know Marcus personally, but you know someone, or you may have experienced something similar personally that screams out that we are all living on borrowed time.

Are you familiar with the term antinomy? An antinomy occurs when two agreed upon truths seem to conflict. It's absolutely true that you should plan and prepare for tomorrow, and it's absolutely true that you must live for today. What most of us forget to do is to plan for today. How do you do that in your personal finances? The first step is to scrap whatever retirement plan that you have. Don't throw anything away; just scrap it in your mind for the moment. Now take a look through your Personal Principles again. How many of those Principles appear to have long term implications? Mid term? Short term?

The majority of financial planning recommendations pertain to the long term category, but most of the stuff we do in life exists in the short and mid term. And recognizing that money plays a role in each of the goals that are likely to spring from your Personal Principles, how would you know how to prioritize? The chances are good that you err on one side or the other. We mentioned the gentler terms of spender and saver, but there are two extremes on each end of that continuum: the spendthrift and the hoarder. On the continuum, where would you put yourself?

```
+----------------------------+-------------------+-----------------------------+
Spendthrift              Spender           Saver                    Hoarder
```

You noticed that there's not a "perfect" in the middle, didn't you? That's because most of us are pretty recognizable. I've looked at hundreds of personal financial statements, and there is no perfect equilibrium. My financial planning colleagues and I are no exception.

If you have a good chunk of money saved in your 401k, but you have very little margin in your checking and savings accounts and a couple of retail store credit cards with balances, and you always pick up the tab, you're a Spender. If you aren't even contributing enough to your 401k to get all the matching contribution from your employer, you've changed banks several times to maximize the first time forgiveness on overdraft fees, your tax return is already spent for next year, and you put your vacations on your credit card, you're a Spendthrift.

If you max out your 401k, contribute to an IRA and have adequate emergency reserves, but you also give your spouse a lecture once a month when you review the household budget, you're a Saver. If you have been certified by every on-line calculator that you are on track to be able to retire— twice—but have the personality of Ebenezer Scrooge (pre-conversion) and set your thermostat on 59 degrees in the dead of winter and scoff at anyone who appears to show any sign of imprudence, you're a Hoarder.

Once you've determined where you are on this continuum, you'll know how to craft your short, mid, and long term fulfillment plan because you'll be able to identify your strengths and weaknesses. You may naturally be gifted in the area of saving for a rainy day far in the future, but you need help opening up the coffers to enjoy a more extravagant family vacation. Or, you might show a natural inclination to take care of yourself and those in your circle today and next year, but it will take discipline to see meaningful amounts of your paycheck going into an account you can't spend. You're to be commended for your strengths, but we all need help on our weaknesses.

One of the most practical tools to be used in planning for the short and mid term is the liquid investment account that we've mentioned in other chapters. Many, many people—often times, even savers and hoarders—have a cash reserve (large or small doesn't matter) and then every other dime is tied up in some sort of investment vehicle designed for long term planning. 401ks, IRAs, 529s, and the like. But there's nothing in between. All they have is cash earning next to nothing (very short term in design) and money with financial handcuffs that is solely designed for the long term and will penalize you for taking distributions.

If all you have is short and long term savings, you have already ruled out some of the more interesting and exciting options in life that might come your way. A fundamental career change? Can't afford it. A year-long home-schooling adventure around the world? No chance. The purchase of a rental real estate property or second home? You see where I'm going with this. The regular old liquid investment account is the ideal mid term investment mechanism. This account should be more aggressively invested than your emergency cash and more con-servatively than your inherently long term accounts.

Look back over that list in the last paragraph for a moment. I see all of those interesting mid term savings items as representing genuine wealth, but be wary that many financial planners will see these as being out-of-the-box. Worse yet, they probably have an economic bias to dissuade you from any of the above courses of action. But this is your plan, not theirs. You should be saving for the mid term even if you can't imagine how you'd use it. If you never do find a valuable use for this money, you simply add it as a complement to your longer term retirement savings.

Economic Bias Alert!

Most of the self-proclaimed "retirement experts" make their living off of the sale or management of securities (like stocks, bonds, and mutual funds) and/or insurance products like annuities. But these aren't the only valuable assets pertinent to one's retirement. Real estate is the most often underestimated and misunderstood asset in retirement planning. Real estate agents are motivated financially to understand real estate, but most financial advisors have no financial incentive to properly plan with real estate in the context of a retirement plan. Because of this Economic Bias, real estate and other non-liquid assets, like an interest in a business, are glossed over or ignored by retirement planners.

Displaying even more Economic Bias is the common practice of recommending that retirees sell their illiquid assets and maintain their mortgages to optimize the assets that can be managed by the advisor. If a second home is sold for a handsome profit, that creates cash to be invested for a commission or fee. Or a client wants to pay off a mortgage to create more cash flow in retirement, but that may mean using money that is currently in an investment generating revenue for the advisor. The result of this Economic Bias is that financial advisors have a tendency to be anti-real estate and pro-mortgage.

But what if there isn't enough cash flow to go around to fund your short and mid term fulfillment plan in addition to your long term objectives? It is a virtual guarantee that you will have to make compromises in your pursuit of your fulfillment plan. Your financial advisor might tell you that you're obligated to plan for your future retirement first. There is an argument to be made for full recognition of your long term goals, because it is those that will require a lifetime of diligent saving to achieve. But before you sign away 100% of your monthly discretionary income to get locked away in an account where you can't get it, I suggest you go back to your Personal Principles and see how you've chosen to prioritize your life. Do you remember the example I used in Chapter Two? Working more to get to your long term goal of reaching "the number" in your long term savings may conflict with your Personal Principle of being accessible to your family.

The other key to finding peace with your short, mid, and long term fulfillment plan is considered by many to be a four letter word—WORK. One of the more difficult tasks for anyone to pull off emotionally or financially is going from fulltime work to fulltime retirement. Interestingly, both medical doctors and independent thinking financial planners acknowledge that these pictures of retirement may not actually be medically or financially advisable. In a *BusinessWeek* article by Anne Tergesen, *Live Long and Prosper. Seriously,* she describes the results of studies done at the University of Michigan, National Taiwan University, and Johns Hopkins University where doctors concluded that retirees that kept working showed signs of better health than those who stopped working completely.

What if you're at a dead end? What if you've already reached the point where your health has made it impossible to increase your income through work, and the income you're receiving from Social Security, pension, and investments simply isn't enough. What then? The single most impactful thing that you can do to improve your financial standing in retirement is—MOVE. You see, your financial standing in retirement is relative, based on your geography. I live in the northern suburbs of Baltimore, where the median home costs $485,200, according to a great online tool at www.bestplaces.net. It also tells me there that the cost of living in my zip code "is 35.95% higher than the U.S. average."

If I wanted to move to Charlotte, North Carolina, I'd find that the median home price is $174,810 and that the cost of living is 9.3% below the U.S. average. Gee, if I took my net worth to the city of Charlotte, I'd get a lot more bang for my buck! But what if I moved down the Washington, DC, beltway to Chevy Chase Village, where the median home costs over a million dollars and the cost of living is 112% higher than the U.S. average? I'd have less money there, but if I moved to Tulsa, OK, where my co-author, Jim Stovall, lives, I'd again get more out of every dollar.

The chances are that wherever you live, you could immediately compound your retirement savings and lifestyle if you are willing to move. When you take a lifetime of savings, pension, Social Security, and real estate from one area to another, you could reasonably go from barely making it financially to being quite comfortable. I don't want you to move if you don't want to or have to, but this possibility gives you options if you feel stuck. If you're thinking about moving, in addition to the website mentioned already, www.retirementliving.com is another excellent resource that will show you, among other things, a tax comparison tool for each state.

At the beginning of the chapter, I posited that we could all use the insight that I've been gleaning from college students a year or two away from graduation. Students generally aren't looking for a way out, and they don't have a very high opinion of that which we've come to label as retirement. There is no written or unwritten law that says this optimism can't accompany us in the later stages of life. You can see retirement as yet another commencement. Instead of feeling the pressure to work like crazy for another two, five, or ten years to stay on track with a computerized projection of retirement, consider instead taking a step down in compensation to create your dream job and work at it with no desire to quit. Instead of going from full-time work to full-time retirement and putting your productive psyche and your nest-egg into shock, work part-time doing something you love, giving your body and mind, as well as your personal financial statements, a chance to ease into so-called retirement.

Timely Application:
Fulfillment Plan

This chapter's Timely Application is three parts.

The first part is for all readers of any age, and it is an exercise to help elaborate on the sentence that you completed at the beginning of the chapter. It helps frame what your current perspective of retirement as a concept is, what your strengths and weaknesses are in handling short, mid, and long term planning, and what YOUR Fulfillment Plan would ideally look like.

The second and third parts of this exercise are for readers that find themselves within striking distance of a transition towards some form of retirement. The Retirement Income Sources application will help you determine what your sources of income will be in retirement. Then, contrast your expected income with a Retirement Budget to complete this chapter's exercises.

Visit www.thefinancialcrossroads.com to find a template to use in creating your own Fulfillment Plan.

Tim Maurer

This chapter could have been another one of those lessons on delayed gratification and compound interest that you've heard or read a hundred times. Know that I believe very strongly in the power of both, but life is not the linear projection that we sometimes make it out to be. You don't even know how hard it is for me to close out this chapter on retirement planning without telling you how much you need to save each month to make $1, $2, $5, or $10 million. I am, after all, a financial planner! But much like politics, we as financial planners can make those numbers say whatever we want. And not surprisingly, when people follow generally prudent principles of living within their means, the simple, grandfatherly wisdom of saving 10% and giving 10% of your income will adequately provide an eventual retirement lifestyle similar to your current.

Give up on planning only for your future. Question what you think you—and your advisors—know about financial and retirement planning. Don't sacrifice your present, where you'll be spending the majority of your days on this earth, for blind faith in a projection of the future that may (or may not) come to pass. Take joy in knowing that you can work, instead, on a plan that will bring financial fulfillment to all of your days by aligning your short, mid, and long term financial plans with your Personal Principles.

Fulfillment Plan

Retirement is…

Spending/Saving Continuum Self Analysis

Spendthrift	Spender	Saver	Hoarder

	Short	Mid	Long	
I'm best with…	☐	☐	☐	term planning.
I'm worst with…	☐	☐	☐	term planning.

During my retirement, this is...

…where I want to live:

At my current home

In a lower cost of living area

Closer to family

…how I want to live:

Family…

Leisurely…

Charitably…

…what I want to do:

Play golf at Pebble Beach

Travel to Spain

Go fly fishing twice a week

Retirement
Income Sources

Primary Retirement Income Sources

SOURCE	YOU	SPOUSE
Social Security		
Pension Income		
Expected personal savings @ retirement		
	X 5%	X 5%
	$0.00	$0.00
TOTAL	$0.00	$0.00

Other Income Sources

SOURCE	YOU	SPOUSE
Part Time Job		
Annuity Payments		
Other_____		
Other_____		
Other_____		
Other_____		
TOTAL	$0.00	$0.00

TOTAL	$0	$0
RETIREMENT INCOME	$0	

Retirement Budget

Category	Current Monthly Spending	Expected Retirement Spending
Alimony		
Auto Insurance		
Cable TV		
Child Support		
Dividends		
Dry Cleaning		
Entertainment		
Fast Food		
Gifts		
Groceries		
Home Insurance		
Internet/TV		
Land Phone		
Mobile Phone		
Mortgage		
Property Taxes		
Rent		
Restaurants		
Taxes		
Utilities		
Water Bill		
Other:		
Other:		
Other:		
Other:		
Other:		
Other:		
Other:		
Other:		
Other:		
Other:		
Other:		
TOTAL	$0	$0

THE ULTIMATE GIFT

*In the end, a person is only known by
the impact he or she has on others.*

Jim Stovall

"**A** lasting relationship with a woman is only possible if you are a business failure."[i] Despite lousy pick-up lines like that, J. Paul Getty had—and lost—five wives. Maybe it was because he was rich? Actually, he wasn't just rich. *Fortune* magazine named him the richest living American in 1957. He is rumored to have made his first million in 1916—two years after completing college—and subsequently pseudo-retired in 1917 to live the high-life in sunny L.A.

George Getty, his father, apparently never much approved of his son's style and told him that he expected him to destroy the family company before he died. His father was wrong about his son's business acumen, but the fractured relationship did pass from George to J. Paul, then to his six sons. True to form, J. Paul Getty refused the initial request of his son, Jean Paul Getty, Jr., for ransom money when his grandson, Getty III, was kidnapped. "The boy's grandfather only changed his mind after one of the boy's ears was cut off and sent to a newspaper," reported the BBC News.[ii] Some legacy.

Contrast that with the scene I witnessed at the funeral of a close friend's father in 2008, in the middle of the darkest days of the financial crisis. The room was filled with friends, family, and employees of the deceased, and I recall feeling as though time had stopped for that couple of hours. Not one person interrupted to check the BlackBerry to see which bank had failed that morning or how far the market had tumbled. Real life had taken over. Honor and respect was paid by all to this man who'd left such an impression on so many. Even the priest conducting the service shared stories of what he had learned from this man, but the indelible impression that the experience left on me was the sight of his adult children.

Arms locked with his sisters, my friend shared a number of stories that tactically recognized the love that his father had for each of the sub-groups that came to honor him that day. But the eulogy concluded when the son and daughters publicly recognized that there was never any doubt that, above all, the chief love of his father's life was his wife, their mother. There may never be an article in Forbes chronicling this man's collection of material possessions, but his legacy has already taken hold. I met him only once, very briefly, but after attending his funeral, I want to live up to his legacy. How many others who were there—and more so, those who had known him for years or were raised in his family—have received a deposit into their character?

At the very least, the financial planning to-do of having estate planning documents drafted is an exercise in informing your state of residence how to dole out your stuff when you're gone. At most, it is a life-giving exercise that changes lives— yours included.

Despite the profound and often solemn tone that accompanies most discussions of after-death planning, you needn't leave your sense of humor at the door. On actual tombstones reads the following:

At rest beneath this slab of stone,

Lies stingy Jimmy Wyett.

He died one morning just at ten

And saved a dinner by it.

Here lies my wife in earthly mold

Who when she died and naught but scold

Good Friends go softly in your walking

Lest she should wake and rise up talking

Timeless Truth

All of us are a part of the unbroken chain of humanity that reaches back before recorded history and stretches into the murky, unknown mist of the future. People have gone before us who have impacted us, and we are continually impacting others, both now and after we are gone.

If you have ever read anything I have written before this book, it is likely you've read my novel The Ultimate Gift or seen the 20th Century Fox movie of the same name. I have written over a dozen books, but that one seems to have a life of its own. There are millions of copies in print, in dozens of languages.

Through The Ultimate Gift book and movie, I have become an unintentional icon in the estate planning field. I thought I was writing a simple story about a billionaire who wanted to pass on his values, and not just his valuables, after his death. Somehow, that simple story connected so strongly among estate planners, attorneys, and financial advisors, that hundreds of these professionals began sharing The Ultimate Gift book and movie with their clients.

I am glad my colleague, friend, and co-author, Tim Maurer, has provided his professional expertise in this estate planning chapter. It is one of the most critical, strategic planning exercises you will ever undertake, because you've got to get it right the first time.

You'll never have a second chance to do your estate plan over. By the time someone discovers there's something wrong with your will, trust, or other element of your estate, it's too late. You will be dead and gone and unable to redo one of the most important things in your life.

As critical as the estate planning process is, I believe that money is the least valuable thing you will leave behind. In fact, if you read The Ultimate Gift book or watch the movie, you will begin to understand that leaving behind piles of money without the corresponding knowledge and wisdom to manage it, is like giving a loaded gun to a child. Your best intentions can result in a disaster.

Put some thought and effort into your estate planning. Be sure it is done properly, and double check it. Review it often, and update it as conditions change.

> If you leave behind the wisdom, experience, and knowledge this life has given you in addition to your resources, you will not have passed this way in vain.

Jim Stovall

This book is an analysis of the intersection of money and life, and there is no financial planning topic for which the nuanced juxtaposition is less understood or more important than in estate planning. It is also a topic that attracts a lot of attorneys, so your co-authors are compelled to give the following disclaimer to keep our behinds from being sued:

All of the recommendations contained herein are merely suggestions for your consideration that should be weighed by you and your estate planning attorney and acted upon in your own judgment forthwith. We are trained in said subject matter, but are not appointed as legal counsel in any state nor do we purport to be attorneys licensed to draft or administer wills, powers of attorney, health care powers of attorney, or advance directives at the behest or on behalf of any party other than our own persons.

Since most estate planning documents are written in tone and text more difficult to follow than our disclaimer, it is our goal to provide a bridge from the legalese jargon (that actually does play a role) to a more down-to-earth understanding of what is important and why. The most official estate planning term that I must introduce to you in the interest of facilitating our discussion is—bucket. It's an especially appropriate term considering the subject matter. One kicks the bucket when passing away. One creates a bucket list—now made famous by Jack Nicholson and Morgan Freeman for their aptly named movie, *The Bucket List*—of things you intend to do before you kick the bucket. But in the context of our discussion, the bucket will be the name we give to "places" or "things" that house or hold assets other than people. You'll see what I mean.

For starters, here is an outline of the primary estate planning documents that almost everyone should have:

- Will

- Durable Power of Attorney

- Advance Directive(s) (or Health Care Power of Attorney and Living Will)

It is estimated that 80% of Americans—give or take—don't have the most basic of estate planning documents, the will. If you think you're off the hook because you fall into the 20% who do have a will, I encourage you to read further. Most of the hundreds of wills that I've read in my career were unsatisfactory. Typically, they were thrown together when a couple, blessed with children, decided to go on vacation to Cancun without the kids and one of their friends said, in jest, "I hope your will is done!" The husband and wife suffered enough guilt that they called the first attorney they could think of and had simple wills drawn up.

For parents with young children, the most important directive in these documents has nothing to do with financial assets; it is the establishment of guardianship for their children in the case that both parents leave this earth. Here are the primary positions that parents can and should designate even before they meet with the attorney:

- Guardian: The designee charged with the day-to-day care of your minor children

- Trustee: The designee given the authority to steward the funds left behind for the purpose of caring for your minor and adult children

- Personal Representative or Executor: The designee given the duty of guiding your estate through the probate process

Probate is the name given to the process of transitioning assets from the estate to its intended recipients. The estate is the bucket holding the deceased's assets until they are transferred to the beneficiaries. Prior to the disposition of the assets, the estate acts as "the owner." If you chuckled because you've always associated the word estate with the ultra-wealthy and you don't see yourself in that category, consider this a promotion; in the eyes of the law, the assets you leave behind are an estate, too.

The Personal Representative (PR), or Executor in some states (same job, different name), watches over the estate bucket. The will sets forth the rules describing how the PR should handle that bucket. It typically suggests that debts can be paid from it as well as the costs for burial and final arrangements, for example. The personal representative is the first person who has work to do after someone passes away, and they direct traffic through the probate process. Many estate planning attorneys handle estate administration and will offer to handle the duties of the PR or executor. There is nothing wrong with this—most lay people are not qualified to properly probate an estate, and will likely seek legal counsel anyway—but do recognize that the attorneys don't do it for free. Estate administration is a valuable service, but one that can be very profitable as well.

The most important office that parents of young children have to fill is the guardian. The guardian is given the enormous responsibility of taking care of your minor children, effectively becoming their parents. This should be the person or couple that you believe will do the best job of molding the character of your children. It doesn't take long for this to become a political decision. You may be afraid that if you don't ask your parents to be guardians, they will be offended. You may have already accepted the role of guardian for your best friends and feel tension if you don't reciprocate. Recognize and stamp out any of this type of mental clutter around this decision. If needed, it will be the most important decision you've ever made, and it shouldn't be influenced by the thoughts, implications, or influence of any outside party. The objective should be to find the person or people you believe will most closely align with your Personal or Family Principles discussed in Chapter Two.

Grandparents are often the first that come to mind for young couples with young children. It is true that there is a high likelihood that Granny and Gramps would instill in your children your values. It's also true that they are the first people that come to mind when you and your spouse want to get away for the weekend. But remember what they look like after you get back from the weekend. They may not tell you, but after watching your two, five, and seven-year-olds for a three-day weekend, it takes Granny and Gramps another three days to recuperate. They would never say no if you ask them, but they're happier being grandparents now and probably don't have the energy or desire to be full-time parents again.

"I want to keep it in the family," is an oft-heard refrain in my conversations with couples. I think this can be an ideal circumstance for some, but there are other considerations that may actually take precedent. Remember to first consider if the Personal Principles are in alignment, but also consider the geography. If your kids are a bit older, and attending school where they are deeply embedded with friends (that you like), it may make their lives without you much easier if they can stay in that environment.

Statistically speaking, being asked to be the guardian for someone's children is largely ceremonial, but it is an honor worthy of a heartfelt invitation over dinner. Allow the individual or couple the time and space to consider your invitation, because if lightening strikes, it will be a major undertaking indeed. You, as the will planner, should also consider the financial and logistical set up of your prospective guardian(s). If they would have to put an addition onto their home, for example, you can add provisions into the will that would help facilitate that.

The final primary designation that you'll want to make is the trustee. The trustee is the individual(s) who will steward the money you leave behind to provide for your family in the absence of your paycheck. Enter another bucket—the trust. The trust is the bucket into which the assets flow that you intend to be there to care for your heirs. Trust is another word that most people associate with significant wealth, but I'm not talking about a "trust fund" here—which incidentally can be a very useful tool for families with significant means. A testamentary trust is a bucket that doesn't come into being until you cease to be. In fact, in most situations, the testamentary trust is only triggered at the death of the second spouse, or in an accident resulting in simultaneous deaths. In your will, you write the rules for this trust that will house the assets that you've earmarked for your heirs, including your life insurance proceeds.

Let's bring back into the picture the *Leave it to Beaver* couple from our life insurance calculation to illustrate the function of a testamentary trust. Ward and June went to Cabo San Lucas for their 20th anniversary. They're fishing for marlin 20 miles off the coast when a squall overtakes the boat, and Ward and June meet their end. Between the two of them, they had $1.5 million of life insurance alone. The life insurance goes into the testamentary trust for the benefit of their two children, ages 10 and 15. Beaver and Wally are in no shape to handle the large sum left behind by their parents, and Ward and June knew that. They figured that Eddie Haskell would convince Wally and Beaver to buy motorcycles and fund the startup of an illegal gambling ring, so they put a trustee in charge of the money and set specific provisions in place to ensure that the money is there only for their benefit.

The money is set to stay in the trust bucket to be used for the health, education, maintenance, and support (also known as HEMS provisions). The HEMS provisions are broad enough that the funds could be used to pay for the boys' undergraduate and graduate education, the down payment on a new home, or even the start-up money for a new business. The trust stays unified to be used fairly in the Trustee's discretion until Beaver reaches age 25. At that time, the pooled trust splits into two—one for each of the boys. The trustee is then instructed to give each of the boys a principal distribution of one-third of the trust at age 30, one-half of the remaining principal at age 37, and 100% of whatever's left in the bucket at age 45.

You know your children better than any financial planner or attorney, so be creative in how you determine how you'd like the proceeds to be distributed. Your planner or attorney may help you think of contingencies that you hadn't considered, though. While spreading the distributions of principal over an extended schedule is certainly designed to protect the money from the child, it is also designed to protect the money for the child. For example, in the case where a child has a marriage fail early on, the provisions in the trust may help shelter your estate for the benefit of your children and grandchildren.

Many think that they can make quick work of their estate planning by making the same trustworthy person the Personal Representative, Guardian, and Trustee. While this has the appeal of simplicity, consider the benefit of establishing a system of checks and balances by dispersing the duties. The PR will normally have a short-term job, but should be someone who has an eye for detail. The person you would deem ideal to raise your children may not be the most financially responsible person you know, so it can often make sense to split those duties.

If you are a single individual without children, you may think that making a will just isn't as important for you. Ironically, it may be even more important, because you have no default beneficiaries. Although the laws are different in each state, spouses and children are likely to be the default beneficiaries when someone dies intestate, the applicable term when one dies without a will in place. If you are single with children, the stakes are also high, especially if there are specific custody issues that apply. Who then, does not need a will? Someone who owns little or nothing and has no dependents in his or her care.

The will stipulates how things should happen when you die, and the Durable Power of Attorney (DPOA) gives instructions on how your assets should be handled in the event that you are unavailable or unable to act while alive. It is especially important in the case that you are disabled and not capable of making decisions. The DPOA will give direction to the individual(s) whom you make your attorney-in-fact. A "springing" document will not take effect until certain criteria are met, usually that you have been deemed unable to make decisions by specified medical authorities. While this seems only logical, it can create inconvenience when action needs to be taken immediately. A springing document may require your family physician and the attending physician at the hospital to certify your incapacity. With the fear of lawsuits in the medical realm at an all-time high, you can imagine the difficulties that come into play with a springing power of attorney.

A document that is "effective upon signing," is empowered as soon as the documents are signed. Well-written documents are extremely powerful—for all intents and purposes allowing your designee to wipe you out financially if they devise some nefarious plan—but my layman's, non-legal, please-don't-sue-me opinion is that you should only pick someone in whom you have implicit trust, and then, trust that person.

A document that is effective upon signing can be a great convenience as well. If you are in the midst of buying or selling a piece of real estate while on a Tahitian holiday, your attorney-in-fact can help seal the deal for you. If your spouse makes most of the financial decisions in your household, your DPOA can allow your spouse to call your financial advisor or banker and give instructions on your behalf; however, in order for these conveniences to be available, it is very important that you register your powers of attorney with your banks and financial institutions. If you walk into your local bank branch, show the teller a 10 page legal document and ask for all the cash in an account that is not in your name, things are not likely to go how you planned. After you complete the documents, send copies to your banks and financial institutions which will have their attorneys review them for efficacy and approve (or deny) them for use.

Not all Durable Powers of Attorney are created equal. You might think that a simple document declaring that so-and-so has the right to act on your behalf in all matters would get the job done, but legal documents follow decades—sometimes centuries—of legal precedent that seek to find a balance between terms that are generically too broad or too rigidly specific. Ideal documents will likely be several pages long and specify financial provisions allowing for certain types of gifting, and especially, powers enabling your attorney-in-fact to make decisions regarding your IRAs, 401ks, or other retirement plans.

The Terri Schiavo case brought to the entire country's consciousness the issue at hand with the last of our primary estate planning documents, the Advance Directive, or as it's known in some states, the Health Care Power of Attorney and the Living Will. Schiavo's case was an extremely private family matter that was dragged into the media spotlight for many years. Terri Schiavo had suffered respiratory and cardiac arrest in 1990, and after years of attempts at rehabilitation, was diagnosed as being in a persistent vegetative state, a medical term defined by Mosby's Medical Dictionary as "a state of wakefulness accompanied by an apparent complete lack of cognitive function, experienced by some patients in an irreversible coma." Effectively, the body has the ability to be maintained, but brain function is lost, and not expected to return.

In the Schiavo case, Michael Schiavo, Terri's husband, claimed that it was Terri's wish that she not be kept alive if found in a persistent vegetative state, but her parents insisted she be kept alive indefinitely. If Terri Schiavo had drafted a living will declaring how end-of-life medical decisions should be made, the painful, public ordeal that Michael Schiavo and Terri's parents endured would never have happened. In its absence, the family battle played out in public from as early as 1993, when Michael first entered a do-not-resuscitate order, until 2005 when a court ordered that life-sustaining measures for Mrs. Schiavo should cease. We seek in no way to impose any particular belief on you regarding these decisions, but urge you to make them for yourself so that no one else must.

An advance directive is a legal document that comprises two other forms, a health care power of attorney and a living will. While the durable power of attorney stipulates who may act in your stead in matters of assets and liabilities if you are unavailable or unable to act, the health care power of attorney gives someone else the ability to make medical decisions for you in the case that you are unable. If you suffered a disabling injury and were unresponsive, who would make the decision to pursue the elective surgery? Your health care power of attorney designates that person. The living will portion of your advance directive spells out in plain language how you would like your end of life medical decisions to be made if you reach a persistent vegetative state.

The advance directive can also be written to be effective upon signing or springing, requiring a doctor or two to confirm that you are actually unable to make decisions. I have spoken with medical professionals who have indicated that springing advance directives can bog a process down at a moment where time is of the essence. When completed, the advance directive can be submitted to area hospitals to ensure that in the unlikely case that it is needed, it will be optimally empowered. This is also the single document that a young adult, without assets for which to write a will or durable power of attorney, should definitely have. Once you pass the age when your parents must make your medical decisions, a young adult should have an advance directive declaring who should be responsible to make those decisions. You can learn more information about your state's advance directives at **http://www.caringinfo.org/stateaddownload**.

Estate planning documents that you write on the back of a napkin may work in the movies—and in theory—but in practice, you should have official documents drafted. Documents that you found online for free or purchased for $19.99 from a spam email are not guaranteed not to work, but let's just say that they're worth precisely what you paid. These are the most important documents that you'll ever write, so don't be a cheapskate and look for the most inexpensive way to accomplish this.

I also don't recommend going to your sister-in-law or the guy on your softball team because you know she or he is a lawyer. They may very well do you the favor of creating some estate planning documents from an old boiler-plate they dust off, but the chances are good that the documents won't be much better than the online resources available. Like doctors, attorneys have specialties. You wouldn't go to your family doctor for laser eye surgery, nor would you ask an orthopedic surgeon to give you a colonoscopy. There are attorneys who specialize in estate planning. I recommend asking your financial planner or CPA to refer you to a few, and then interview them yourself. Estate planning attorneys inside of large law firms are likely to cost more than a smaller practice specializing in estate planning. I also recommend asking for flat-fee pricing so you don't have to worry about skimping on good questions for fear that you're on the hourly-billing clock.

These three estate planning documents—the will, durable power of attorney, and advance directive—are very important and surprisingly powerful when properly drafted. For that reason, it is mandatory that you set aside the time and effort required to ensure that you understand what you are doing. But despite their great importance, it's time to tell you the most important estate planning document—even more important than the three above—the beneficiary designation form. Your 401ks, 403bs, IRAs, Roth IRAs, 529s, life insurance policies, and more have designated beneficiaries or successor custodians that outrank your will. That's right; your beneficiary designations will trump your will, if different.

Many a divorcee has learned this lesson the hard way. Mr. Johnson got caught having a long-term affair with his secretary. Mrs. Johnson got a very good divorce attorney and got her fair share on her way out the door (actually, she got the door). Mr. Johnson felt that the financial punishment didn't fit the crime, so he was sure to redo all of his estate planning documents to ensure that if he dropped dead, the former Mrs. Johnson wouldn't get a penny. Then, he was struck by lightening in the middle of his backswing on the 13th hole at Pebble Beach, and met his untimely end.

His will had everything going to the secretary, but Mr. Johnson forgot to change the beneficiary on his 401k, his IRA, and his insurance policy, the value of which made up 70% of his entire post-divorce estate. The former Mrs. Johnson was still listed on each of those as beneficiary, so regardless of what the will says, as soon as she finishes the bronze plaque that will be placed on the 13th hole at Pebble Beach in memory of her late ex-husband, she'll be meeting with her financial planner to figure out how to spend his money. A beneficiary designation trumps a will, and the titling on an asset trumps a beneficiary designation, so after you complete your estate planning documents, you must ensure that the beneficiary designations and titling of your assets are in alignment with the wishes in your will.

So how should your beneficiary designations read once you've completed the will? Should the beneficiary designation on your life insurance and retirement accounts be a person, the trust bucket, or the estate bucket? Opinions vary widely on this, and choices will also differ depending on the laws of your state, but let's review the available options.

If you are married, it will be the intent of most estate plans to have everything pass from one spouse to the other upon a single death, the most likely scenario. The "Simple Will" tells the courts to take whatever's mine and give it to my spouse, and vice versa. Similarly, the primary beneficiaries on most retirement plans and insurance policies for each half of a married couple should be the other spouse, so that, in the case of death, the surviving spouse has immediate access to the family assets. The more difficult question arises: who or what should be the secondary or contingent beneficiary in the will, and then for the retirement plans and life insurance policies?

The tug-of-war in this decision-making process is between the control camp and the save money camp. The control camp tends to be represented by attorneys and the save money camp, by accountants. First, the simpler example of life insurance. If you and your spouse die simultaneously, the benefit of life insurance is to care for your children or other dependents. The trust bucket has the rules you've set forth giving you control beyond the grave to finance your children in a way fitting with your Personal Principles. The simplest way to ensure that this works as planned is to designate no contingent beneficiary. In that case, the life insurance proceeds will go into the estate bucket, and the will directs the funds from the estate bucket into the trust bucket. This is the simplest way to ensure that the money gets where you want it to go without complication.

But why not send the life insurance proceeds directly to the trust bucket? You can. This becomes an even more attractive option as the size of the estate grows. You may ask the attorney for verbiage to be listed in your contingent beneficiary space to direct the insurance proceeds directly to the trust bucket, bypassing the estate bucket. The advantage to this method is that the money goes directly into the trust, bypassing the probate process. Additionally, since the Personal Representative, the attorney, or both will likely be taking a fee based on the size of your probate estate (the stuff that ends up in the estate bucket), eliminating the life insurance proceeds from that process should decrease the associated costs. The disadvantage is that you're adding a layer of complexity, and each time that happens, the risk of a mistake increases.

So for most of your assets, the objective is to get them into the hands of direct beneficiaries and/or the trust; in both cases, you are controlling the process with the estate planning documents and beneficiary designations. But in dealing with retirement accounts, the Feds already have a set of rules in place for how distributions should be made. Here is where the set of rules that you've created and the set of rules that the Feds have created tend to conflict. According to the Feds, here is how distributions are taken from the following retirement accounts:

For 401ks, 403bs, other corporate retirement accounts, and IRAs, beneficiaries have the right to take full distribution immediately if they choose, and pay the tax in the year in which the distribution is taken, but beneficiaries may also have the ability to stretch those distributions out over their own life expectancy. Again, distributions from 401ks, 403bs, and IRAs (with the exception of Roth IRAs) are taxed—even to beneficiaries; therefore, it is very possible that being forced to take a full distribution from an inherited IRA or 401k could cause a serious tax problem for a beneficiary.

For beneficiaries who don't need the money and would prefer to spread the tax burden over their lifetime, the life expectancy distribution is an excellent option that has become unofficially known as the "Stretch IRA." Similar distributions are allowed in 401ks, although the life expectancy table may not be as favorable as in an IRA. Special dispensation is made for spousal beneficiaries. A spouse can choose to allow the IRA to be treated as an inherited IRA as any beneficiary would, and take the distributions based on his or her own life expectancy; but the surviving spouse also has the ability to choose to roll the deceased spouse's IRA into his or her own IRA.

The advantage of consolidation is simplicity—the surviving spouse need not worry about two different accounts and required distributions from both, but the consolidated IRA will be treated as if there were no death, and the surviving spouse beneficiary will be subject to the normal distribution rules (no distribution without penalty before 59½ and mandatory required distributions at age 70½). The advantage to a spouse who keeps his or her deceased spouse's IRA separate, as an inherited IRA, is that a spouse under the age of 59½, who may need funds from the IRA on which to live, would be able to take those distributions free of penalty.

With all those rules, you can probably see how things can get a little hairy when you try to incorporate your rules with those of the IRS. If you make your spouse the primary beneficiary and "the estate" your contingent beneficiary, explicitly or by default, and then the cruise ship with you and your spouse goes down, you will have voided all the IRA tax privilege for your heirs. Effectively, tax will be paid on the entire amount as it is distributed all at one time to the estate. Your trust will now be able to control the leftover funds, but after almost half of the IRA is slashed in taxes, your heirs have a lot less money; however, if you keep your heirs listed as direct beneficiaries of your 401ks and IRAs, they would have access to the funds once they reach the age of majority. Do you see the battle between control and save money?

For the broad cross-section of Baby Boomer parents—and younger—for whom this would be a concern, consider the following suggestion. If, heaven forbid, you and your spouse "go" simultaneously, leaving your children behind, it is likely that the majority of your estate will be your life insurance and real estate proceeds. Your 401ks, 403bs and IRAs are of reasonable size, but still less than your life insurance, the purchase of which was to care for your family in your absence, and your real estate. You can maintain control over those IRA assets while your beneficiaries are still minors. Minors can't inherit an IRA anyway, so you'll want to make the person you've chosen as your trustee the custodian for your minor children. But when they reach the age of majority (21 in most states), they will have full control of how they spend the money.

Therefore, consider taking advantage of the control outlined in your trust with your life insurance, real estate and personal assets, and opt for the save money method with your retirement plans by making your children direct beneficiaries, allowing them the option of stretching that IRA out over time. If your kid decides to blow it all on his 21st birthday and throw a party with gold-plated beer kegs and U2 as the night's entertainment, the IRA will be gone, but the trust bucket will still have control of the bulk of your estate. If, however, your children are wise enough to listen to the good advice of your trustee and stretch their distributions out over their lifetime, all the better. It is possible to maintain elements of the tax privilege and the control you desire by creating a trust that is specifically designed to work with IRA assets, but it is much more complicated and costly, and you'll recall that added complications increase the risk of something not working in the future.

Latin may be a dead language, but it's alive and well in the legal realm. In order to properly complete your beneficiary designations, you need to understand the difference between per stirpes and per capita. Most beneficiary designations, if not otherwise noted, will default to per capita. Consider another Cleaver scenario. Later in life, Ward has already passed on. June lives at a retirement community, and Wally and Beaver are married with children of their own. Beaver, ever the good son, drives to pick Mom up to take her to lunch, but he's blindsided by a truck that ran through the red light, and pronounced dead on the spot. June, upon hearing the news, dies of cardiac arrest.

If June's beneficiary designations are per stirpes, Wally would receive his half and Beaver's lineal descendents—his children, not his wife—would receive the other half. If listed as per capita, and Beaver predeceases June, the remaining beneficiaries would split the accounts; in this case, Wally would get 100%, since there were only two of them. If there were three children, instead of the account or insurance policy proceeds being split 1/3, 1/3, 1/3, it would be split 1/2, 1/2 between the living beneficiaries.

Since most of your beneficiary designations will default to per capita, it is very important that you specify per stirpes if it is your intent to have your respective grandchildren receive the inheritance of any child that predeceases you. Some IRA custodians may even refuse to do it, because it creates more work and legal compliance for them; but most will comply, and it is a common practice with most insurance companies.

Whether you are talking about the personal representative, guardian, and trustee in your will; your designation for attorney-in-

fact for your durable power of attorney; your designation of health care attorney-in-fact; or your beneficiaries, you should ALWAYS list a primary designee and at least a contingent designee in the case that your primary is unwilling or unable to fulfill his or her duty.

We have mentioned the process of probate several times, and it deserves another look. As mentioned, each state has its own process, and some are more notorious than others. The primary negative implications of probate are the cost and the lack of privacy. Considering the cost, some states have caps on the amount that a personal representative or executor—often an attorney—can charge to walk an estate through the probate process. Examine these costs to see if yours is an estate with notably onerous probate costs. Elvis didn't do proper estate planning, and his estate was hammered by the probate process, making his private life public for the whole world and eating up much of his estate in fees and taxes.

One technique that is becoming more widely known for individuals and families attempting to avoid probate is the drafting of a Revocable Living Trust (RLT). Unlike the testamentary trust bucket which doesn't exist until you don't, the RLT is a bucket that is supposed to own your stuff while you're living. The idea is that you title all of your worldly possessions in this trust while you're still alive so that when you die, there is nothing left to go through probate. The trust lives on. There are some states in which optimal estate planning practically requires a revocable living trust, but most can avoid probate without paying significantly more to create a revocable living trust.

Your retirement accounts and life insurance policies already have beneficiary designations. As long as you designate a person or trust directly, those assets will avoid probate. Your liquid investment accounts without beneficiary designations can have "beneficiary designations" by having a Transfer On Death (TOD) feature added to the account. Your bank accounts, similarly, can be fitted with Payable On Death (POD) designations. Even your home can pass free of probate with a Life Estate Deed, which transfers the property directly to a beneficiary of your choice with a valid death certificate.

Economic Bias Alert!

The revocable living trust is an excellent estate planning tool for many reasons, but you should not assume that it's the right vehicle for you simply because you heard an attorney on the radio, TV, or in a seminar tell you that its benefits are for everyone. The people for whom an RLT is most appropriate are those who own property in multiple states (so they don't have to go through probate in more than one state).

The truth is that some attorneys create what are referred to in the industry as "Trust Mills." They preach the gospel of the RLT and claim that its benefits are to be enjoyed by everyone. The chances are that anyone who takes that broad of a view is less of a counselor and more of a salesperson.

The cost of an RLT can be double or triple the

cost of only a will. Additionally, the ongoing maintenance of an RLT is quite work intensive, requiring you to re-title all of your assets to be owned by the trust, a process referred to as "funding" a trust. An un-funded trust is a very expensive, worthless document.

If you went to a seminar where an attorney espoused the benefits of a revocable living trust and paid for your lunch, the chances are that you've uncovered an estate planning Economic Bias.

While most families will be well served with a simple will that directs one's assets to primary and contingent beneficiaries, or the slightly more complex will with a testamentary trust, if your net worth is already in the millions, you've been blessed financially and cursed to deal with state and federal estate tax. Federal estate tax, in the year 2009, is levied on estates in excess of $3.5 million, but with the proper estate planning, a married couple can shelter up to $7 million from federal estate tax. Most people won't have this problem, but those who do face one of the more egregious taxes the IRS levies—45% of everything over the limit. That tax is on top of any state estate tax, state inheritance tax, and federal income tax, so it's possible for a single individual with all of her $10 million of wealth in an IRA to have up to 90% of her estate over $3.5 million eradicated by taxes.

To make matters more confusing, the estate tax is currently set to be repealed completely in 2010 and then "sunset" back to a $1,000,000 exemption (versus the $3.5 mil in 2009) in

2011. Majority opinion is that Congress will deal with it before we celebrate New Year's Day 2010. The detailed complexity and dynamic nature of this niche realm of financial planning led us to stop short of addressing it comprehensively in this book, but we've included an Estate Planning Appendix on our website, www.thefinancialcrossroads.com, where we'll offer some sophisticated financial planning strategies, legal opinions from attorneys, and updates on the federal legislation surrounding estate tax planning.

As you go through the process of considering the many decisions you have to make surrounding your estate plan, it is best to create a Survivor Guide to accompany your documents. This is not an official legal document, but a booklet that articulates important information like the following: the names and contact information of the folks closest to you, churches and associations of which you're a member, memorial plans, names and contact information for your financial planner, attorney, accountant, and insurance agent, as well as additional information or personal wishes that didn't make it into your estate planning documents.

Timely Application
Legacy Plan

Begin or revisit your personal estate plan by completing the Legacy Plan exercise. Included is an estate checklist to ensure that you have the necessary documents updated with the appropriate provisions inside of them. As you work through the process of getting your documents in line with your Personal Principles, develop your survivor guide which should accompany your estate planning documents to provide additional details of your wishes to those you leave behind. You'll find a downloadable booklet on our website for your Legacy Plan.

My co-author, Jim Stovall, has changed the way that five million readers, and Lord knows how many movie goers, understand the word legacy through his book, and subsequent movie, The Ultimate Gift. If you haven't read it yet, I encourage you to do so. It is a fast, refreshing read that would act as a great launching point for a legacy plan that goes well beyond the numbers.

For those who are encouraged to take additional steps to ensure that they leave a legacy, not just an estate, the themes exhibited in The Ultimate Gift are now available as tools that you can find at www.theultimategift.com.

Visit www.thefinancialcrossroads.com to find a template to use for your Estate Checklist and Survivor Guide.

Tim Maurer

Your estate planning documents will, hopefully, reflect your wishes, but they will never articulate in your words what you want your legacy to be. These financial planning recommendations are more meaningful than your investment asset allocation or the amount of personal liability protection, and I encourage you to go beyond thinking about your estate to consider your legacy. Even if you are penniless and in your twenties, you're making a mark on this world, and careful consideration about how you'd like to leave it is a worthwhile pursuit.

---

[i] This was from *Divorce With Decency* by Bradley Coates

[ii] A much admired American expat examined in BBC News *Profile: Sir John Paul Getty II*

Legacy Plan

Information

YOU

Name:	
Address:	
City:	State:	Zip:
Social Security:	Phone:
Employer:	E.Phone:
Employer contact:	

SPOUSE

Name:	
Address:	
City:	State:	Zip:
Social Security:	Phone:
Employer:	E.Phone:
Employer contact:	

Estate Check List

	YOU	SPOUSE
Documents:	☐ Will Last Revision:Date___ /___ /___ ☐ Power of Attorney ☐ Advance Directives	☐ Will Last Revision:Date___ /___ /___ ☐ Power of Attorney ☐ Advance Directives
Executor/ Personal Representative	Name: Phone: Address:	Name: Phone: Address:
Guardian:	Name: Phone: Address:	Name: Phone: Address:
Trustee:	Name: Phone: Address:	Name: Phone: Address:

Chapter
seventeen

EVERYONE IS BIASED

This is like déjà vu all over again.

Yogi Berra

"Everyone is biased." Those were the words of a mentor of mine shortly after I entered the business of financial advising. I had already been working in the financial industry for several years, but this was the second time that my idealistic view of the objective, trusted financial advisor received a healthy dose of reality. The first time was about three years earlier. I had just finished celebrating my rite of passage into the stock brokerage world—successful completion of the "Series 7" examination that allows one to sell stocks, bonds, mutual funds, options, and various other securities to the public—when I left my entry-level back office job at a reputable brokerage firm to join a successful team of stock brokers at another firm as a "junior broker."

The celebration continued as I settled into my new office (with walls) and my 100% raise. Now I was ready to conquer the financial world. I intended to set up shop as a financial doctor and wait to see wealthy patients line up at my door eagerly awaiting my professional diagnosis and walking away with a prescription of financial wisdom.

I showed up the first day, bright and early, in my token blue pin-striped suit, starched white shirt, and bold power tie. I sauntered into the team leader's office to await my very first "Morning Call." I listened intently and began feverishly taking notes as a man's voice rang through a small box detailing the economic events and non-events that were expected to influence the stock and bond markets that day, as well as the state of the current "inventory" that the company held.

As the call wrapped up with a dose of encouragement—akin to a team chant before a football game—I took a deep breath, a final swig of coffee, and moved forward onto the edge of my chair, eagerly awaiting the golden wisdom from my suspender-bound leader as I set out to save the populous from their deviant financial ways. He stood up, glanced out over the magnificent view of the Baltimore harbor visible from his corner office, and invited me to walk across the hall to get comfortable in my new confines.

He grabbed a three-ring binder, six inches thick, and opened it to the first page. Then he told me to write down the only note he had taken during the morning call: "BGE 6.5% Preferred." My mission was to call the first number attached to the first name (of many) on the first page (of many) and begin a conversation to help bring whoever answered the phone to the conclusion that they could simply not go another day without putting some of their hard earned money to work for them in this bargain basement deal with an unbeatable yield on this new issue of the bedrock Baltimore utility company's preferred stock.

I was told to start by putting a smile on my face, because my joy would better translate through the other end of the phone. I should talk and talk and talk until the voice either transitioned into a static dial tone or submitted to my plea to "talk to the resident expert" in house (my team leader), at which point I should put them on hold and alert the big shark that we had a fish on the line (I'm not stretching the metaphors here; that's really how they talked).

This was my dream?? Several weeks later, driving home from a client lunch with my leader, I got up the nerve to ask him a question, the answer to which I was dying to know: "What drives you? A genuine interest to guide a client to the path of financial success or a pure love of the sale?"

I appreciated his honesty as he let out a "hrmph" and retorted, "The sale—of course! If this business dried up, I'd sell snow cones to Eskimos!"

He was the resident trainer for the company's new breed of financial advisors that would guide (or pester) the residents of the Baltimore metropolitan area. I talked to him a few days later and told him that I felt we had a "philosophical disconnect" in the way we viewed the business. He agreed, saying, "Yeah, some people just aren't cut out for the phone," and we parted on good terms.

The celebrated entrance into the business I had dreamt about since the eighth grade ended in disappointment after only two months. I regrouped and accepted a job as an equity trader on the trading floor of a regional brokerage firm.

Fast forward three years. I was back in the game with

more experience and only slightly less naivety. I had joined a company that convinced me they were dedicated to the financial planning process, a large insurance company said to be transitioning from a single line of business to a comprehensive planning process to include investment and other financial analysis.

I was teamed up once again, this time with a thirty year veteran of the insurance business. He was (and still is) a good man, well-intended, and a leader in the community. Having one of many heart-to-heart conversations on the road home from an appointment, I shared with him my view of the importance of pure objectivity in the planning process—that we must be advocating on the client's behalf, in search only of the products that would best serve their needs.

He saw through my veiled attempt to suggest our process should be less insurance heavy and spoke those words that have rung in my head ever since, "Everyone is biased. There is no true objectivity." His bias just happened to lean towards the value of permanent insurance products. One year later, I had to move on once again. Not able to change the world in which I existed professionally, I had to find another one.

Several years and two more companies later, with Certified Financial Planner™ certification and seven industry licenses behind me, I have arrived at some important conclusions:

First, the behemoth financial industry, including the major brokerage firms, insurance companies, and banks, is inherently set in a way that puts the company first, the broker of products and services second, and the client's interest no higher than third.

Second, that industry implicitly promotes itself as the fiduciary of the public, placing their clients' interest above all. This is a dangerous impression because, as employees of these companies, the advisor's primary duty is to represent their company while clients are encouraged to believe (through an endless marketing campaign) that their interest is coming first. Put to the test, the vast majority of brokers and sales people—or advisors and consultants, as they are often termed these days—would not be able to sign (per their own compliance departments) a pledge that they will place the interest of their clients above all, even though many of them want to.

Finally, everyone does carry a certain bias, but the interest of the client will best be preserved in environments that do not encourage behavior to the contrary. Different professionals in any line of highly regulated business, such as doctors, lawyers, architects, or engineers, may have differing and even opposing opinions and may legally support their opinions and encourage clients to act accordingly. The problem in the institutional financial industry is that it calls itself advisory, but is actually a sales operation—a veiled misrepresentation.

This is not a "whistle-blowing" or "tell-all" of a repentant, once-wayward soul. It is also not meant to decry every advisor, stock broker, or insurance representative at the establishment companies that are worthy of criticism. Some of the best financial minds and well-intended individuals I know work for these companies and work hard for their clients despite the institutional pressures to do otherwise.

This is a bringing of truth to light; a guide for what you should know and probably don't about the financial advisory business; an explanation of exactly what a fiduciary is, why it's important, and how it is different from the premise under which most business in the financial industry is conducted; and suggestions for how you can find an advisor that has the best of intentions and—as important—the freedom, encouragement, and mandate, all the way up the corporate ladder, to act on them.

Timeless Truth

All of us deal with professionals in our lives. We hope these are highly-trained, ethical, and responsible people. If we stop to think about it, we realize that they make a living from serving us. Your doctor is a highly-trained professional whose job is to assess your situation, review the medical landscape relating to treatment options, and then provide you with the best option considering your personal needs and situation.

Your doctor gets compensated, and we hope well compensated, for providing this service. He or she may receive more or less compensation depending on the treatment option they advise you to take; however, we have been conditioned to believe that these highly-trained, ethical people adhere to their oath and put our needs ahead of their own compensation.

Occasionally you will become aware of a story in the media reporting the deplorable and unethical behavior of a specific doctor. This story only makes the news because it is relatively rare that a medical professional abuses the confidence they have been given.

Most professionals in the financial industry are honorable and ethical; however, you need to understand their motivation. One of my mentors always reminded me "everyone in business has an angle. This is good. The people you need to watch out for are those whose angle you do not recognize or understand."

Every product or service, including this book, is sold with a profit motive. The most ethical of salespeople have a motive to sell you their product or service. For this reason, they are forced to believe or at least act as if everyone could benefit from what they are offering. Charlie Munger, Warren Buffett's partner, often says, "To a man with a hammer everything looks like a nail." To an insurance salesperson or stockbroker, everyone looks like a client. Just because someone has a title before their name or initials after their name, doesn't mean they are not a salesperson.

In the famous movie, Wall Street, Michael Douglas playing Gordon Geckko delivers the immortal words "Greed is good." Martin and Charlie Sheen, father and son, play father and son characters in the movie. At one point in the film the son, who is a junior stock broker making cold calls to get new clients, attempts to correct his father by telling him that he is a broker not a salesman. His father reminds him, and hopefully us, when he says, "If you call strangers on the phone and ask for money, you're a salesman."

You must understand how your financial advisor makes a living and what effect his or her motivations may have on you and your family's financial future.

Jim Stovall

So, how do you find a good advisor if you don't have one? And how do you determine if the one you have is good or not? We'll begin to answer that by telling you a bit more about the Big 3—banks, brokerage firms, and insurance companies— and the instrumental role they've played in shaping the financial advisory business. As they are often quick to remind us, the Big 3 have been around forever. One of the newest firms, the result of a merger of two of the firms which made headlines for struggling through the financial crisis, has a new slogan: "A new wealth management firm with over 130 years of experience." They advertise that they, alone, have 18,000 financial advisors. It is thought that there are upwards to half a million individuals calling themselves some creative variant of a financial services professional, and most of them work for the Big 3.

A little history first. The Glass-Steagall Act of 1933 was passed after the collapse of much of the banking system. When enacted, it effectively put each of the Big 3 in a silo, and allowed them only to conduct their primary line of business. So banks could be banks and only do banking—not offering brokerage services or insurance products, and so on. This act remained in place until it was repealed in 1999. After the repeal of Glass-Steagall, it was once again a free-for-all. It's hard to tell which company is what any more, because when you go into the bank, they offer to sell you life insurance and open an IRA. Much in the same way, insurance sales people are also selling investment products, and brokerage firms also offer to be a one-stop-shop. Here we are, only a decade removed from the repeal of the Glass-Steagall Act, and we're again talking about new regulation for the financial industry after a near-collapse of the banking system.

And I'm not sure that the industry has actually received the message just yet. In *The Wall Street Journal*, Friday, July 31, 2009, the front page headline reads, "Bank Bonus Tab: $33 Billion." Here is how the article starts:

> Nine banks that received government aid money paid out bonuses of nearly $33 billion last year—including more than $1 million apiece to nearly 5,000 employees—despite huge losses that plunged the U.S. into economic turmoil.

Wait—weren't these the companies that needed a bailout from U.S. taxpayers just to stay afloat last year? The article goes on to say, "Six of the nine banks paid out more in bonuses than they received in profit." All I can say is, hmmmmmmmm.

Despite their attempts to convince us otherwise, the Big 3 are each still loyal to their primary line of business. While bankers, brokers, and insurance agents are now called financial advisors, financial consultants, wealth managers, or financial planners, a bank financial planner is still pushed to bring deposits to the bank and sell mortgages, a broker/financial advisor is still expected to pitch the proprietary investment product or service, and the insurance financial planner is required to sell insurance.

The deviation into other product lines is called "cross-sell," and the motivation to do it is enormous. Advisors in each model are given statistics that suggest that if a customer has purchased one product—a mutual fund, let's say—they have a 50% chance of remaining a customer. If, in addition to that mutual fund, they also purchase an insurance policy, there's a 70% chance of keeping the customer. But, if they also have their bank account or mortgage with us, there is a 90% chance that they'll stay.

So what the heck is financial planning then?? Financial planning, as a profession, is actually very young. It's said to have emerged, "with a meeting of 13 individuals at Chicago's O'Hare Airport in 1969," according to Investment Advisor magazine.[i] The first class of the College of Financial Planning graduated in 1973. With a history of no more than 40 years, it's understandable how the profession has faced difficulty in differentiating itself from the Wall Street institutions that date all the way back to 1790.[ii] This has been especially difficult as the Big 3 have worked very hard to promote themselves as financial planners.

I have worked for each of them as a financial advisor, and my experience was that financial planning was not the end, but a means to the end of product sales. Have you had a broker, banker, or insurance agent provide you with a financial plan? It may have even been surprisingly inexpensive or free. And I would be willing to bet, if you received a financial plan from a brokerage firm, that the actionable recommendations were spearheaded by having them manage your investments. A financial plan done by someone who is employed with or contracted by an insurance company doubtless resulted primarily in a recommendation for life, disability, or long term care insurance. To understand why independence from any parent company that sells financial products is so important, we need not look any further than the medical profession. Would you be uncomfortable if your family doctor worked for the pharmaceutical company, Pfizer? You shouldn't accept anything less of your financial advisor.

How then are the various types of financial planners compensated? Although they can be broken down into subsets, the following are the three broad methods of compensation for financial advisors: Commission-only, Fee-based and Fee-only. Commission financial personnel only receive their compensation from the commissions resulting from the sale of financial products. The Series 7 investment license, as well as licenses for life and health insurance, do not authorize one to advise clients. They only license someone to transact a product sale; therefore, commission advisors do not have the ability to charge fees for advice. They are compensated only when they sell something.

Economic Bias Alert!

The Economic Bias of a commission-only financial advisor is quite high, because they only "eat what they kill." Every morning that you wake up as a commission salesperson, you are unemployed and required to go find new business so that your income stream continues. Even for the most well-intended commission advisor, this reality will have an inevitable impact on his or her judgment because if you don't buy, they don't get paid.

While this next question is sure to raise some eyebrows, you should ask—point-blank—what amount of commission is being paid on the product that they're recommending. Would it surprise you that the sale of a $100,000 annuity could result in a $10,000 commission, split by the salesperson and his or her sponsoring company? It should surprise you, and understanding this will help you gauge whether or not the product you are purchasing is made for you, the consumer, or for the selling company and salesperson.

Fee-based advisors are thought by most to be synonymous with fee-only advisors, but there is actually a world of difference between the two. Fee-based advisors derive a meaningful portion of their compensation from fees that they charge for financial planning recommendations and/or from the management of investments. But a fee-based advisor may also receive commissions from transactions. These transactions often come from the sale of mutual funds, but most often from annuities and insurance, products known for especially high commission rates. When an advisor manages investments for a fee, he or she is required to have a Series 65 or Series 66 license, making them an Investment Advisor Representative (IAR) of a Registered Investment Advisory (RIA) firm.

When you have this license, and if you are being compensated by fees, the services for which you are taking the fee must be provided on the fiduciary level. While legal definitions of this word vary, the basic gist is that an advisor is required to act in the client's best interest. While it may surprise you that this is not a standard to which all in the financial industry are held, commission transactions do not require the salesperson to act as a fiduciary. This becomes a very gray area for those in the fee-based world and those who are clients of fee-based advisors, because an advisor who takes a fee for one service is required to act as a fiduciary in the provision of that service, but can then take the fiduciary hat off to sell a product for a commission through another service.

Economic Bias Alert!

Due to increased scrutiny on advisors whose compensation is purely gained from commissions, the fee-based realm of financial planning has been growing very fast. But the Economic Bias of a fee-based advisor may be even more dangerous than that of a commission-only advisor. The reason is that their label of fee-based gives consumers the impression that their advisor is always acting in a fiduciary capacity, but since the fee-based advisor also has the ability to take commissions on the sale of products, the consumer never really knows whether they are talking to an advisor or a product pusher.

And, from my own experience, I can tell you that a fee-based advisor is absolutely encouraged by their sales manager and company to sell products for a commission. If you are paying a fee for some of your investment management, but you have also purchased an insurance policy or annuity from your advisor, you have a right to ask how he or she is compensated on those products so that you have the complete picture on the Economic Bias in play.

I've talked to colleagues in the fee-based realm, in which I functioned for several years, and I have encouraged them to move from fee-based to fee-only for the freedom of conscience that I've experienced. But the refrain I hear from most is, "Well, the vast majority of my compensation is from fees, but I'm simply not willing to give up those big life insurance and annuity commissions. Somebody's going to get that commission, so why not me?" I don't judge, because I have thought and said the same thing, but having moved from commission-only to fee-based to fee-only, I can declare without hesitation that there is a difference in the way I approach client recommendations now that I take no commissions at all, and the only people who don't seem to believe that are the ones still accepting commissions.

A fee-only advisor can only receive compensation from fees. No commissions or referral fees are allowed if you call yourself fee-only, and that term has been institutionalized by the National Association of Personal Financial Advisors. NAPFA-registered advisors are put through a rigorous path to membership. One must have the appropriate credentials and experience, and must also have an actual financial plan that they've written pass a peer review. NAPFA advisors are also held to the highest standard in the industry for continuing education, and are required to sign a fiduciary pledge that they will act only as a fiduciary 100% of the time (ruling out the fee-based method of planning).

Within the fee-only realm, there are various methods of compensation. Some advisors do hourly-only work, and there is a network of hourly advisors across the country called the Garrett Planning Network. This is an excellent organization founded by Sheryl Garrett to provide access to fee-only planners for individuals and families who aren't looking for a perpetual relationship or investment management services, but instead want to talk to a professional planner who will render advice on an hourly basis. Some fee-only advisors charge flat fees for comprehensive or modular financial plans, but there are also fee-only advisors who, in addition to providing comprehensive personal financial advice, also manage investments for clients. The most common way that these planners are compensated is on an Assets Under Management (AUM) basis, but some do charge an annual retainer. With AUM, you'll pay a fee of 1% to 2% (typically) to have your investment assets managed. A flat retainer may also be charged that is revisited and adjusted on an annual basis for comprehensive services and/or investment management.

Economic Bias Alert!

Fee-only advisors are not exempt or immune from Economic Bias. Remember, everyone brings some bias to the table, and once you understand what it is, you're a better informed consumer. Fee-only advisors who solely offer services on an hourly basis still have the same bias of anyone who does hourly work. Their bias may encourage them to stretch the length of their work. Fee-only, hourly-only planners function as fiduciaries, so it would be against their code to stretch their work, but that doesn't mean the bias doesn't exist.

Planners who only do flat-fee work have a bias to do less or faster work allowing them to search for the next person willing to hire them for a flat-fee. Similarly, a retainer-based practice also faces this inevitable Economic Bias.

Finally, and probably the most notable and important of the three to recognize, is the Economic Bias of a fee-only planner who does manage investments for a percentage fee. If the planner is charging 1.5% to manage your investments, how might he or she approach your dilemma over whether or not you should take money out of investments to pay off your mortgage? If you take the money out, the advisor has fewer assets to invest on which you can be charged a fee—effectively, they just got a pay cut! The bias of fee-only advisors is the lowest in the industry, but no one is without Economic Bias entirely.

As mentioned earlier, there are estimates that suggest that over 500,000 people in the U.S. alone call themselves financial something-or-others. As of June 30, 2009, there were 59,662 Certified Financial Planner™ certificants, 27,500 members of the Financial Planning Association, 2,093 National Association of Personal Financial Advisors members, and only 1,269 that are NAPFA-Registered Financial Advisors. That tells me that there are tons of people out there who would like you to think that they are your financial advisor, but only a relative handful that are qualified to do so as true professionals.

But what does that word professional really mean? Does it have any importance at all, or has it been overused into vernacular oblivion? I've had the privilege of getting to know Dick Wagner over the last few years. He has been recognized by the CFP® Board, the FPA, and NAPFA nationally as one of the thought leaders in the industry. I call him the conscience of the financial planning profession. It has now been 20 years since Dick's seminal paper, "To Think...Like a CFP" was published in the Journal of Financial Planning. CFP stands for the Certified Financial Planner™ practitioner—one who has been licensed by the CFP® Board to hold the credentials. The CFP® credential is now appropriately recognized as the minimum standard for a financial planner, but when Dick originally wrote his article, it was not yet a recognizable standard. Dick was calling financial planners to task.

Dick was and is a CFP® practitioner, but he started his career in law. The name of his article, "To Think...Like a CFP," was a play-on-words from the movie, *The Paper Chase*, which chronicled the life of a young law student. As an attorney steeped in legal professionalism, Dick postured that financial planners needed to break from the sales realm and become true professionals, a pursuit which demanded, "principles over apparent self-interest." For financial planners to be genuine professionals who could be called upon to guide people in their personal finances, they must see the interest of their clients over their own. That is the true definition of a fiduciary.

I've used the word fiduciary now a number of times, but I haven't explained why it is so central to this discussion. There are three different legal standards to which those in the financial realm are held, the highest of which is fiduciary. As mentioned, a fiduciary is legally bound to act in the client's best interest. The next tier down is suitability. Suitability is the standard required of those who take commissions on investment products—stocks, bonds, options, mutual funds, and variable annuities, among others. The suitability standard requires that the salesperson sell a product that is generally considered to be suitable for that individual at that time. It does not create an advisory relationship and only has reign over a transaction at a moment in time. So, as long as the product sold at the time was suitable, the selling agent or broker's responsibility has ended. Finally, we have caveat emptor—"buyer beware"—that reigns over most insurance product sales, with the exception of those which have a variable investment component. Insurance is regulated on a state-by-state basis, and as long as a product has been approved by the state's insurance commissioner, the selling agent has very few restrictions on to whom the product can be sold...kind of like shopping at the five-and-dime.

How then, can you determine how to find a truly professional advisor, or if you already have an advisor, how do you know that he or she is a professional? Here are six criteria to which a truly professional advisor should be held. Your advisor should be:

Educated

• Minimum of a Bachelor's Degree; preference for advanced degree—Master of Business Administration (MBA), Master of Science in Finance, or Master of Financial Planning (very few exist)—and/or financial planning specific certificate(s)

Credentialed

- CFP®, Certified Financial Planner™, *is the* financial planning credential

- CPA, Certified Public Accountant, *is the* accounting credential, and an excellent addition to your financial planner's resume

- CFA, Chartered Financial Analyst, is a very demanding credential, specific to investment analysis

- JD, Juris Doctorate, indicates you're working with an attorney; very demanding degree, often accompanying planners who specialize in estate planning

- CIMA, Certified Investment Management Analyst, is awarded by the Institute for Certified Investment Management Consultants

- AIFA® and AIF®, Accredited Investment Fiduciary Analyst and Accredited Investment Fiduciary are two newer credentials that are growing in reputation dealing specifically with investing as a fiduciary

- ChFC, Chartered Financial Consultant, is good but should be in addition to CFP® credential and probably indicates insurance sales background

- CLU, Chartered Life Underwriter, almost always indicates insurance sales background and should be combined with CFP® for credibility

There is a veritable alphabet soup of letters that people put behind their names, but any of them that are not preceded by CFP®, CPA, CFA, or JD are either less than central to the practice of financial planning or masking a lack of appropriate credentials.

Experienced

• Minimum of 5 years experience and working in conjunction with senior planner or minimum of 10 years, and still ideally partnering with a more seasoned planner

Independent

• Should not be working for one of the Big 3, but also be wary of "Independent Broker Dealers" which carry the word independent, but often reflect the sales practices of the Big 3

• Purely independent financial planning and Registered Investment Advisory (RIA) firm optimal

Fee-only

• Steer clear of conflict-of-interest by steering clear of commissions

100% Fiduciary

• Contrasted with part-time fiduciaries in the fee-based model or no-time fiduciaries in commission-only realm

There is no panacea or bias-free utopia in financial planning. I am part of the National Association of Personal Financial Advisors (NAPFA) as well as the larger Financial Planning Association, and several sub-associations, groups and think tanks, and the discussion of how we can improve compensation models is endless, and will be, because we'll never find something that will be optimal for every single client and advisor. The best advisor decision starts with you. Review the different variants listed above and determine what is best for you. An excellent online resource is available for you at www.focusonfiduciary.org. This is a website designed by NAPFA to help consumers differentiate between advisors and salespeople. Also keep your eye out for a coalition that has been formed with the CFP® Board, the FPA, and NAPFA to ensure that the fiduciary standard becomes the minimum standard for financial advisors in the wake of the financial crisis.

Timely Application
Fiduciary Questionnaire

Go to the Focus On Fiduciary website to learn more about why this word is so important in your quest for the right financial advisor. You can also navigate directly to http://www.focusonfiduciary.org/Fiduciary_Questionnaire.pdf to find a downloadable, printable questionnaire that you can ask your advisor or a prospective advisor to complete for you. At the end of the questionnaire is a Fiduciary Oath that you should ask your current or prospective financial advisor to sign, showing their willingness to put your interests ahead of their own.

Visit www.thefinancialcrossroads.com where you'll find a link to the Fiduciary Questionnaire.

Tim Maurer

I know that some of my fee-only brethren will cringe when I say this, but a traditional stock broker may very well be the best option for some people. They like the whole "hot-tip" mentality and like having someone to call to say, "Hey, what do you think of this one?" And for someone who has become a do-it-yourself financial expert, going directly to an insurance agent to buy insurance makes perfect sense. There is absolutely nothing wrong with being a stock broker or insurance agent. What is wrong is putting on the façade of a fiduciary when sales is the primary objective.

I warn you in advance that most companies in the financial realm will not allow their employees to sign the fiduciary pledge because they're not willing to take on the liability risk. It is a shame, because I know that there are many good advisors who would prefer to act as a fiduciary. But from your perspective, it should be a no-brainer. Picture for a moment that the "perfect" financial advisor for you has been duplicated. One of the two works for an independent company that conducts all business as a fiduciary; the other works for a firm that is not willing to allow the perfect advisor to commit to working only in your best interest. Which one do you choose?

Finally, I encourage you to look for more than a compensation structure in your ideal partner in personal finance. I asked Dick Wagner, the industry thought leader I mentioned earlier, "What is the point of having a financial planner?" He said, "The point is to help people relate to the force of money in their lives." There are brilliant technical financial planners that could strategize until your eyes glaze over but couldn't identify with you enough to actually improve your life. And that is the point—for your life to be in some way unburdened or improved. That is going to require more than having the right investment allocation or retirement projection; it requires a relational connection and a deeper understanding that numbers aren't the end, but the means. I encourage you to interview planners until you find one that is willing to learn about you, your Personal Principles and Goals as part of his or her advisory process.

[i] This quote came from an article in Investment Advisor in 2005, and was written by Kathleen McBride

[ii] This is from an excellent book written by Charles Geisst and released in 1997 entitled *Wall Street, A History.*

Fiduciary Questionnaire

Why do you need to *Focus on Fiduciary*?

Because Financial Advisors adhering to a Fiduciary Standard act in the client's best interests. These advisors are not Stock Brokers or Registered Representatives who benefit from selling you an investment or financial product. Fee-Only Financial Advisors adhere to a Fiduciary Standard and sell only one thing—their knowledge.

Do you want to know if your Financial Advisor, or prospective Financial Advisor, holds to a Fiduciary Standard? Just have them complete this quick questionnaire and compare the answers with the provided answer key. You'll be happy you did!

1.   How are you and your firm compensated?

- Fee-Only
- Fee-Based
- Fee-Offset
- Commissions

2.   Do you have an agreement describing your compensation and services that will be provided in advance of the engagement?

- Yes
- No

3.   Do you have a minimum fee?

- Yes (If yes, please explain)
- No

4.   If you earn commissions, approximately what percentage of your firm's commission income comes from?

_____% Insurance products
_____% Annuities
_____% Mutual Funds
_____% Limited Partnerships
_____% Stocks and bonds
_____% Coins, tangibles, collectibles
_____% Other:_____

5.　　　Does any member of your firm act as a general partner, participate in, or receive compensation from investments you may recommend to me?

- Yes
- No

6.　　　Do you receive referral fees from attorneys, accountants, insurance professionals, mortgage brokers, or others?

- Yes
- No

7.　　　Do you receive on-going income from any of the mutual funds that you recommend in the form of "12(b)1" fees, "trailing" commissions, or other continuing payouts?

- Yes
- No

8.　　　Are there financial incentives for you to recommend certain financial products?

- Yes (If yes, please explain)
- No

9.　　　Are you currently engaged in any other business, either as a sole proprietor, partner, officer, employee, trustee, agent or otherwise? (Exclude non-investment related activities which are exclusively charitable, civic, religious or fraternal and are recognized as tax-exempt.)

- Yes (If yes, please explain)
- No

10.　　Will you sign the Fiduciary Oath below?

- Yes
- No

FIDUCIARY OATH
The advisor shall exercise his/her best efforts to act in good faith and in the best interests of the client. The advisor shall provide written disclosure to the client prior to the engagement of the advisor, and thereafter throughout the term of the engagement, of any conflicts of interest which will or reasonably may compromise the impartiality or

independence of the advisor. The advisor, or any party in which the advisor has a financial interest, does not receive any compensation or other remuneration that is contingent on any client's purchase or sale of a financial product. The advisor does not receive a fee or other compensation from another party based on the referral of a client or the client's business.

What the Fiduciary Oath means to you—the client

- I shall always act in good faith and with candor.
- I shall be proactive in my disclosure of any conflicts of interest that may impact you.
- I shall not accept any referral fees or compensation that is contingent upon the purchase or sale of a financial product.

_____

Signature

The following answer key will provide you with the recommended answers to the questions contained within the Fiduciary Questionnaire. By comparing the answers provided to you by the advisor with these recommended answers, you will be able to better understand whether or not the advisor in question holds to a Fiduciary Standard.

1. How should a financial advisor charge for services? The members of NAPFA firmly believe that financial advisors should charge Fee-Only. Although NAPFA recognizes that financial planners can provide services on a commission basis, it is NAPFA's core position that a Fee-Only engagement removes the potential conflicts of interest that are inherent in a commission relationship.

   Fee-Only Financial Advisors put their client's interests first and, therefore, hold to a Fiduciary Standard.

2. Prior to formalizing a relationship, a financial advisor should always provide you information which clearly discloses how she/he will be compensated: Fee-Only, Fee-Based, commissions only. Ask for this information prior to commencing a relationship, and if there are any corresponding conflicts of interest presented by the compensation arrangement, be aware that your interests might not always be placed ahead of the advisor's.

   Financial advisors who have no apparent conflicts of interest are more likely to be considered a Fiduciary.

3. Financial advisors may charge a minimum fee for services they render. If you have limited financial planning needs and/or a small portfolio, paying a minimum fee may not be in your best interests. If that is your situation, search for an advisor who will provide you professional advice on a flat-fee, project, or hourly basis.

4. While NAPFA encourages you to consider using a Fee-Only Financial Advisor to minimize the potential for conflicts of interest, you may instead select an advisor who accepts commissions. Financial advisors who are compensated based on commissions should be able to explain how they are compensated and identify what percentage of their compensation is derived from the sale of various commission-based investment products and/or securities trading.

   Financial Advisors who do receive commissions but cannot account for how they are compensated should raise serious questions from the consumer. NAPFA recommends Fee-Only financial advisors to eliminate as many conflicts of interest as possible.

5. Ask your prospective financial advisor if she/he is limited to presenting certain types of investments or investment products to you. If so, inquire why she/he is limited, and how this might affect the success of attaining your goals and/or the amount of fees to be paid.

6. As you work with a financial advisor, other needs revolving around important financial issues will become evident. Certain advisors, for example, recommend attorneys, accountants, insurance agents, and mortgage brokers to their clients. You should inquire whether the financial advisor will receive a referral fee for the recommendation. If the financial advisor does receive a referral fee or some other type of compensation from the professional(s) that she/he may recommend to you, you should seriously consider this conflict of interest prior to engaging the recommended professional.

   Financial Advisors receiving a referral fee from other professionals for referring your business may not be acting in your best interests. A true Fiduciary will not receive any compensation from any outside sources.

7. Some mutual fund and investment product sponsors pay 12b(1) and similar fees. A financial advisor who receives 12(b)1 fees or "trailers" is not a Fee-Only Financial Advisor. Trailing fees may negatively affect you, because typically the product sponsor charges shareholders higher fees and then pays a portion of the money to the financial advisor on an ongoing basis.

NAPFA recommends Fee-Only Financial Advisors to ensure a Fiduciary relationship.

8. Commission-based advisors may receive higher commissions on certain products they sell than on others. This may influence their decision to recommend investment products that are not in your best interest. Ask your prospective financial advisor how his/her recommendation might affect the success of attaining your goals and/or the amount of fees to be paid. Fee-Only advisors do not have this conflict of interest; they are able to recommend investments based solely upon your specific needs.

    NAPFA recommends Fee-Only Financial Advisors to ensure a Fiduciary relationship.

9. By knowing what other business ventures a financial advisor is involved in, you will better understand if there are any conflicts of interest with regard to the advice that you might receive. This is especially important if the advisor is involved with any other investment-related entity. Ask for a detailed account of how that relationship will impact the advice she/he will provide you. The outside relationship may be in conflict with your personal interests.

10. Accountability is important in financial planning. While there are many people in the financial services industry who profess to have the client's best interests at heart, they still may make recommendations that present a conflict of interest. NAPFA requires all of its members to sign a Fiduciary Oath; this helps to ensure that each client's best interests, not the advisor's, are always a priority.

If your Financial Advisor, or prospective Financial Advisor, satisfactorily answered these questions according to the NAPFA-recommended answers, then that Financial Advisor most likely holds to a Fiduciary Standard. This means he/she is placing your interests ahead of their own.

To learn more about a Fiduciary Standard and the Focus on Fiduciary campaign, please visit www.FocusonFiduciary.org or call 800-366-2732.

This message is brought to you by the National Association of Personal Financial Advisors (NAPFA) Consumer Education Foundation.

Chapter
eighteen

YOUR STORY, YOUR PLAN

> Any change, even a change for the better, is always accompanied by drawbacks and discomforts.
>
> *Arnold Bennett*

We have made reference in other parts of the book to the oft quoted phrase about death and taxes. I enjoy history, so I had to trace its origin. It appears that Daniel Defoe, in 1726, was the first to make this now famous claim, albeit more eloquently: "Things as certain as death and taxes, can be more firmly believed." Much closer to the modern day phrase, however, was Ben Franklin's redux in a letter to Jean-Baptiste Leroy in 1789, in which he said, "In this world nothing can be said to be certain, except death and taxes." Regardless of the veracity of this line of thought, I find it all quite depressing. But I do think that we could turn this into a phrase in which we'd all agree: *One guarantee in this world is change.*

Do you embrace, reject, resist, or retreat from change? The fact that you purchased this book tells me you probably don't reject it. That you read this far tells me you probably don't resist it. The question now, however, is whether you will embrace it or retreat from it. The easier path is to retreat, because as Arnold Bennett tells us, "even a change for the better, is always accompanied by drawbacks and discomforts." Regarding the intersection of money and life, there are two different types of change: fundamental change and practical change. In a perfect world, fundamental change happens first and practical change follows almost effortlessly. But fundamental change does not always come easily. Often times, practical change precedes fundamental change as we allow a discipline to shape our view fundamentally.

A fundamental change is seeing the world as a risk manager; practical change is altering your insurance policies. Fundamental change is shifting from a retirement plan to a fulfillment plan; practical change is taking degree or certificate college courses that could lead to a job change. Fundamental change is seeing your estate plan as a legacy plan; practical change is updating your will.

Practical change is cutting up the credit cards, your path to *more*; fundamental change is genuine contentment with *enough*. Practical change is beginning a giving program; fundamental change is having less of an attachment to material things. Practical change is writing your Personal Money Story; fundamental change is realizing its significance. Practical change is dealing with the dollars and cents in life; fundamental change is life itself.

Timeless Truth

We live in a world that, when it's all said and done, there's a lot said and very little done. You will not succeed in money or in life based on what you know. Taking action will not guarantee success either. Gaining enough knowledge to take the right action is what will bring that which you seek.

We live in an information age. We no longer suffer from the desires and hunger to know more. Instead, we seek to make sense and prioritize the myriad of facts and details before us.

After reading this book, you certainly will not know how to do everything it takes to be successful, but this is not an excuse to do nothing.

My co-author and I have tried to give you a glimpse into the kindergarten-through-graduate-school view of money and life. Far from being the last word on the topic, we are helping you to find the first word along your path. It is not our aim to give you all the answers but, instead, to frame the questions so you can define success with respect to your money and your life.

You know that the journey of a thousand miles begins with one step. In this book, by the very nature of the topic, we were forced to give you an overview of the entire journey. While it seems daunting if you attempt to swallow it whole, all you need do now is commit to take the first step.

I have written a number of books and, hopefully, will write many more. For the most part, those books start and end with a topic or story fully explored. Your money and your life defy that kind of experience. We do not share an author/reader relationship. We are fellow travelers along the road to our own destinies.

My co-author and I cannot tell you the definition of success for you and your family. In this book, we have shared some common ingredients that will be a part of every successful recipe. Do not look at these financial concepts as something that restricts your life and freedom. Instead, these concepts, tools, and principles will give you freedom, promise, and possibility.

For over a decade, I have written a syndicated column that shares timeless principles with people around the world. Each of these hundreds of columns contains different information, but they all conclude with the simple statement "Today's the Day!" I feel this is the all-encompassing, critical message to leave with my readers, because it doesn't matter what you know. It matters what you do. And when we look at doing things in this world, the only day that matters is today.

Jim Stovall

As we've learned, financial planning is not just about dollars and cents. It starts with the recognition of the role that money plays in our lives, the history that we have with money, and then reshaping our view of its purpose as a means, not an end. Then, we have the privilege of making a declaration of what will mark our lives—our Personal Principles—followed by the establishment of specific, measurable, attainable, and meaningful goals that are based on those principles. This step may also involve testing and eliminating any goals that we had previously set that do not align with our principles or meet the necessary goal criteria.

The establishment of our Personal Financial Statements is where life planning begins to merge into traditional financial planning. A successful cash flow mechanism is at the heart of every good financial plan, whether your income is $10,000 per year or $10 million. Our financial statements will show us whether we are living with enough or for more. Real investing doesn't begin until our assets begin to dwarf our debts, and the elimination of all debt should be a stated goal of every financial plan.

Debt is not an investment and neither is insurance. Insurance is a valuable tool, but one that should be used by a wise risk manager who seeks to avoid, reduce, and assume risk prior to insuring. Life insurance is one of the simplest parts of the financial plan that is made the most complex. Don't let it be. Invest with investments and insure with insurance. The time you save in life insurance planning can be applied to ensuring that you're not leaving catastrophic risks uninsured with the most ignored of all insurance—home and auto. Take advantage of the most tax efficient account allowed by the IRS, the Health Savings Account, and fear not the most complex of insurance products—disability income and long term care insurance—because too many don't know they need them until it's too late.

View investing also as a risk manager, not fearful of risk, but calculating. Don't trust "the market" to be a benevolent force that will deliver your hopes and dreams; that's your job. But remember that the clearest investment minds manage risk, not returns, with full recognition that it is easier to lose money than it is to make it back. Don't stop rooting for the home team, the U.S.A., but recognize that the best investment gains of the next century lie south and far east of our borders. Annuities— don't buy them, but be careful getting out. Don't pursue investment strategies for the primary purpose of tax privilege, but take full advantage of free money (401k employer match), tax-deferred contributions (401k), and especially, tax-free opportunities (Roth IRA).

Education is invaluable, but not priceless. If you compromise your own financial health for the sake of your children's education, you do them a great disservice, because they may have to bail you out in your retirement years; a much more expensive proposition than paying off a student loan. The three-legged stool of retirement is now a pogo stick, but don't panic, because you should have a fulfillment plan, not a retirement plan. You don't need to be happy about spending a pretty penny to sit down and talk about your demise with an attorney, but it doesn't have to cost you a fortune, and those documents are the most important you'll ever write, when you need them. And be picky about who you choose to partner with you as your advisor. The vetting process won't be easy, but it will be worth it.

Economic Bias Alert!

Do you remember the news from the last chapter? Everyone is biased, and we all exhibit a personal Economic Bias as well. Your authors have an Economic Bias. Yes, it's true. We'd like people to buy this book—there, we've said it!

But you have a personal Economic Bias as well. You'll have a tendency to go through a book like this and be receptive to the recommendations that aren't going to cost you anything. You may be a young parent whose #1 financial planning priority should be to get a will done, but you know that it's going to cost several hundred dollars. Or, you may know that you have to get around to paying off those credit cards because it will put you on the path to financial freedom, but you don't do it because it means that you won't be able to take the vacation you want. That's personal Economic Bias, and like all Economic Bias, it's not evil or bad—it just is—and you'll be better off when you acknowledge it.

As you'll see if you fan the pages of this book that you've already read, financial planning contains a lot of infomation, and this book only attempted to highlight the most important themes of personal finance. That is why it is imperative that you have a way to collect and organize the information in your financial life. Think back to when I told you that you can always take principal that you've put into a Roth IRA back out with no taxes or penalties at any age. That information is only valuable if you know how much you've contributed in the first place. Like dieting, brushing your teeth, and budgeting, information management is relatively painless if you discipline yourself to do it as you go, but very difficult to catch-up on after years of neglect. The maintenance of this information can be done by you, manually or electronically, or it is a service that some financial planners provide.

So what now?? If you've been keeping up with the Timely Applications using our online exercises, you probably have a head start, but it would be very difficult to keep everything organized and moving in a purposeful, prioritized direction. That is why our final Timely Application is designed to help you organize and prioritize all this information into your own personal Action Plan.

Timely Application
Action Plan

The Action Plan is broken down categorically into the various sections of the book. As you organize your Timely Applications, you'll be able to carry the actions that you'd like to take over to the Action Plan. Each section will give you an opportunity to describe the Fundamental Change that you want to improve your life as well as the Practical Change steps that you intend to take. Beside each action in each section, you'll be able to name a responsible party to complete the action. It may be you or your spouse, or it may be an action that an estate planning attorney or financial planner will complete.

Then, you'll have a column in which you'll be able to prioritize all of these actions. Even if you have the money to implement everything at once, you definitely don't have the time. If you don't prioritize, you may be overwhelmed with the task at hand and give up. Finally, you'll have a column to write in a date when it's completed. Give yourself the chance to feel that endorphin rush of checking off a to-do. You deserve it!

Visit www.thefinancialcrossroads.com to find a template to use in creating your own Action Plan.

Tim Maurer

The Timeless Truths will endure, but the Timely Applications will perpetually change. We would like to partner with you as you navigate the financial landscape. You have likely visited the website to retrieve Timely Application exercises, so you've probably noticed that the website also hosts an ongoing discussion of personal finance topics that are always in a state of flux. We invite you to dialogue with us on our blog where we'll keep you updated on things that are changing in the financial world. As we emerge from this Great Recession, we will see numerous changes in the financial industry that will impact our lives.

We invite you to bring your questions to the blog regarding how to implement strategies outlined in the book, but also questions that we may not have addressed that impact your personal finances. We would love to hear your success stories as you implement your Action Plan but also struggles that arise. We also invite you to share the frustrations you face in completing the Timely Application exercises. Stumbling blocks are the norm—not the exception—because life is not lived out in the black-and-white letters on these pages. We will continue to walk through this with you in the form of an ongoing conversation on our website and blog. And we know that the best applications are created in practice, so if you find potential improvements to any of the Timely Application exercises, we welcome and invite those suggestions and will implement them for everyone's benefit.

Your Personal Money Story is already partly written. It may be a rags-to-riches story, it may be a riches-to-rags story, or it may be a rags-to-rags or riches-to-riches story. But remember that the riches part of your story is not the primary indicator of success, nor is a story lacking riches a failure. True wealth—

contentment—is success. You can have wealth with millions or hundreds, and the beauty of that is that you can have it today. A friend of mine closes his emails with the following phrase: "Keep moving forward." Whether you have more money than you could ever spend in this lifetime or a negative net worth and mounds of debt, that recommendation applies to all.

Please stay in touch and in conversation with us, because this book is not our last word on the subject, nor can it be. Very little in the realm of personal finance is a matter of right-and-wrong. It is a blend of science and art, or, MONEY and LIFE.

You can be very successful in this world, be admired by everyone, have endless possessions, a lovely family, success in your work, and have everything the world can give, but behind it all, you can be completely lost and miserable. If you have everything the world has to offer you, but you do not have love, then you are the poorest of the poorest of the poor.

John O'Donohue

ACTION PLAN

Life Planning

Fundamental Change: I will understand my past with money and the underlying values and life goals upon which my financial decisions are based.

	Practical Change(s)	Responsible Party	Priority (A,B,C,1,2,3)	Date Completed
1	Share Personal Money Story with spouse	Me	C	10-Dec
2	Establish personal principles and goals	Both	A	
3				
4				
5				
6				

Personal Financial Statements

Fundamental Change: I will control my money instead of being controled by it.

	Practical Change(s)	Responsible Party	Priority (A,B,C,1,2,3)	Date Completed
1	Establish personal financial statements	Me	A	5-Dec
2	Use Mint.com or ynab.com	Me	A	5-Dec
3				
4				
5				
6				

Debt Management

Fundamental Change: I will enjoy "enough" in the present and future instead of forever chasing "more".

	Practical Change(s)	Responsible Party	Priority (A,B,C,1,2,3)	Date Completed
1	Eliminate bad debt, high interest first	Both	A	
2	Pay off HELOC	Both	B	29-Dec
3				
4				
5				
6				

ACTION PLAN

Estate Planning

Fundamental Change:

	Practical Change(s)	Responsible Party	Priority (A,B,C,1,2,3)	Date Completed
1				
2				
3				
4				
5				
6				

Retirement/Fulfillment Planning

Fundamental Change:

	Practical Change(s)	Responsible Party	Priority (A,B,C,1,2,3)	Date Completed
1				
2				
3				
4				
5				
6				

Financial Advisors

Fundamental Change:

	Practical Change(s)	Responsible Party	Priority (A,B,C,1,2,3)	Date Completed
1				
2				
3				
4				
5				
6				

ACTION PLAN

Risk Management

Fundamental Change:

	Practical Change(s)	Responsible Party	Priority (A,B,C,1,2,3)	Date Completed
1				
2				
3				
4				
5				
6				

Portfolio Management

Fundamental Change:

	Practical Change(s)	Responsible Party	Priority (A,B,C,1,2,3)	Date Completed
1				
2				
3				
4				
5				
6				

Taxes

Fundamental Change:

	Practical Change(s)	Responsible Party	Priority (A,B,C,1,2,3)	Date Completed
1				
2				
3				
4				
5				
6				

Notes

Notes

Notes

Notes

Notes

Notes

Notes

Notes

Notes

Notes

Notes

Notes